THE

C0-AJW-234

OnWine

AUSTRALIAN WINE ANNUAL

2001

Published in Australia 2000 by

Jeremy Oliver Pty Ltd trading as OnWine Publications
565 Burwood Rd
Hawthorn, Victoria, 3122
Australia
Tel: 61 3 9819 4400
Fax: 61 3 9819 5322

Printed by	Times Printers Pte Ltd Singapore
Designed by	Artifishal Studios Melbourne, Victoria, Australia
Programming and Layout by	Virgil Reality Melbourne, Victoria, Australia
Cover photograph by	Peter Russell
Distributed to book retailers in Australia by	Pan Macmillan Free call 1800 684 459 Free fax 1800 241 310
Distributed to wine retailers in Australia by	Tucker Seabrook Tel: 02 9666 0000 Fax 02 9666 0011

Copyright © Jeremy Oliver 2000

ISBN 0-9587213-4-3

Introduction

'Growing pains, growing pains, always in a hurry . . .'

warbles Tim Finn on his Escapade LP. Could have been singing about Australian wine, which in recent times has taken to resembling a juggernaut struggling to control its own progress. One minute we're talking about a glut of chardonnay so big that Olympic swimming pools seem even smaller than Ian Thorpe makes them appear. We're facing record vintages but aren't quite sure who's going to drink what we make.

Next minute the vintage is down on expectations, chardonnay is not only in short supply but is being planted again, and Jacob's Creek is on allocation to its many export markets. The big worry is now the domestic market, which at time of writing almost seems to have forgotten that wine exists.

'It remains to be seen if it's worth the worry . . .'

Hardly. Wine is that sort of an industry you could worry yourself to death over, yet it's always going to be there in the morning. This is clearly the view adopted by the Australian Federal Government which, in its infinite wisdom, as part of an overall tax reform process, actually increased the tax hike on the wine industry. Insult is only added to injury, since the very tax which perpetrates this crime against all reasonable sensibility is called the Wine Equalisation Tax. The writers of 'Yes, Minister' couldn't have scripted it better.

Yet the industry will get over it, the public will ultimately forget, just like they did after each additional tax hike after the first impost of wine sales tax in 1984, less than eighteen months after the then Australian Prime Minister said there would never be a tax on wine. No, Prime Minister?

But with a tax regime equivalent to a sales tax of around 45% how will Australia ever make the most of its extraordinary asset its wine industry represents? Will our rural areas ever be able to maximise their opportunities for tourism, employment and development? How many rural-based industries add the sort of value to a primary product that the wine industry does? What is it about wine that so distorts the way our politicians view it and treat it? Do they think we're having a better time than they are?

Australian wine is one of our country's greatest advertisements for travel and trade, yet at home it's treated like a milk cow munching on the longest of Long Paddocks. Unlike the brewing industry, against which it is traditionally compared, wine is made only after a high-quality primary product has been successfully grown and harvested. You don't just turn on a tap for your most basic raw material as you do in a brewery; you have to grow it.

Few industries reflect the free market like Australian wine. Few industries move with such predictable unpredictability from one end of a spectrum to another, oblivious to the lost opportunities to plan its development along the way. Take the way winegrapes have been planted here over the last five years. White and red grapes were planted at roughly equal rates until 1996, when the pendulum first swung in favour of red. In 1997 our plantings of over 10,000 ha included more than 8,600 ha of red grapes, and there was a similar proportion of red grapes in slightly reduced plantings the following year. Whites were totally neglected, creating the potential shortfall now being realised. Grapes, most of which are red, are being planted so quickly that there are serious concerns as to whether wineries can buy enough tanks in time to process and store them. What happens if the world market suddenly switches its preference to white wine? When many large vineyards were planted in the 1970s in the Hunter Valley, most were to red grapes. About a year later wine-drinking Australians discovered chardonnay, big time. They had to pull the red vines up again.

'Growing pains, growing pains, always in a hurry...'

Without implementing a government-controlled system based on European models, it's virtually impossible for this industry to regulate itself. It doesn't even really know the extent of vine plantings until several years after many vineyards have been put in the ground! I wouldn't advocate for a moment that we followed the European leads, but like many others I was horrified over the recent episode which saw a couple of disgruntled American winemaking students nearly turn this industry on its head.

A large South Australian winery, it was alleged, was using illegal additives and unethical practices which involved the use of red tannins to give colour to poor red wines made from cheap white grapes, and ethanol to increase alcoholic strengths. The winery had its export licence revoked for a short period after an investigation determined that silver nitrate, a legal wine additive in several countries, had been used. None of the other accusations were substantiated.

None of which makes me sleep any easier if, that is, I thought it worth the worry. How does a large and high-profile Australian winery have in its chemical store a banned additive? If it is seen to be present at one, what's preventing it from being present, even used, at others? The industry has to tighten its controls. It's reached the stage where there's too much at stake for some cowboy winery to damage the economic viability of others. I don't claim to have the answer, but the first step is surely to acknowledge the extent of the problem.

And to paraphrase the rest of Mr Finn's message, you don't regret the time you spend figuring out how to do things better. Too right, Mr Finn, too darned right.

So, welcome to the fourth edition of *The OnWine Australian Wine Annual*. It's filled to the brim with more wineries than I ever thought could be crammed into 320 pages, with more new wineries and new wines than ever before. It's been a pleasant challenge to compile this edition, since one of the obvious joys has been to taste the reds from 1998, while last year I was forced to wade through those of 1997. You will see what I mean when you try them yourself. I hope that you enjoy using this book and that it helps you find more pleasure than ever before from Australian wine.

Acknowledgments

As ever, this book could not have been published without the help of some very talented, and indulgent people. My sincere thanks to Frank Ameneiro, Toby Hines, Robyn Lee, Wendy L Mahoney, Stephen O'Connor, Virgil Reality, Jon Williams and to my tolerant wife, Jennifer.

Contents

How to use this book

Finding the wine or winery

It's dead easy to find the listing you're after in *The OnWine Australian Wine Annual*. Each winery or brand of wine is presented in alphabetic order. Under the winery heading, each of its wines or labels is then listed alphabetically. To find Rosemount Estate Roxburgh Chardonnay, for example, simply search for the start of Rosemount Estate's entries, which begin on page 240, after which it's easy to scroll alphabetically down the pages to the Roxburgh Chardonnay, whose listing appears on page 242.

Winery information

The OnWine Australian Wine Annual presents each winery's actual physical address, wine region, telephone number and facsimile number. On those occasions where the entries refer to just a vineyard whose wines are made elsewhere, the address supplied is for the vineyard itself. If you're thinking of visiting a vineyard and wish to be sure whether or not it is open for public inspection, I suggest you telephone the company using the number provided.

Each winery included is accompanied by a listing of its winemaker, viticulturist and chief executive, plus brief details concerning any recent changes of ownership or direction, key wines and recent developments of interest.

The Wine Ranking

The OnWine Australian Wine Annual provides the only current Australian classification of nearly all major Australian wine brands determined on the most important aspect of all: quality. Unlike the very worthwhile Langtons' Classification of Distinguished Australian Wine, which presents a more limited overview of the super-premium market and which is largely based on such aspects as resale price and performance at auction, the Wine Rankings in *The OnWine Australian Wine Annual* are not influenced in any way by price or other secondary factors. Being a secondary market, the auction market is usually slow to respond to the emergence of new quality wines, while in some cases, the first release of the Penfolds Yattarna Chardonnay being a fine example, it can produce excessive prices grossly disproportionate to true wine quality.

The Wine Ranking is your easiest and most convenient guide to wine quality. This book accords to the best wines in Australia a Wine Ranking numeral between 1 and 5, based on the scores received out of 20 in my tastings, which are printed adjacent to each entry. The scores from 20 printed in this edition usually relate to the most recent occasion on which I have tasted each wine. Any wines with a Wine Ranking must have scored consistently well in these tastings, so each wine allocated one deserves to be taken seriously, irrespective of whether it is 1 or 5.

To provide a rough basis for comparison, a Wine Ranking of 1 is broadly equivalent to a First Growth classification in France. A large number of wines are included in this book which are not given Wine Rankings, since the minimum requirement for a ranking of 5 is still pretty steep.

Here is a rough guide to the way Wine Rankings relate to scores from 20, and how they compare to different medal standards used in the Australian wine show system:

Wine Ranking	Regular Score in Jeremy Oliver's Tastings	Medal Equivalent
1	18.8+	Top gold medal
2	18.3–18.7	Regular gold medal
3	17.8–18.2	Top silver medal
4	17.0–17.7	Regular silver medal
5	16.0–16.9	Top bronze medal

It is worth noting that wines scoring an average of 15.5 out of 20 in Australian wine shows are awarded a Bronze Medal, those that score 17 are awarded Silver Medals and those that score 18.5 are awarded Gold Medals.

As far as this book is concerned, if a wine improves over time, so will its Wine Ranking. Similarly, if its standard declines, so will its ranking. Since Wine Rankings are largely a reflection of each wine's performance over the last four years, they are unlikely to change immediately as a result of a single especially poor or exceptional year.

Why I don't print meaningless wine prices

It is meaningless to print a current price for each vintage of every wine included in this book. Retail prices vary so dramatically from shop to shop that there is no such thing as a standard recommended retail price, even for current release wines. Price guides become even more trite for older releases, since too many factors come into play – was the wine bought by retailer at auction for resale? In what condition is the bottle? How has it been stored? How keen is the buyer and how desperate is the vendor? What margin does the retailer (or restaurateur) wish to apply and for how long have they had the stock? Since no system has yet been invented which even vaguely approximates the price of older wines and which takes into account all of the factors above, I don't use one. For what value is there in providing worthless information?

Current price range

In this book I offer a simple key to help you determine at a glance the approximate retail price of each wine. The Current Price Range, presented in symbol form as described below, provides a reasonable price range for the currently available vintage of each wine, costed at full retail margin.

This price estimation is an approximate guide only and may alter during the period in which a particular vintage wine is for sale. It is largely based around or just under a wine's suggested retail price and does not take into account any special offer or significant discounting.

A wine's Current Price Range can easily be decoded using the table below.

Current Price Range	$5 - 11	$12 - 17	$18 - 25	$26 - 39	$40+
Symbol	$	$$	$$$	$$$$	$$$$$

When to drink each wine

To the right hand side of every page of wine listings is a column which features the suggested drinking range for every vintage of each wine included, within which I would expect each wine to be drinking at its peak. These drinking windows are my estimations alone, since it's apparent that different people enjoy their wines at different stages of development. Some of us prefer the primary flavours of young wine, while others would rather the virtually decayed qualities of extremely old bottles.

The drinking windows reflect my belief that if a wine shows the necessary potential to develop in the bottle, it should be given a chance. It's a day-to-day tragedy how few top Australian cellaring wines of all types and persuasions are actually opened at or even close to their prime.

For quick and easy reference, a broad indication of each vintage's maturity is provided with a simple colour background. The chart below illustrates how the colours indicate whether a wine is drinking at its best now, will improve further if left alone, or if it is likely to be past its best. A '+' symbol after an entry suggests potential for improvement beyond the later date.

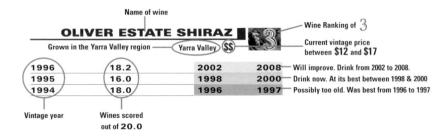

Australia's perfect 1's

Of the thousands of table wines made in Australia today, I have allocated a highest possible Wine Ranking of 1 to a mere seventeen. These are the wines that time and again perform to the highest standard. Each has its particular stamp, its special quality and personal identity. To a major degree, each wine reflects the character of the individual or company whose name it carries. Each certainly reflects vintage variation from year to year, usually without compromising the special qualities associated with the label.

I believe these are the modern benchmarks, the wines against which others can be measured. As a group they are continually improving, but together they define the limits of contemporary Australian wine.

Bannockburn Chardonnay

Gary Farr's complex and ever-so-classical chardonnay: low-yielding fruit from the Bellarine Peninsula given the full Burgundian treatment.

Bass Phillip Reserve Pinot Noir

Australia's best and longest-living pinot noir: a frustratingly rare, full orchestra wine capable of stunning evolution and expression. From Gippsland, by Phillip Jones.

Best's Thomson Family Shiraz

Sourced from some of Australia's oldest shiraz vines, this wine is about intensity and purity of dark spicy fruit, style, elegance and a wonderfully tight-knit and fine-grained backbone.

Cullen Cabernet Sauvignon Merlot

An essay in concentration and refinement from Margaret River. The piercing intensity, classically refined structure and enormous potential of Vanya Cullen's premier wine leaves little to the imagination.

De Bortoli Noble One

From the Riverina comes Australia's best and most consistent dessert wine: this sumptuous, concentrated elixir by Darren De Bortoli is an essay in the marriage of late-harvest semillon with noble rot.

Giaconda Chardonnay

My pick as Australia's finest chardonnay, extraordinarily structured and complete, expressing a heritage more Burgundian than Australian. From Rick Kinzbrunner at Beechworth in Victoria.

Grosset Polish Hill

A modern icon in Australian wine, Jeffrey Grosset's standout Clare Valley Riesling stretches the limits of what this most traditional of Australian wines can achieve.

Henschke Hill of Grace

In a country full of spectacular single vineyard shiraz wines, Steven Henschke's signature wine from this individual Eden Valley vineyard is the best and most important.

Howard Park Cabernet Sauvignon Merlot

Simply a dream cabernet created by John Wade, sourced from a number of growers in the Great Southern and Margaret River, Western Australia's two most important wine regions.

Leeuwin Estate Chardonnay

At the forefront of Australian chardonnay since its first vintage in 1980, this luscious and long-living Margaret River wine by Bob Cartwright has been for many palates the real 'white Grange'.

Moss Wood Cabernet Sauvignon

A true perfectionist, Keith Mugford makes this classically restrained, reserved and long-living cabernet sauvignon, a cornerstone of Margaret River's reputation for red wine. The latest releases see more richness and more oak.

Mount Mary Cabernet 'Quintet'

An inspiration by John Middleton in Victoria's Yarra Valley. The nearest Australian wine to a premier Bordeaux red and a global standard in its own right.

Penfolds Bin 707 Cabernet Sauvignon

The most eloquent expression of Penfolds' approach to red wine, but directed towards cabernet sauvignon. John Duval and his team direct the pick of their entire South Australian cabernet crop towards Bin 707.

Penfolds Grange

Australia's definitive red wine, a model of style, consistency and quality ever since its inception by Max Schubert in 1951. Based on Barossa Valley fruit, with contributions from other South Australian regions, plus cabernet sauvignon.

Petaluma Chardonnay

Brian Croser's highly intellectual approach to chardonnay now pays full dividends in a tightly crafted, infinitely complex and sophisticated wine sourced from a variety of 'distinguished sites' in the Piccadilly Valley.

Petaluma Coonawarra

While its regional origins may be the subject of present debate, there's no denying that with the release of the 1997 and 1998 vintages, Petaluma's Coonawarra has joined the elite.

Pierro Chardonnay

The role model for so many of Australia's more opulent and hedonistically proportioned chardonnays, this stunning expression of Margaret River chardonnay is made by Mike Peterkin.

The OnWine Wine of the Year

In the December 1998 – January 1999 issue of *Jeremy Oliver's OnWine Report* I introduced the first OnWine Wine of the Year, Rosemount Estate's stunning Mountain Blue Shiraz Cabernet Sauvignon 1996. From the first edition of the third volume of the *OnWine Report* I have nominated a Wine of the Edition for each issue, from which I have chosen the OnWine Wine of the Year, also featured in the July – August 2000 issue of the OnWine Report.

While the Wine of the Edition does not necessarily represent the best wine I have tasted since the previous issue, quality clearly remains paramount. Significantly, the wine must be commercially available at time of publication and represent some special characteristic of individuality, achievement, maturity or longevity. Wines selected must make a statement about style, terroir and winemaking direction.

I now introduce the finalists for the OnWine Wine of the Year, and the winner itself.

Wine of the Year:

Cullen Cabernet Sauvignon Merlot 1998
(May/June 2000)

A benchmark cabernet by Vanya Cullen of rare poise and suppleness. Its minty cassis and mulberry fruit integrates perfectly with cedary and vanilla oak, while the fineness of its firm tannins and the smoothness of its palate serve as a winemaking yardstick. It's a rare delight today to find a cabernet blend that offers almost indescribable depth of flavour while retaining unmistakable elegance and fineness. It would do a lot of Australian winemakers a great deal of good to taste this sort of wine today. Three thousand châteaux in Bordeaux can't be wrong!

Finalists:

Ashton Hills Reserve Pinot Noir 1997
(October/November 1999)

Stephen George has created perhaps the most varietally complete South Australia pinot noir yet. The best from an exceptionally consistent sequence of vintages since 1993, this is a wild, briary wine with many, many layers of red and black cherry fruit. Its earthy, floral and musky complexity lends it the multi-dimensional character you expect in top Burgundy. It's supple, willowy and concentrated, smooth as silk yet it's certainly no lightweight. There's a hint of mint, plum and beetroot, while its spices are as exotic as they are aromatic. Its excellent length, weight and balance of tight-knit extract will see it mature for several years.

Delatite VS Riesling 1999
(March/April 1999)

A cracker of a riesling grown and made at the Ritchie family's Delatite vineyard and winery near Mansfield in the Victorian highlands. Delatite's first riesling plantings were towards the top and bottom of the steep ironstone hills of its vineyard. In the extremely dry 1999 season winemaker Rosalind Ritchie noticed that its fruit was substantially different from that grown on younger vines over the rest of the property. Made separately, the VS Riesling has a complex, musky perfume of lime/floral riesling and an underlying mineral scent. It's long and austere yet delivers a fleshy concentration of bright citrus fruit before a lingering savoury finish of wet slate and tangy acidity. It could be left with confidence until 2007-2011 or even further.

Penfolds Eden Valley Reserve Riesling 1999
(December 1999/January 2000)

Penfolds' first Eden Valley Reserve Riesling boasts a depth of perfume and musky aromatics that leave most rieslings trailing in its wake. Furthermore, its superb length of concentrated essential riesling fruit finishes with refreshing and tingling acidity. Sure, it's marginally sweet, but as far as I am concerned, a perfectly valid expression of the variety. It's bursting with citrus rind and deciduous fruit aromas and its fleshy, juicy mouthfeel has something Alsatian about it that I rather enjoy. Unlike the steelier rieslings bottled under the Leo Buring and Lindemans labels, this isn't a super long-term wine, suited to drinking now or after another five years.

Petaluma Coonawarra 1992
(October/November 1999)

A re-release of Petaluma's Coonawarra blend of cabernet sauvignon and merlot from 1992, this long-term wine is now beginning to express some of the fleshiness and creaminess it will acquire with future cellaring. Unusual for a Petaluma, it reveals a brambly, almost wild and meaty expression of blackberry fruit, supported by cedary and vanilla oak, some leathery bottle development and a faint background suggestion of eucalypt. It's restrained, stylish and very reserved, with a nutty, savoury finish and long, dry finish of tight tannins.

Tim Adams The Aberfeldy 1998
(July/August 2000)

A first-rate shiraz which flies directly against the over-ripe and over-oaked wines so popular today, The Aberfeldy is a selection from an individual Clare Valley vineyard of considerable age. Built around a firm, tight-knit backbone it's deep, dark and heady, opening layer after layer of wild, brambly dark berry fruits and dusty vanilla oak. Its length and potential to develop in the bottle are exceptional, while its retail price of around $45 is simply no reflection of its quality.

2000 Australian vintage report

It was a tough, demanding vintage whose 1.15 million tonnes finished a little less than 15% below expectations of 1.3 million tonnes, but Australia did harvest more red winegrapes from 2000 than it did in the record-breaking 1999 season. Much of the shortfall in tonnage affected white grapes, especially chardonnay, which has had the immediate effect of shelving any talk about an Australian chardonnay surplus, for the time being at least. Personally, I favour the view that it's time for Australians to begin planting chardonnay again, especially in quality areas. For the first time in recent years the mix of red to white grapes harvested was about 50:50, a dramatic change from the 1999 ratio of 60% white grapes.

Poor fruit set across most major regions was the initial factor which reduced yields, followed by an especially hot January – February period which reduced berry sizes. From a quality perspective, grapes tended to ripen too quickly, causing sugar levels to far exceed flavour development and creating serious headaches for those wondering when to harvest fruit. Then heavy rains in late February brought fruit splitting problems and fungal disease issues. Fortunately the later and more southerly regions got out of jail with a late Indian summer prior to harvest, keeping disease and splitting problems down to a minimum. Despite mixed news from much of the continent, the Hunter Valley and Margaret River both experienced nigh-perfect vintages, especially for red wines.

New South Wales

While the Hunter Valley literally had the Vintage of the Century, with few able to decry this claim at this early stage, Mudgee's hopes for 2000 were washed away with rains prior to and during harvest. Early-harvested whites could be okay. Both the Upper and Lower Hunter Valleys experienced some of their driest, hottest and potentially greatest years on record, with shiraz surpassing expectations even for 1998. The semillons may be too rich to be classic. While the Riverlands, responsible for much of Australia's cheaper chardonnay, cabernet sauvignon and shiraz, didn't fare as badly as some regions, crops were certainly down and quality below par. Cowra's vintage caught some of the rain and crops are leaner and tighter than usual.

South Australia

South Australia's best wine regions bore much of the brunt during this difficult vintage, especially the Barossa Valley and McLaren Vale, where many crops were reduced by as much as 40-60% and even then had a tough time ripening their reduced yields. Accelerated ripening under extreme heat made it virtually impossible to harvest shiraz and cabernet with their usual richness, while the late arrival of Tropical Cyclone Steve then dumped over two inches of rain on the McLaren Vale's stressed and soft-skinned fruit, bringing on downy mildew. Some parcels of Barossa cabernet from Lyndoch do however show significant potential. Clare experienced much the worst of South Australia's heat and many growers didn't have the water to keep their riesling and shiraz vines ticking. Yields are down, but reds could be powerful and concentrated, provided they're not too jammy. Fortunately, the Adelaide Hills and Eden Valley both fared better, avoiding the extremes of heat, producing some very promising cabernet and shiraz. Coonawarra and the state's southeast around Padthaway and Wrattonbully also had an easier time ripening shiraz and cabernet fruit in cooler conditions, even if poor crop levels made it hard to find cabernet grapes at some Coonawarra vineyards. Wrattonbully shiraz could be exceptional. Langhorne Creek was another region to experience a difficult year, although the vigorous young red vines planted over the last five to seven years helped pull through with some sound wines. South Australia's Riverlands enjoyed one of its better red vintages.

Tasmania

If there was a state to prosper from 2000, that state is Tasmania. Although the south and east of the state is still enduring its worst drought ever – a factor which doubtless has contributed to reduced yields – Tasmania's summer and autumn were close to perfect, consistently warm without ever becoming really hot. Naturally enough, winemakers are excited about quality, as many regions doubtless experienced their best, if earliest, vintages ever. Pinot noir fared particularly well, with intense colours and flavours.

Victoria

Victoria's 2000 vintage was another early one, brought on early by the heat. Viticulturally the challenge was to harvest fruit that was not excessively jammy and porty, especially north and west of the Great Divide, while even in some of the cooler regions like the Yarra Valley and Mornington Peninsula it appears that some growers were caught napping by the heat and harvested too late. Yields in the Yarra Valley were by-and-large well below normal despite a generally dry and disease-free season. Look to the cooler sites for the better pinot noirs in both regions. Under its third consecutive season of drought, Geelong's fate will be determined by how well growers managed to protect their grapes against the heat with whatever water they had remaining. Low crops from central and western Victoria are likely to produce portier, jammier shiraz and cabernet than usual, while the Sunraysia area reports some of the best reds for around twenty years, although Grape Vine Yellows (GVY) were observed through sections of chardonnay vines. Similarly, the rich reds and fortified muscats and tokays from the state's northeast simply revelled under the hot sun.

Western Australia

Vintages like 2000 remind you how big WA actually is. While Margaret River experienced an ideal red wine vintage with a warm start and a lingering, dry Indian summer to put the finishing touches to the ripening process, the cooler, more southerly and later parts of the Great Southern region had a forgettable time. However riesling, cabernet sauvignon and possibly shiraz from the northerly extremes around Frankland River could be exceptional. Most importantly, Margaret River cabernets from 2000 should be muscular and first-rate, even from the more southerly extremes of the region. Provided the fruit was adequately shaded, its chardonnays and semillon sauvignon blanc blends should look smart as well, if fleshier than usual. Shiraz has ripened well, without the green edge usually seen in the region. Pemberton and Manjimup's season was drier than 1999 and while the hot summer should remove the green edges from its red wines, it could be a top chardonnay vintage there. The Swan Valley received a drenching in January, producing lighter reds and crisp whites, some with botrytis.

Seasonal variation and quality

It's clear just by glancing through this book that the same grapes from the same vineyard invariably produce very different wines from year to year. Although vintage variation in Australia is merely a fraction of that encountered in most European wine regions of any quality, it is still a significant variable which demands consideration when making informed buying decisions.

Even in the event that all other variables are consistent from year to year, which they are certainly not, weather provides the greatest single influence in wine quality and style from season to season. Weather can influence wine in an infinite number of ways, from determining whether conditions at flowering are favourable or not, all the way through to whether final ripening and harvest occur in the warmth of sunshine or through the midsts of damaging rains. If viticulturists were to turn pagan, it would be to a god of weather that they would build their first shrine.

Weather-influenced seasonal variation is nearly always more pronounced and more frequent in the cooler, more marginal viticultural regions. While Australia is principally a warm to hot wine producing nation, a significant proportion of the country's premium wine now comes from cooler regions in the southwestern and southeastern corners of the continent. The spectrum of diverse weather encountered in these regions far exceeds that of the traditional Australian wine growing areas like the Barossa Valley, McLaren Vale, central Victoria and the Clare Valley. Paradoxically it seems, the best years in cool climates are actually the warmer seasons which accelerate the ripening period, creating a finer acid balance, superior sugar levels, flavours and better-defined colours.

Variety by variety, this is how Australia's premium wine grapes are affected by seasonal conditions:

White wines

Chardonnay Cool years cause chardonnay and most white varieties to accumulate higher levels of mineral acids and to result in lean, tight wines with potential longevity, provided they have sufficient intensity of fruit. Cool year chardonnays can display greenish flavours and can resemble grapefruit and other citrus fruit, especially lemon. Warmer year wines become richer and rounder, with fruit flavours more suggestive of apple, pear, quince and cumquat. In hot seasons, chardonnays become faster-maturing wines with flavours of peach, cashew, melon and tobacco.

Riesling Although riesling does not need to ripen to the sugar levels necessary for a premium chardonnay, cool-season riesling tends to be lean and tight with hard steely acids, possibly lacking in length and persistence of flavour. Better rieslings from superior years have succulent youthful primary fruit flavours of ripe pears and apples, with musky, citrus rind undertones. Significantly broader and less complex than wines from better seasons, warmer year rieslings tend to mature faster, occasionally becoming broad and fat on the palate after a short time.

Sauvignon Blanc Cool season sauvignon blancs tend to be hard-edged wines with steely acids, with over-exaggerated and undesirable herbaceous flavours suggestive of asparagus and cat pee, a description for which I have yet to find a polite alternative nearly as succinct. The warmer the season the riper the fruit becomes and the less grassy and vegetal the aroma. The downside is often a reduction in the intensity of the wine's primary fruit flavours. Expect sweet blackcurrants, gooseberries and passionfruit from sauvignon blancs in good seasons, with at least a light capsicum note. Warmer seasons create broader, occasionally oily and less grassy wines, with tropical fruit flavours suggestive of passionfruit and lychees.

Semillon Semillon tends to react to cooler seasons by creating very tight, lean wines with more obvious grassy influences but without much in the way of primary fruit character. On occasions these rather one-dimensional young wines can develop stunning flavours in the bottle over many years, as classically unoaked Hunter semillon shows time and again.

Red wines

Cabernet Sauvignon A late-ripening grape variety which reacts very poorly to cool, late seasons, cabernet sauvignon has traditionally and wisely been blended with varieties like merlot (in Bordeaux) and shiraz (commonly, until recently in Australia). Cool season cabernet sauvignon makes the classic doughnut wine: intense cassis/raspberry fruit at the front of the palate with greenish, extractive tannin at the back and a hole in the middle. Under-ripe cabernet sauvignon has less colour and a thin, bitter finish. Its tannins are often greenish and under-ripe, tasting sappy or metallic, while its flavour can be dominated by greenish snow pea influences more suggestive of cool-climate sauvignon blanc.

Warmer seasons create much better cabernet, with genuinely ripe cassis/plum flavours, a superior middle palate and fine-grained, fully-ripened tannins, although a slight capsicum note can still be evident. In hot years the wines tend to become jammy and porty, suggestive of stewed, cooked fruit flavours and lacking in any real definition and fineness of tannin.

Pinot Noir Pinot noir does not react well to very cool seasons, becoming herbal and leafy, with a brackish, greenish palate and simple sweet raspberry confection fruit. Warmer seasons produce the more sought-after primary characters of sweet cherries and plums, fine-grained tannins and spicy, fleshy middle palate. Too warm a season and the wine turns out to be undefined, simple and fast maturing, often with unbalanced and hard-edged tannins.

Shiraz Thin and often quite greenish – but rarely to the same extent as cabernet sauvignon – cool-season shiraz often acquires leafy white pepper characters, with spicy, herby influences. Provided there's sufficient fruit, which may not be the case in wine from cool seasons, it can still be a worthwhile wine, although not one likely to mature well in the bottle, especially with metallic, sappy and green-edged tannins. Warmer years create shiraz with characteristic richness and sweetness, with riper plum, cassis and chocolate flavours and fully-ripened tannins. Hot year shiraz is often typified by earthy flavours suggestive of bitumen and leather.

Trends in Australian wine

I've no doubt that the best Australian wines made today are the best Australian wines of all time. Trouble is, there should be more of them. Sadly, our winemakers appear to be too easily distracted from what they should be doing. Take our white wines, for instance, from 1999 in particular. Not a great vintage in most regions, but winemakers just can't blame the weather for some seriously under-performing whites, especially from riesling and chardonnay.

Were they all spending too much attention on their reds? If so, they're working too hard, for despite a generally magnificent Australian red wine season in 1998, there are still far too many red wines whose making miserably fails to realise the potential of this special vintage.

There are problems with many contemporary Australian reds, issues that surely relate to who and what is able to influence our winemakers. Too many Australian red wines are made from fruit which has travelled well beyond normal ripeness, be it flavour or physiological. Not only do these wines taste of shrivelled, dried out fruits such as prunes and raisins, but they lack life and freshness, the sort of vitality which can make even ten year-old wines taste young. These wines taste old when they're released, flat and tired, and typically beefed up by oak which has to be applied in excess to give them any sort of palate sweetness at all. Claiming longevity, their makers are surely horrified to observe how quickly these 'souper-wines' peak and plummet.

Makers also need to rediscover the benefits of maintaining better microbial control over the making and presentation of their wines, for the pendulum towards 'natural winemaking' has swung too far. Too many reds are now too 'feral' and reductive in their youth and don't improve. The winemaker's typical defence is that these wines taste more complete and complex while young and besides, the media loves them. Seduced by obvious concentration, oblivious to alcoholic strengths bordering on the levels usually associated with fortified wines and 'complexity' resultant from slack winemaking, many wine critics are indeed guilty as charged, especially some of the more influential figures in the US media, at whose feet some of the blame for the sheer waste of a decade of fine seasons can surely be laid. Some makers of what have become expensive Australian wines patently make their reds to suit such commentators, all the while entirely prepared to lose credibility within the domestic Australian market in the sure and comfortable knowledge that their wines can and do fetch spectacular prices in the US.

Surprisingly this trend, which began with shiraz, is now flowing in the cabernet direction. Too many makers appear convinced that the more their cabernet resembles their shiraz, the quicker it will sell. Too often cabernet is also picked too ripe, before being pumped up with alcohol, oak and tannin so that any semblence it might have had to fineness, elegance or trueness to type has vanished long before bottling. Since vine plantings in Australia over the last four years have favoured red grapes and our irrigated river areas, these concerns are now even tipping over into less expensive bottled wines and are no longer restricted to certain idiosyncratic red labels.

Australian wine makers need to work harder to fully grasp the opportunity facing them. They'll have to pay more attention to detail as fruit is ripening and after it arrives in the winery. Perhaps they might even look again at the old filter gathering dust in the corner of the winery…

Tasting wine

Wine tasting is essentially a play in three parts in which the third part – the tasting itself – is only entered into after a sight and a sniff. We begin by looking at the wine. Use a clear glass, shaped like a tulip and without cuts or grooves. ISO standard glasses are easy to find and strongly recommended. Grab the glass by the stem – that way the bowl stays clear and you won't warm wines above their serving temperature with the heat of your hand. Fill your glass to its widest point (actually very low for a tasting glass) and you're ready to go.

Tilt the glass against a white background, preferably in a well-lit place. The colours in the wine should now be easier to detect. White wines tend to begin life with a green colour, after which with age they move to straw and then yellow, finally to a yellow-amber and brown, at which stage it is usually time to return them to the earth from whence they came. Wood-matured whites are often released with a more advanced colour, resulting from the slow and controlled oxidation they experience in the casks, which is a form of ageing itself.

Reds begin purple, moving to purple-red, red, red-brown, and finally to that tawny brown, usually suggesting that the teeth have well and truly fallen out.

Now check for clarity and brightness. All wines should be filter-bright, as the expression goes, apart from some exceptions from unfiltered pinot noir (rare) and unfiltered chardonnay (rarer). A wine should not look cloudy, hazy, ropy, muddy or any of the colours not previously mentioned. Test this by holding up your glass and looking straight through it from (a) the sides and (b) the top. Bits of cork, crystal or sediment (usually the same colour as the wine itself) in the wine are no cause for alarm. Simply take a little care in pouring or decanting to avoid confronting them later on in the glass.

The nose is next. If you've seen the concentrated sniffing of professional tasters at work you could be forgiven for thinking there was something pretty hypnotic in those glasses. This bit looks terribly impressive, but it works.

Hold the glass by its stem and swirl the wine around once or twice. Put your nose right inside (remember, you didn't fill it to the top) and take a large sniff before the wine has stopped moving. Isn't that more intense? And don't worry, you will soon get used to the way people start looking at you.

A wine's smell can be divided into those flavours derived from its 'grapiness' or 'aroma', and those flavours which result from the wine's own development in the bottle by new flavouring compounds formed as other flavours break down and recombine within the wine, collectively known as the 'bouquet'. Young wines show a dominance of 'aroma' in their nose, while older, more developed wines can reveal almost 100% bouquet. The aromas and bouquets of classic grape varieties, like cabernet sauvignon and riesling, are remarkably consistent from wine to wine and can become quite identifiable by the drinker. It just becomes a matter of becoming familiar with what to look for.

As wine ages, its bouquet becomes less assertive as its different components blend together in a harmonious way. With excessive age, it goes flat, loses its quality and tends to become dominated by a single flavour. Wines that are too old have a dull, toffee-like nose, or may even smell like vinegar, in which case it has gone acetic.

The nose is a great aid in the detection of winemaking faults, for smells of decaying vegetables, old socks, burnt rubber, onion-skins or foreign objects often signal disaster. Some faults are tolerated a little more than others, largely because different people have a different threshold level to different smells, while some of us are more tolerant of slight imperfections if the ultimate impression is generally pleasing.

Finally, have a taste. Do this with confidence and a degree of aggression. Take a good mouthful of wine; there's no sense in mucking around with a polite sip. Purse your lips slightly and suck in a little air, which will evaporate volatile wine flavours and shoot them up to the olfactory centre underneath your brain, which is where you detect smell. Once again, it's like turning up the intensity of flavour.

The tasting ability of your mouth is extremely restricted, and most of the perception of wine flavour takes place as I have just described. Apart from being able to detect hot and cool flavours like curry and mint, the tongue can only distinguish four things: sweetness at its tip, saltiness at its front sides, acidity along the sides and bitterness across the very back.

Fruit flavours are generally tasted towards the front of the mouth, where you can also detect if the wine is sweet or dry. Acidity and sweetness are frequently capable of rendering the other less noticeable, often to the point when you wonder if the other is there at all. It is also possible to mistake a wine's fruitiness for sweetness, which is a trap when trying to describe them.

Acid is essential in all wine – for in addition to the freshness and tang it gives to round off flavour, it is also a preservative against bacteria. Wines which lack acid taste fat, flabby and overly broad, before falling away and finishing short in the mouth. Try to think of acid as the punctuation which finishes the taste.

Tannins can be derived from the skins, stalks and seeds of grapes, and some can be picked up from new oak barrels if the wine is matured or fermented in wood. Although wood tannins are generally softer, both are generally detected by the rasping, bitter taste (more of a sensation, really) that puckers up the inside of your mouth as they corrode away the proteins of your mouth lining. Don't be too worried, nobody has ever required surgery as a result.

Wines should deliver some magnitude of impact from the front of your palate – around your teeth – all the way along the palate to the back of your tongue. Furthermore, the flavour should persist after the wine has been swallowed or, if it's the expected protocol, spat out.

Finally, you should be left with the impression that all of the different facets of the wine, both textural and flavour-related, are in some form of harmony and balance. As such, there shouldn't be any single feature, such as oak for instance, which over-dominates any other. Neither should tannin, acid or any other aspect of the wine. Fruit is of course a legitimate exception to this and is the only facet of a decent wine which can lay an unchallenged claim to centre stage. Fine wines are indeed, as the cliché suggests, a harmonious balance of its constituent components. Although they may seem excessively tannic to drink at a young age, even the traditional Australian cellaring red wines based around shiraz and cabernet sauvignon must be in excellent balance not only to survive, but actually to improve with the test of time.

Investing in wine

While I continue to believe that only a small number of people will actually make a regular and consistent profit from wine investment, the number of opportunities for people to invest in wine is increasing with each passing week. In Australia, at least, the last four years have seen a plethora of new wine auction houses, some of whose offerings I would regard with considerable scepticism. More recently, the Internet has facilitated a further invasion of what Langton's and Oddbins would once have regarded as their sacred turf.

You can now bid, tender or make outright purchases of wines from the comfort of your own workstation. The possibilities are already seemingly without limit, so one can only imagine the innovative new ways to buy wine that will surely emerge over the next twelve months.

Recent experiences of mine involving buying wine at auction and from commercial wine cellaring operations reinforce the concerns that should be at front of mind for every wine buyer and investor. Irrespective of its label or price, wine is a perishable thing that is only as good as the way it has been kept and transported. I have lately paid large amounts for now-prestigious Australian wines for the corporate tastings I conduct, only to be horrified at the condition of an alarmingly high proportion of the bottles opened, many of which were not even that old. A high percentage revealed the dullness, flatness and prematurely advanced nature I know comes directly from poor cellaring conditions in which bottles have been left to age amid fluctuating temperatures. The results are lethal, permanent. But how do you tell which bottles have been affected before you open them? Other than being alert to bad ullage levels for the wine's age, there's little you can do other than to trust the source you're buying from. But do they really know where their stock came from? Or do they care?

I have every reason to expect that a frighteningly large amount of the huge volumes of wine now appearing on the secondary market have been kept in conditions far below ideal. You might be able to pass on bad stock for a while, but sooner or later someone is going to drink it, someone is going to get badly burned and want recompense. Just watch the collectors and auction houses start ducking for cover when that happens. Buyers have a right to demand a wine's cellaring history, just as they ask for the pedigree of a dog or a stud bull.

It's no accident at all that I list a number of professional wine cellaring facilities in this book. Their role within this industry will surely expand as buyers demand the accountability they aren't getting today.

In facing the question of whether or not to invest in wine, little has really changed at all. To do it effectively you need to be resourceful, patient and well equipped. The amateur collectors who are placing their superannuation in Australian wine face considerable disappointment if they lack the resources to care for it properly. As I have discussed, you can't just shove it in the garage and start counting the dollars. Because the demand for blue-chip investment wines far outweighs their supply, you will have to take risks on other wines currently rated well below their status. Clearly, you need to know what you are doing. How on earth the syndicated wine investment schemes are ever going to collect enough of the super-premiums they need to justify their existence to their stakeholders, I have little to no idea.

Bounding to the rescue are Langton's Fine Wine Auctions. Australia's market-leading auction house has released its third Classification of Distinguished Australian Wine, a document which has increased in size by 39% since its previous edition published just four years ago in 1996. With 89 different wines on its new list, Langton's is doing what it can to encourage investors to buy more widely, in the directions it recommends. Given Langton's considerable influence in the pricing of wines on the secondary market, were I to be a wine investor I would follow their picks very closely.

As for future price trends, I can't see any reason why the market should take a backward step. A wobble in domestic Australian sales would surely be countered by the increasing proportion of Australian auction wine bought overseas. With the increasing role played by the Internet in this regard, that will only increase. There's still no real reason for the market-leading wines like Grange, Hill of Grace, Mount Mary and Giaconda to drop in price. A realistic approach to Grange prices in future might be to expect a steady and continued increase in the worth of properly cellared stocks, but at a rate much slower than that witnessed in recent years.

As I suggested in last year's edition, there is certainly a spate of new so-called 'ultra-premium' super-cuvée wines, as companies seek the prestige and kudos that accompanies a label that performs like a star at auction. Hardly a week passes by without the emergence of a new sixty-plus dollar label, most of which lack requisite quality, pedigree and longevity. Everyone wants to own the next Penfolds Yattarna, Petaluma Tiers or Clarendon Hills' Astralis. But irrespective of their quality or lack of it, time alone will tell if these wines will be taken as seriously as their makers expect them to be. I can't help the feeling that this bubble will surely burst.

Nobody knows for how long the Australian market can continue to absorb the skyrocketing prices of premium wine. But I have seen the expressions on the faces of regular buyers as they discover new price increases and the time is fast approaching when they won't wear much more. Not only do I still anticipate the emergence of a 'new' class of quality wine priced between $20 and $30, but I expect a great deal more activity in imported wines priced between $30 to $60, as buyers look for better value. Just look at what's coming out of Italy and southern France right now; it's already happening.

I'm equally astonished by the prices fetched at auction for bad years of highly rated Australian labels. Who buys these wines? Do they drink them afterwards, or do they just re-introduce them to the auction houses a few years later? How many owners have some of these bottles actually had?

There are still bargains in Australian wine, at all quality levels. One of the worst parts of my job, which is to identify what they are, is that almost every day I am called by someone I don't know wanting to find what wines he (it is always a he) should buy in order to make an immediate killing on the auction market. I hate it and sometimes don't know what to say or how to say it.

Were I a betting man, I'd still take note of the very affordable prices for imported wines at auction and retail today, and stock up on those. Not a day goes by without them looking more and more competitive against the better level of Australian product. It's inevitable that more Australians will taste quality imported wine over the next few years and then it's just a matter of time before they want to buy it themselves. Australian wine could even lose some important and influential segments of its own market.

Commercial cellaring facilities

Archaeologists of the future may well wonder why so few dwellings made in this day and age are equipped with wine cellars or even have the potential to store wine adequately. Wine drinking, wine buying and wine collecting are at a premium, but what do we do with our newly acquired collection of drinkable classics?

Fortunately an increasingly large number of professionally operated wine cellaring operations are opening their doors. Several of these offer temperature and humidity-controlled conditions, while others offer a fully computerised stock management schedule with ongoing valuations.

Here's a state-by-state listing of several commercially operating wine storage centres:

New South Wales

Anders Josephson Private Wines, Gwanda Bay Manor, Gwandalan, NSW, 2259, (02) 4972 5100

Langton's Fine Wine Auctions, 52 Pitt St, Redfern, NSW, 2016, (02) 9310 4231

Millers Wine Storage, 866 Bourke St, Waterloo, NSW, 2017, (02) 9699 2300

Wine Ark, 1/3 Esther St, Surry Hills, NSW, 2010, 0417 698 860

Queensland

Millers Wine Storage, 98 Montpelier Rd, Bowen Hills, Qld, 4006, (07) 3257 3224

Millers Wine Storage, 6 Newcastle St, Burleigh Heads, Qld, 4220, (07) 5593 5993

Wineaway, Unit 3 Abbotsford Business Centre, Taylor St, Bowen Hills, Qld, 4006, (07) 3852 1891

South Australia

Adelaide Lock-Up Self Storage, cnr Adam & Holden Sts, Hindmarsh, SA, 5007, (08) 8346 4948

Glen Ewin Cellars, Lower Hermitage Rd, Houghton, SA, 5131, (08) 9380 5657

Victoria

Chequered Flag Stables, 5-7 Manikato Ave, Mordialloc, Vic, 3195, (03) 9587 6168

Keystorage, 60 Dawson St, Brunswick, Vic, 3056, (03) 9388 0788

Langton's Fine Wine Auctions, 69 Flinders Lane, Melbourne, Vic, 3000, (03) 9662 3355

Liquid Assets, 100 Nicholson St, Abbotsford, Vic, 3067, (03) 9415 8801

Millers Wine Storage, 601 Little Collins St, Melbourne, Vic, 3000, (03) 9629 1122

WineCare Storage Centre, 28 Transport Drive, Somerton, Vic, 3062, (03) 9308 7500

Western Australia

Australasian Wine Exchange, 263a Hay St, Subiaco, WA, 6008, (08) 9388 8455

John Coppins, 502 Stirling Hwy, Cottesloe, WA, 6011, (08) 9384 0777

Australian wineries, wines and vintages

Region: Great Southern Winemakers: Michael Staniford, Rod Hallett
Viticulturist: Wayne Lange Chief Executive: Merv Lange

Alkoomi is one of the oldest and most important vineyards at Frankland River, to the far north of the Great Southern area of Western Australia. Its long-living, steely Riesling and tight-knit, fine-grained Cabernet Sauvignon are its two flagship wines.

Alkoomi

Wingeballup Road
Frankland WA 6396
Tel: (08) 9855 2229
Fax: (08) 9855 2284

CABERNET SAUVIGNON

Great Southern $$$

1998	17.8	2010	2018
1996	14.8	2001	2004
1995	15.0	2003	2007
1994	16.8	2002	2006
1993	16.4	1998	2001
1992	16.6	1997	2000
1991	16.7		2003+
1990	17.2		2002+
1989	16.5		2001+
1988	16.0	2000	2005

CHARDONNAY

Great Southern $$$

1998	16.3	2000	2003
1997	17.9	2002	2005
1996	16.5	1998	2001
1995	16.0	1997	2000
1994	17.2	1999	2002
1993	17.9	1998	2001
1992	18.0	1997	2000
1991	18.5	1999	2003

RIESLING

Great Southern $$

1999	16.5	2001	2004+
1998	17.3	2006	2010
1997	17.6	2005	2009
1996	17.4	2004	2008
1995	17.4	2000	2003+
1994	18.5	2002	2006
1993	16.3	1998	2001
1992	17.6	1997	2000
1991	17.5	1996	1999

All Saints

All Saints Road
Wahgunyah Vic 3687
Tel: (02) 6033 1922
Fax: (02) 6033 3515

SAUVIGNON BLANC

Great Southern $$$

1999	16.0	2001	2004
1998	16.5	2000	2003
1997	17.2	1998	1999
1996	15.9	1997	1998
1995	16.2	1996	1999

Region: NE Victoria   Winemaker: Peter Brown
Viticulturist: Peter Brown   Chief Executive: Peter Brown

All Saints occupies a marvellous site alongside the banks of the River Murray at Wahgunyah, where its historic castellated winery is a well-known landmark. Its white wines are fresh, fruity and zesty, but recent red releases push the limits of oak influence, perhaps at the expense of some concentrated old vine fruit.

CABERNET SAUVIGNON

NE Victoria $$$

1998	15.2	2003	2006
1997	16.0	2002	2005
1996	16.3	2001	2004
1995	16.6	2003	2007
1994	16.7	2002	2006
1993	15.0	1998	2001
1992	17.0		2004+
1991	16.6	1999	2003

LATE HARVEST SEMILLON

NE Victoria $$

1997	14.5	1998	1999
1996	18.1	2001	2004
1995	16.4	2000	2003
1994	17.3	1996	1999
1993	17.6	1998	2001

MARSANNE

NE Victoria $$

1998	15.2	2003	2006
1997	16.2	1999	2002
1996	16.5	2001	2004
1995	15.8	1997	2000
1994	17.2	1999	2002

MERLOT

NE Victoria $$

1998	16.8	2003	2006
1997	15.0	1999	2002
1996	16.6	2001	2004
1995	15.9	1997	2000

SHIRAZ

NE Victoria $$

1998	16.2	2003	2006
1997	16.4	2002	2005
1996	16.0	1998	2001
1994	17.9	2002	2006+
1993	17.3	2001	2005
1992	16.4	2000	2004
1989	16.5	1997	2003

VINTAGE PORT

NE Victoria $$$

1996	16.8	2004	2008
1994	15.6	2002	2006
1992	17.0		2004+

Region: Lower Hunter Valley Winemakers: Bill Sneddon, Steve Langham
Viticulturist: Bill Sneddon Chief Executive: Wally Atallah

Allandale is a consistent maker of honest, reliable varietal wines
of which the occasional example, like the 1996 Matthew Shiraz
and minerally 1999 Chardonnay are really quite special. Like
several other Hunter-based wineries, Allandale is now sourcing red
grapes from other regions, identifying such blends on their labels.

CABERNET SAUVIGNON

Mudgee, Hilltops (formerly Lower Hunter Valley) $$

1997	15.0	2002	2005
1996	14.5	1998	2001
1994	17.0	1999	2002
1991	17.0	1999	2003
1990	14.0	1992	1995

erley
Road
WA 6282
) 9755 2288
) 9755 2171

CHARDONNAY
Lower Hunter Valley $$$

1999	16.8	2004	2007
1998	14.5	1999	2000
1997	15.7	1998	1999
1996	16.8	1998	2001
1995	17.8	2000	2003
1994	16.6	1996	1999
1993	17.0	1998	2001

MATTHEW SHIRAZ
Lower Hunter Valley $$$

1998	14.8	2000	2003
1996	17.1	2001	2004
1994	14.7	1996	1999
1993	16.0	1998	2001
1991	17.0	1996	1999
1990	17.0	1992	1995

SEMILLON
Lower Hunter Valley $$

1998	15.9	2000	2003+
1997	16.7	2002	2005
1996	17.8	2004	2008
1995	17.0	2000	2003
1993	18.3	2001	2005
1992	17.5	1994	1997

Region: Margaret River Winemakers: Eddie Price, Greg Tilbrook
Viticulturist: Philip Smith Chief Executive: Eddie Price

Home to one of the best winery restaurants in the Margaret River region, Amberley is a maker of delightfully fragrant and zesty white wines of which the Semillon Sauvignon Blanc is the finest example. The Semillon and Chenin Blanc can be fresh and grapey. Warmer seasons like 1996 also see some richness and ripeness in Amberley's Cabernet Merlot and Shiraz red wines.

CABERNET MERLOT
Margaret River $$$

1998	15.3	2003	2006
1997	18.1	2005	2009
1996	17.0	2004	2008
1995	15.8	2000	2003
1994	16.1		2006+
1993	17.4	2001	2005
1992	17.6	2000	2004
1991	16.6	1999	2003

CHARDONNAY

Margaret River $$$

1999	16.0	2001	2004
1997	15.6	1998	1999
1996	15.2	1997	1998
1995	16.2	1997	2000

SEMILLON

Margaret River $$$

1999	15.7	2000	2001
1998	16.5	2003	2006
1997	15.0	1998	1999
1996	16.7	2001	2004
1995	16.5	1997	2000
1994	17.3	1999	2002
1993	16.6	1998	2001
1992	16.0	1997	2000
1991	16.2	1992	1993

SEMILLON SAUVIGNON BLANC

Margaret River $$$

1999	17.2	2004	2007
1998	17.3	2001	2004
1997	16.6	1998	1999
1996	18.5	1998	2001
1995	14.6	1996	1997
1994	16.8	1996	1999
1993	16.7	1998	2001

SHIRAZ

Margaret River $$$

1998	14.7	2000	2003
1997	16.8	2002	2005
1996	18.0	2004	2008
1995	14.8	1997	2000
1994	14.0	1996	1999

Andrew Garrett is one of the Mildara Blass stable and can usually
be relied upon for fruity, clean table wines sourced from South
Australia's better areas. The wines are made for early drinking and
other than the Cabernet Merlot are best opened young.

BOLD SHIRAZ

McLaren Vale $$

1998	15.5	2000	2003
1997	16.0	1999	2002
1996	15.7	1998	2001
1994	16.3	1996	1999
1993	17.3	1998	2001
1992	17.1	1997	2000
1991	16.8	1996	1999

CABERNET MERLOT

Coonawarra, Adelaide Hills, McLaren Vale $$

1998	15.6	2003	2006
1997	16.0	2002	2005
1996	15.0	1998	2001
1994	16.6	2002	2006
1993	16.7	1998	2001
1992	17.0	1997	2000
1991	16.8	1996	1999

CHARDONNAY

McLaren Vale, Padthaway $$

1999	15.0	2000	2001
1998	16.5	1999	2000
1997	16.0	1998	1999
1996	15.0	1997	1998
1995	17.6	2000	2003
1994	15.8	1996	1999

SAUVIGNON BLANC SEMILLON (FORMERLY SAUVIGNON BLANC)

Padthaway $$

1999	14.0		2000
1998	17.5	1999	2000
1996	14.8	1996	1997
1995	16.5	1996	1997

Region: Clare Valley Winemaker: David O'Leary
Viticulturist: Peter Pawelski Chief Executive: Terry Davis

It's taken just a few years for Annie's Lane to become one of the
best of Mildara Blass' brands. Winemaker David O'Leary
consistently provides pristine varietal wines at surprisingly low
prices. I strongly recommend the Shiraz and Riesling.

CABERNET MERLOT

Clare Valley $$$

1998	17.2	2003	2006
1997	16.0	2002	2005
1996	15.0	1998	2001
1995	18.3	2003	2007

CHARDONNAY

Clare Valley $$$

1999	16.8	2001	2004
1998	16.2	2000	2003
1997	16.9	1999	2001
1996	18.3	1998	2001

RIESLING

Clare Valley $$

2000	16.8	2002	2005
1999	14.8	2000	2001
1998	18.4	2003	2006+
1997	17.2	2005	2009
1996	18.3	1998	2001

SEMILLON

Clare Valley $$

1999	16.0	2004	2007
1998	17.6	2000	2003
1997	16.0	1999	2002
1996	18.2	2004	2008

SHIRAZ

Clare Valley $$$

1998	17.0	2003	2006
1997	16.8	2002	2005
1996	17.0	2001	2004
1995	16.4	2000	2003

THE CONTOUR SHIRAZ

Clare Valley $$$$$

1997	18.2	2005	2009
1996	18.6	2004	2008+
1995	17.3	2003	2007

Region: Adelaide Hills Winemaker: Stephen George
Viticulturist: Stephen George Chief Executive: Stephen George

Having one of the finalists in this year's OnWine Wine of the Year, my respect for Ashton Hills as a leading maker of Australian pinot noir increases each year. Its Obliqua cabernet blend is made along similar lines, creating a distinctive and different style, while the whites are similarly individual in their outlook.

CHARDONNAY

Adelaide Hills $$$$

1998	15.6	2000	2003
1997	17.2	2002	2005
1996	15.4	1997	1998
1995	17.0	1996	1997
1993	18.5	1998	2001
1992	15.4	1997	2000

OBLIQUA

Adelaide Hills $$$

1997	16.2	2002	2005
1996	16.7	2004	2008
1994	17.6	1999	2002
1992	16.2	1997	2000
1991	18.6	1999	2003
1990	18.3	1998	2002

PINOT NOIR

Adelaide Hills $$$$

1998	16.8	2000	2003
1997	18.9	2002	2005+
1996	18.6	2001	2004
1995	18.3	2000	2003
1994	18.6	2002	2006
1993	18.3	1998	2001

RIESLING

Adelaide Hills $$

1999	17.9	2004	2007+
1998	18.1	2006	2010
1997	18.4	2005	2009
1996	17.2	2004	2008
1995	15.0	1997	2000
1994	18.3	1999	2002
1993	18.3	1998	2001
1992	16.5	1997	2000
1991	18.0	1996	1999
1990	17.0	1995	1998

SALMON BRUT

Adelaide Hills $$$$

1995	17.0	1997	2000
1994	15.1	1996	1999
1993	16.4	1998	2001
1992	14.0	1994	1997

Region: NE Victoria Winemaker: Allan Hart
Viticulturist: Mick Clayton Chief Executive: Terry Davis

Its renewed focus on its resources of old vines shiraz has seen Baileys take great strides with the 1920s Block Shiraz, a thick, sinewy wine built for the long term. The initial release of 1904 Block Shiraz from 1998 lacks immediate charm but will cellar well.

1920S BLOCK SHIRAZ

NE Victoria $$$

1998	18.2		2010+
1997	16.3	2002	2005
1996	16.5	2001	2004
1995	15.8	2000	2003
1994	18.0		2006+
1993	16.2	1998	2001
1992	17.2	2000	2004
1991	18.4		2003+

Exciting times are ahead for Balgownie, the famous central Victorian vineyard and winery initially established by Stuart Anderson in the 1970s. Lindsay Ross has been given full rein to fashion classically rich Bendigo reds from cabernet sauvignon and shiraz, while the recent change in ownership also heralds a return for the idiosyncratic Pinot Noir and sometimes classic Chardonnay. Balgownie's area under vines is increasing dramatically.

CABERNET SAUVIGNON

Bendigo $$$$

Vintage	Score	Drink from	Drink to
1998	17.7	2006	2012+
1997	17.6	2009	2017
1996	18.5		2008+
1994	18.0		2006+
1993	17.7		2005+
1992	18.3		2004+
1990	18.6		2002+
1989	17.0	1997	2001
1988	18.5		2008+
1987	16.0	1995	1999
1986	18.0		1998+
1985	17.0		2005+
1984	15.0	1992	1996
1983	14.0	1988	1991
1982	14.5	1987	1990
1981	15.0	1993	1998
1980	19.0	2000	2005
1979	14.5	1984	1987
1978	18.0	1990	1995
1977	16.0	1985	1989
1976	19.0		1996+

SHIRAZ

Bendigo $$$

Vintage	Score	Drink from	Drink to
1998	16.9	2003	2006+
1997	18.2		2009+
1996	18.0	2004	2008+
1995	18.5		2007+
1994	17.3	2002	2006
1993	18.2		2005+
1990	18.4		2002+
1989	16.0	1994	1997
1988	18.0	1993	1996
1987	16.0	1992	1995
1986	17.0	1991	1994
1985	16.0	1993	1997
1984	15.0	1989	1992

Region: Geelong Winemaker: Gary Farr
Viticulturist: Lucas Grigsby

The enduring quality of its Pinot Noir and Chardonnay establishes
Bannockburn as an icon in Australian wine, while the small-release
(and not inexpensive) Serré and SRH premium wines simply add
lustre to its glowing reputation. Gary Farr says the Geelong climate
presents him with a greater challenge with Shiraz than with Pinot
Noir, a wine he also makes using Burgundian techniques. The most
recent releases were almost entirely made from fruit sourced from
other regions after a hailstorm decimated the vineyard in 1997.

Bannockburn

Box 72 Midland Highway
Bannockburn Vic 3331
Tel: (03) 5281 1363
Fax: (03) 5281 1349

CHARDONNAY

Geelong $$$$

1998	18.0	2003	2006
1997	17.8	2005	2009
1996	18.6	2001	2004
1995	19.1	1997	2000
1994	18.7	2002	2006
1993	18.9	2001	2005
1992	18.5	2000	2004
1991	18.3	1996	1999
1990	18.5		2002+
1989	18.6	1997	2001
1988	18.6	1996	2000

PINOT NOIR

Geelong $$$$

1998	17.3	2003	2006
1997	19.1	2005	2009
1996	18.7	2004	2008
1995	18.4	2000	2003
1994	18.6	2002	2006+
1993	18.4	1998	2001+
1992	16.5	2000	2004
1991	17.9	1999	2003
1990	18.5	1998	2002
1989	18.6	1994	1997
1988	18.7	1996	2000

SERRÉ PINOT NOIR

Geelong $$$$$

1996	19.1	2004	2008+
1995	18.8	2003	2007
1994	18.9	2002	2006+
1993	17.0	2001	2005
1991	13.0	1993	1996
1990	16.5	1998	2002+

SHIRAZ

Geelong $$$$

1998	18.6	2006	2010
1997	18.2	2005	2009
1996	18.1	2004	2008
1995	16.0	2000	2003
1994	18.8	2002	2006
1993	17.2	1998	2001
1992	18.2	2000	2004
1991	18.5		2003+
1990	17.0	1998	2002

SRH CHARDONNAY

Geelong $$$$$

1995	18.5	1997	2000
1994	18.2	1996	1999
1993	19.3	1998	2001

Barossa Valley Estate

Heaslip Road
Angle Vale SA 5117
Tel: (08) 8284 7000
Fax: (08) 8284 7219

Region: Barossa Valley Winemaker: Natasha Mooney
Chief Executive: Bruce Richardson

Its flagship wine, the E&E Black Pepper Shiraz, is a classy modern expression of low-yielding Barossa vineyards to which Natasha Mooney introduces a substantial but balanced degree of American oak. Its recent show success is easy to justify. The Ebenezer wines are generous, flavoursome and uncomplicated.

E&E BLACK PEPPER SHIRAZ

Barossa Valley $$$$$

1997	17.0	2005	2009
1996	18.6	2004	2008
1995	18.2	2007	2015
1994	18.0	2002	2006
1993	18.2	2001	2005
1992	18.4	2004	2012
1991	18.8		2003+
1990	17.0	1998	2002
1989	17.0		2001+

E&E SPARKLING SHIRAZ

Barossa Valley $$$$$

1995	17.6	2000	2003
1994	17.9	1999	2002+
1993	16.8	1998	2001

EBENEZER CHARDONNAY

Barossa Valley $$$

1999	15.3	2000	2001
1998	15.9	1999	2000
1997	16.0	1998	1999
1996	16.0	1997	1998

EBENEZER DRY RED BLEND

Barossa Valley $$$

1998	16.0	2003	2006
1997	14.5	1999	2002
1996	17.6	2001	2004
1994	16.2	1996	1999
1993	14.0	1994	1995
1992	17.0	1997	2000

EBENEZER SHIRAZ

Barossa Valley $$$

1997	16.5	2002	2005
1996	16.6	2001	2004
1995	17.8	2000	2003
1994	17.5	1999	2002
1993	15.8	1998	2001
1992	16.0	1997	2000

Region: Hilltops Winemaker: Jim Brayne
Viticulturist: Murray Pulleine Chief Executive: Kevin McLintock

With each successive release, Barwang's quality becomes less of a surprise and more of an established benchmark. The superbly textured and mealy 1998 Chardonnay and spicy, bony 1998 Shiraz are both outstanding and will develop superbly.

CABERNET SAUVIGNON

Hilltops $$$

1998	17.2	2006	2010+
1997	18.3	2005	2009+
1996	16.0	2001	2004
1995	16.7	2003	2007
1994	17.3	2002	2006
1993	17.6	2001	2005
1992	17.0	2000	2004
1991	18.6	1999	2003
1990	15.8		2002+

CHARDONNAY
Hilltops $$$

1998	18.5	2003	2006
1997	17.2	2002	2005
1996	17.9	2001	2004
1995	16.5	1997	2000
1994	17.5	1996	1999
1993	16.9	1995	1998

SHIRAZ
Hilltops $$$

1998	18.5	2006	2010
1997	18.4	2005	2009
1996	16.3	1998	2001
1995	18.2	2003	2005
1994	17.8	1999	2002
1993	18.3	1998	2001
1992	16.8	2000	2004
1991	17.8	1999	2003
1990	15.5	1998	2002

Bass Phillip

Tosch's Road
Leongatha South Vic 3953
Tel: (03) 5664 3341
Fax: (03) 5664 3209

Region: South Gippsland Winemaker: Phillip Jones
Viticulturist: Phillip Jones Chief Executive: Phillip Jones

Nothing less than exceptional attention to detail and almost impossibly low yields are the reasons for the spectacular consistency experienced with Bass Phillip's various Pinot Noirs. I can't think of too many pinot noir vineyards around the world which perform year after year to the standards maintained by the fastidious Phillip Jones. For the thousands to whom Bass Phillip remains something of an impossible dream, the good news is that future releases will begin to see some of the benefits from new plantings on premium sites near the winery, so volumes of this most scarce of resources can be expected to increase.

PREMIUM PINOT NOIR
South Gippsland $$$$$

1998	18.9	2006	2010
1997	18.7	2002	2005+
1996	18.6	2004	2008
1995	18.6	2003	2007
1994	19.1	2002	2006+
1993	18.6	1998	2001+
1992	18.8	2000	2004
1991	18.0	1996	1999
1990	15.3	1992	1995
1989	18.4	1997	2001

RESERVE PINOT NOIR

South Gippsland $$$$$

Year	Score	Year	Drink
1998	19.0	2006	2010+
1997	19.0	2005	2009
1996	18.8	2004	2008
1995	19.0	2003	2007
1994	19.0	2002	2006
1991	18.8		2003+
1989	18.6	1997	2001
1988	15.4	1996	2000

**Region: Grampians, Great Western Winemakers: Viv Thomson, Michael Unwin
Viticulturist: Ben Thomson Chief Executive: Viv Thomson**

One of the two wines promoted to a Wine Ranking of '1' in this edition is the spectacular Thomson Family Reserve Shiraz, a wine of true style and greatness. It's made from some of the oldest shiraz vines in Australia and presents length, fineness, elegance and longevity rarely encountered today. Its dark, spicy and peppery fruit is beautifully focused. It's also worth noting that the 'standard' Bin 0 Shiraz is not so far behind its more prestigious stablemate and that the 1999 Riesling is a real return to form.

BIN 'O' SHIRAZ

Grampians, Great Western $$$

Year	Score	Year	Drink
1997	17.0	2005	2009
1996	18.5	2004	2008
1995	18.7	2007	2015
1994	16.6	2006	2014+
1993	15.9	1998	2001
1992	18.7	2004	2012
1991	17.6	1999	2003
1990	17.8	1995	1998
1989	16.0	1994	1997
1988	18.0		2000+
1987	15.8	1995	1999

CABERNET SAUVIGNON

Grampians, Great Western $$$

Year	Score	Year	Drink
1997	17.0	2005	2009+
1996	16.6	1998	2001
1995	17.0		2007+
1993	16.2	2001	2005
1992	18.3		2004+
1991	17.2		2003+
1990	17.8	1998	2002
1989	15.0	1991	1994

CHARDONNAY

Grampians, Great Western $$$

1998	15.8	2003	2006
1997	16.5	2002	2005
1996	16.7	1998	2001
1995	18.1	2003	2007
1994	18.4		2006+
1993	16.0	1998	2001
1992	16.6	1997	2000
1991	17.9		2003+
1990	17.5		2002+

PINOT MEUNIER

Grampians, Great Western $$$

1996	15.1	2001	2004
1995	16.4	2003	2007
1994	16.8	2002	2006
1993	15.0	1998	2001
1992	16.8	1997	2000
1991	16.7	1996	1999
1990	16.0	1995	1998
1989	16.5	1994	1997

RIESLING

Grampians, Great Western $$

1999	18.0	2007	2011
1998	16.5	2003	2006
1997	15.0	1999	2002
1996	16.8	1998	2001
1995	18.3	2003	2007
1994	18.4		2006+
1993	15.1	1995	1998
1992	16.8	2000	2004
1991	16.0	1999	2003
1990	17.5	1998	2002
1989	14.3	1991	1994

THOMSON FAMILY SHIRAZ

Grampians, Great Western $$$$$

1997	18.5	2005	2009+
1996	19.4	2008	2016
1995	19.1	2007	2015+
1994	18.7	2006	2014
1992	18.9	2004	2012

Region: Barossa Valley Winemakers: Paul Bailey, Geoff & Robert Schrapel
Viticulturists: Geoff & Robert Schrapel Chief Executives: Geoff & Robert Schrapel

Bethany is a maker of readily approachable and flavoursome Barossa table and fortified wines whose ripe flavours and punchy oak come together relatively early. The GR Reserve Shiraz is soft, luxuriant and silky red which is usually ready to enjoy by release.

CABERNET MERLOT

Barossa Valley $$

1998	16.2	2003	2006
1997	14.7	1999	2002
1996	15.4	1998	2001
1995	16.2	1997	2000
1994	17.0	2002	2006
1993	15.0	1995	1998
1992	16.6	1997	2000
1991	18.0	1999	2003
1990	17.2	1998	2002

GR RESERVE SHIRAZ

Barossa Valley $$$$$

1996	17.2	2001	2004
1995	15.8	2000	2003
1994	17.8	1999	2002+
1992	18.6	2000	2004

RIESLING

Barossa Valley $$

1999	16.7	2001	2004
1998	16.5	2000	2003
1997	14.7	1999	2002
1996	17.0	2001	2004
1995	16.2	2000	2003
1994	16.2	1996	1999
1993	17.0	1995	1998

SELECT LATE HARVEST RIESLING

Barossa Valley $$$

1999	16.5	2001	2004
1998	16.8	2000	2003+
1997	17.2	1999	2002
1996	17.6	2001	2004
1995	16.0	1997	2000
1994	18.2	1999	2002
1993	17.8	1998	2001
1992	17.5	1994	1997

SEMILLON

Barossa Valley $$

1999	16.7	2001	2004
1998	16.8	2000	2003
1997	14.5	1998	1999
1996	14.5	1997	1998
1995	16.3	2000	2003
1994	16.3	1996	1999
1993	18.0	1998	2001
1992	16.8	1997	2000
1991	16.5	1993	1996

SHIRAZ

Barossa Valley $$

1997	15.6	1999	2002+
1996	15.4	1998	2001
1995	16.0	1997	2000
1994	17.0	1999	2002
1993	16.0	1995	1998
1992	18.2	2000	2004
1991	16.9	1999	2003
1990	18.3	1998	2002
1989	17.0	1994	1997
1988	18.2	1996	2000
1987	16.8	1995	1999

**Region: Macedon Winemakers: Stuart Anderson, Michael Dhillon
Viticulturist: Bill Dhillon Chief Executive: Bill Dhillon**

One of the most exciting of small Victorian vineyards, Bindi continues to release cool-climate wines of exceptional quality. Its pinots are very musky, spicy and supple, while the chardonnays are brightly flavoured with citrus and melon fruits, before a taut and mineral finish. The premier 'Block 5 Pinot Noir' and 'Quartz' Chardonnay selections are an amazement for such young vines, while the first releases of Bindi's Macedon sparkling wines are nothing short of spectacular, if almost impossible to find.

CHARDONNAY

Macedon $$$$

1998	16.4	2003	2006
1997	18.1	2002	2005
1996	16.0	1997	1998
1995	18.6	2003	2007
1994	18.3	1999	2002
1993	17.6	1998	2001

PINOT NOIR

Macedon $$$$

1998	17.5	2003	2006
1997	18.4	2002	2005
1996	18.3	2004	2008
1995	18.5	2000	2003
1994	18.5	2002	2006

Region: Bendigo Winemakers: Ian McKenzie, Ken Pollock
Viticulturist: Ian McKenzie Chief Executive: Ian McKenzie

Blackjack is a relatively young maker of fine regional red wines from Bendigo in central Victoria whose depth and richness tends to develop with every passing vintage. The Shiraz shows special promise and is already a reliable candidate for the cellar.

CABERNET MERLOT

Bendigo $$$

1998	16.8	2003	2006
1997	17.0	2005	2009
1996	16.1	2001	2004
1995	15.5	1997	2000
1994	15.0	1996	1999

SHIRAZ

Bendigo $$$

1998	16.8	2003	2006+
1997	17.0	2002	2005
1996	17.0	2001	2004
1995	15.0	1997	2000
1994	16.8	2002	2006
1993	16.5	1998	2001

Region: Langhorne Creek Winemaker: Michael Potts
Viticulturist: Robert Potts Chief Executive: Michael Potts

A plush, smooth and creamy 1997 Bremerview Shiraz is the highlight of a typically ripe, honest and very consistent range of Bleasdale red wines. This vintage also represents the third excellent release on the trot for the premier Frank Potts label.

BREMERVIEW SHIRAZ

Langhorne Creek $$

1997	17.8	2005	2009
1996	16.7	2001	2004
1995	17.0	2000	2003
1993	15.0	1995	1998
1992	16.6	2000	2004
1991	16.7	1999	2003
1988	16.6	1996	2000

FRANK POTTS BLEND

Langhorne Creek $$$

1997	17.2	2005	2009
1996	17.9	2004	2008+
1995	17.8	2003	2007
1994	16.0	1999	2002
1992	14.8	1994	1997

MALBEC

Langhorne Creek $$

1998	16.5	2000	2003
1997	15.5	1998	2001
1996	15.3	1998	2001
1994	16.4	1999	2003
1992	14.9	1997	2000
1990	16.5	1995	1998
1989	16.5	1994	1997

MULBERRY TREE CABERNET SAUVIGNON

Langhorne Creek $$

1998	16.4	2003	2006
1997	16.4	2002	2005+
1996	16.8	2004	2008
1995	15.0	1997	2000
1993	16.0	2001	2005
1992	16.8	2000	2004

Blue Pyrenees Estate

Vinoca Road
Avoca Vic 3467
Tel: (03) 5465 3202
Fax: (03) 5465 3529

Region: Pyrenees Winemaker: Kim Hart
Viticulturist: Kim Hart Chief Executive: Kim Hart

Blue Pyrenees Estate has unquestioned and proven potential to make stylish cabernet blends, chardonnays and sparkling wines from its large and extensively classified vineyard near Avoca. Recent releases haven't lived up to expectations, and the first 'The Richardson' Merlot from 1997 doesn't do the big man justice.

CHARDONNAY

Pyrenees $$$$

1998	16.4	2000	2003
1997	18.0	2002	2005
1996	17.6	2001	2004+
1995	16.6	1997	2000
1994	16.8	1999	2002

RED BLEND

Pyrenees $$$$

1997	16.7	2005	2009
1996	18.1	2008	2016
1995	18.0	2003	2007
1994	18.6		2006+
1993	18.4	2001	2005
1992	17.8	2000	2004
1991	18.3	1999	2003
1990	18.4	2002	2010
1989	16.8	1994	1997
1988	18.5	2000	2008

Region: Mudgee Winemaker: Kevin Karstrom
Viticulturist: Kevin Karstrom Chief Executive: Trina Karstrom

Botobolar is an organic vineyard in Mudgee whose wines depend more than most on seasonal conditions around ripening and harvest. Of course this doesn't prevent it from releasing red and white wines that are simply delicious, if indeed a little different.

CABERNET SAUVIGNON

Mudgee $$

1997	16.2	2002	2005
1992	17.5		2004+
1991	18.0	1999	2003
1990	16.7	1992	1995
1989	17.9	1997	2001

CABERNET SHIRAZ MOURVEDRE (FORMERLY ST GILBERT DRY RED)

Mudgee $$

1996	15.2	1998	2001
1991	16.0	1999	2003
1990	16.8	1998	2002
1989	17.9	1997	2001

CHARDONNAY

Mudgee $$$

1999	14.5	2000	2001
1998	15.0	1999	2000
1997	17.0	1999	2002
1995	15.0	1996	1997
1994	16.6	1996	1999
1993	18.0	1998	2001
1992	17.2	1997	2000

Botobolar

89 Botobolar Road
Mudgee NSW 2850
Tel: (02) 6373 3840
Fax: (02) 6373 3789
E-mail:
botobolar@winsoft.net.au

MARSANNE
Mudgee $$

1999	16.3	2000	2001
1997	15.7	1999	2002
1996	16.8	1998	2001
1995	16.1	1997	2000
1994	16.5	1999	2002
1993	17.8	1998	2001
1992	17.5	1997	2000

SHIRAZ
Mudgee $$

1997	15.2	1999	2002
1996	15.0	1998	2001
1992	18.0	2000	2004
1991	16.0	1999	2003
1990	16.3	1995	1998
1989	18.3	1997	2001

Bowen
Estate

Riddoch Highway
Coonawarra SA 5263
Tel: (08) 8737 2229
Fax: (08) 8737 2173
E-mail: bowenest@penola.
mtx.net.au

Region: Coonawarra Winemaker: Doug Bowen
Viticulturist: Doug Bowen Chief Executive: Joy Bowen

Bowen Estate made a stellar collection of reds from Coonawarra's copybook 1998 season, but none better than the supple and stylish Cabernet Sauvignon, the best for several years from this highly rated winery. Similarly the Shiraz is brightly perfumed and translucently flavoured with pristine spicy berry fruit. I've a feeling though that we have yet to see the best from Bowen Estate.

CABERNET MERLOT
CABERNET FRANC
Coonawarra $$

1998	16.5	2000	2003
1997	16.2	1999	2002
1995	15.8	2000	2003
1994	15.0	1999	2002
1993	16.5	1998	2001
1992	18.0	2000	2004
1991	17.8	1999	2003
1990	18.0	1995	1998
1988	16.5	1993	1996

CABERNET SAUVIGNON

Coonawarra $$$$

Year	Score	From	To
1998	18.7		2010+
1997	16.3	2005	2009
1996	18.6	2008	2016+
1995	15.3	2000	2003
1994	17.1	2002	2006
1993	15.4	1998	2001
1992	18.0		2004+
1991	18.0	1999	2003
1990	18.5	1995	1998
1989	17.5	1994	1997
1988	16.0	1990	1993
1984	18.8	1996	2004

CHARDONNAY

Coonawarra $$

Year	Score	From	To
1998	16.0	1999	2000
1996	16.7	2001	2004
1995	14.9	1997	2000
1994	17.5	1996	1999
1993	17.8	1998	2001
1992	16.6	1994	1997

SHIRAZ

Coonawarra $$$

Year	Score	From	To
1998	18.1	2010	2018
1997	16.5	2005	2009
1996	18.0	2001	2004
1995	17.0	2003	2007
1994	18.0	2002	2006
1993	18.5	2001	2005
1992	18.6	2000	2004
1991	18.3	1996	1999
1990	16.0	1998	2002
1989	17.5	1994	1997
1988	16.5	1993	1996

Boynton's

Great Alpine Road
Porepunkah Vic 3740
Tel: (03) 5756 2356
Fax: (03) 5756 2610
E-mail: boyntons@bright.
albury.net.au

Region: Alpine Valleys Winemaker: Kel Boynton
Viticulturist: Kel Boynton Chief Executive: Kel Boynton

One of Victoria's highest vineyards and wineries, Boynton's is naturally more at the mercy of the elements than other small vineyards located on warmer sites. Given ripe fruit, however, Kel Boynton is more than capable of making very polished and classy red wines of true cellaring potential from several varieties.

CABERNET SAUVIGNON

Alpine Valleys $$$

1998	15.1	2000	2003
1997	17.4	2005	2009
1996	15.7	2001	2004
1995	13.6	1997	2000
1994	18.3	2002	2006
1993	18.2		2005+
1992	17.9	2000	2004
1991	16.0	1996	1999
1990	18.6	1998	2002

CHARDONNAY

Alpine Valleys $$$

1998	16.2	2000	2003
1996	15.4	1998	2001
1995	14.8	1996	1997
1994	16.8	1999	2002

MERLOT

Alpine Valleys $$$

1998	16.8	2000	2003
1997	16.6	1999	2002+
1996	17.2	2001	2004

SHIRAZ

Alpine Valleys $$$

1998	15.8	2000	2003
1997	16.0	2002	2005
1995	14.0	1996	1997
1994	17.6	1999	2002
1993	17.1	1998	2001
1992	17.5	1997	2000
1991	16.3	1996	1999
1990	18.5	1995	1998
1989	18.0	1997	2001

Region: Coonawarra Winemakers: Jim Brayne, Jim Brand
Viticulturist: Bill Brand Chief Executive: Kevin McLintock

Under the watchful eye of McWilliams' chief winemaker Jim Brayne, Brand's is now making the best wine of its life. Not only are the 'commercial' releases from 1998 little short of exceptional value for their price, but the emergent premium labels of Stentiford's Reserve Shiraz, Eric's Blend (of cabernet sauvignon, shiraz and malbec) and Patron's Reserve (cabernet sauvignon, shiraz and merlot) are pushing their way into Coonawarra's elite.

Brand's

Riddoch Highway
Coonawarra SA 5263
Tel: (08) 8736 3260
Fax: (08) 8736 3208
Website:
mcwilliams.com.au
E-mail: brands_office
@mcwilliams.com.au

CABERNET MERLOT
Coonawarra $$$

1998	16.8	2003	2006
1997	16.0	2002	2005
1996	14.9	2001	2004
1995	16.7	2000	2003
1994	16.3	1996	1999
1993	16.0	1995	1998
1992	16.8	1997	2000
1991	18.2	1999	2003
1990	17.4	1998	2002
1988	18.0	1993	1996
1987	16.5	1992	1995

CABERNET SAUVIGNON
Coonawarra $$$

1998	17.9	2006	2010
1997	17.2	2002	2005
1996	14.9	1998	2001
1995	16.1	2000	2003
1994	17.4	1999	2002
1993	18.0	1998	2001
1992	14.8	1994	1997
1991	15.5	1993	1996
1990	16.9	1992	1995

CHARDONNAY
Coonawarra $$

1998	16.0	1999	2000
1997	16.4	1999	2002
1996	15.7	1998	2001
1995	16.4	2000	2003
1994	16.0	1996	1999
1993	17.8	1998	2001
1992	17.8	1997	2000
1991	18.3	1996	1999

SHIRAZ
Coonawarra $$$

1998	17.2	2000	2003+
1997	17.5	2002	2005
1996	16.7	1998	2001
1995	15.7	1997	2000
1994	14.9	1996	1999
1993	16.3	1995	1998
1992	16.8	1997	2000
1991	16.8	1993	1996

STENTIFORD'S RESERVE OLD VINES SHIRAZ
Coonawarra $$$$$

1997	18.6	2005	2009+
1996	18.2	2004	2008
1995	17.5	2000	2003

Region: Langhorne Creel Winemaker: Rebecca Willson
Chief Executive: Craig Willson

Bremerton

Strathalbyn Road
Langhorne Creek SA 5255
Tel: (08) 8537 3093
Fax: (08) 8537 3109
Website:
www.bremerton.com.au
E-mail:
info@bremerton.com.au

Bremerton is a relatively new Langhorne Creek brand with access to large vineyards and considerable potential to expand. Its realistically priced red wines are open, generous and uncomplicated, and will repay some cellaring.

CABERNET SAUVIGNON
Langhorne Creek $$$$$

1998	17.0	2006	2010
1997	15.9	1999	2002
1996	16.8	2004	2008

OLD ADAM SHIRAZ
Langhorne Creek $$$$

1998	16.4	2000	2003
1997	15.2	2002	2005
1996	17.0	2001	2004

Region: Clare Valley Winemaker: Brian Barry
Viticulturist: Brian Barry Chief Executive: Brian Barry

Erratic in 1999 and 1997, Brian Barry's rieslings are usually a Clare Valley benchmark in a softer, more spicy and appley style. Typically firm and robust, the Cabernet Sauvignon is usually made for an extended spell in the cellar.

JUDS HILL CABERNET SAUVIGNON

Clare Valley $$$

1997	14.8	1999	2002
1996	16.8		2008+
1995	16.6		2007+
1994	16.0		2006+
1993	15.2	1995	1998

JUDS HILL RIESLING

Clare Valley $$$

1999	14.5		2000
1998	18.5	2003	2006+
1997	14.6	1998	1999
1996	18.2	2001	2004+
1995	18.0	2003	2007
1994	18.6	2002	2006

Region: Lower Hunter Valley Winemakers: Neil McGuigan, Karl Stockhausen
Viticulturist: Derek Smith Chief Executive: Neil McGuigan

Briar Ridge is one of my favourite Hunter Valley labels. Its Shiraz and Semillon are made in long-living style and are as honest an expression of this region's qualities as you can find. Hunter wine legend Karl Stockhausen still lends his name and his talents to Briar Ridge's best wines.

CHARDONNAY

Lower Hunter Valley $$$

1999	15.0	2001	2004
1998	17.0	2000	2003+
1997	16.5	1999	2002
1996	18.0	2001	2004
1995	18.0	2003	2007
1994	17.2	1999	2002
1993	18.1	1998	2001
1992	15.8	1994	1997

SEMILLON

Lower Hunter Valley $$$

1999	17.8	2004	2007+
1998	18.4	2003	2006+
1997	16.6	1999	2002
1996	17.0	1998	2001
1995	16.8	2003	2007
1994	18.2	2002	2006
1993	18.3	1998	2001
1992	17.6	1994	1997
1991	17.8	1996	1999

STOCKHAUSEN HERMITAGE

Lower Hunter Valley $$$

1998	16.7	2003	2006
1997	18.5	2005	2009
1996	15.3	2001	2004
1995	17.8	2007	2015
1994	16.4	1999	2002
1993	18.0	2001	2005
1992	17.8	2000	2004
1991	17.7	1996	1999
1990	14.5	1992	1995
1989	17.0	1994	1997
1988	16.5	1993	1996
1987	15.0	1995	1999

Region: Various SA Winemakers: Brian Croser, Con Moshos
Viticulturist: Mike Harms Chief Executive: Brian Croser

Bridgewater Mill is a bistro-style multi-regional brand made by Brian Croser's team at Petaluma. It's about to be substantially expanded under a joint venture with the large American wine business of Stimson Lane. The ripe, punchy flavours of the Sauvignon Blanc and Chardonnay are ideally suited to early drinking, while no matter how appealing it may be at release, the earthy, bony Millstone Shiraz does reward a short spell in the cellar.

CHARDONNAY

McLaren Vale, Clare Valley, etc $$$

1997	17.2	1999	2002
1996	15.8	1998	2001
1995	17.1	1997	2000
1994	16.7	1996	1999
1993	18.1	1995	1998
1992	17.0	1997	2000
1987	15.0	1992	1995

MILLSTONE SHIRAZ

McLaren Vale $$$

1997	16.6	2002	2005
1996	17.2	2001	2004
1995	16.5	2000	2003
1994	17.4	1999	2002
1993	17.8	2001	2005
1992	18.1	1997	2000
1991	16.5	1996	1999

SAUVIGNON BLANC

Coonawarra, Clare, McLaren Vale, Langhorne Creek $$$

1999	17.0	2000	2003
1998	16.0		1999
1997	17.5	1998	1999
1996	17.6	1997	1998
1995	16.7	1996	1997

Region: Lower Hunter Valley Winemakers: Iain Riggs, Peter-James Charteris
Viticulturist: Keith Barry Chief Executive: Iain Riggs

Brokenwood's two Hunter semillons and Graveyard Vineyard are modern icons. A recent tasting underlined the cellaring abilities of the Semillon Reserve and the Graveyard, a wine now justly rated amongst Australia's best shirazes. Brokenwood looks elsewhere for much of its Cabernet Sauvignon and Chardonnay.

CABERNET SAUVIGNON

McLaren Vale, Coonawarra, King Valley $$$

1997	17.0	2000	2005
1996	16.3	2004	2008
1994	17.3	2002	2006
1992	18.0	2000	2004
1991	18.1	1996	1999
1990	17.8	1995	1998
1989	17.0	1994	1997
1988	17.0	1993	1996
1987	16.0	1992	1995

CHARDONNAY

McLaren Vale, Cowra, Padthaway $$$

1998	18.1	2000	2003+
1997	18.5	2002	2005
1995	17.6	2000	2003
1994	15.7	1995	1996
1993	18.5	1998	2001
1991	17.5	1996	1999

GRAVEYARD

Lower Hunter Valley $$$$$

1998	19.0	2010	2018+
1997	17.5	2002	2005+
1996	18.0	2004	2008
1994	18.6	2006	2014
1993	16.6	2001	2005
1991	18.8	2003	2011
1990	17.0	1998	2002
1989	18.3	1997	2001+
1988	18.5	2000	2008+
1987	18.4	1995	1999
1986	18.6	1998	2003
1985	16.7	1990	1993

SEMILLON

Lower Hunter Valley $$$

1999	17.6	2001	2004+
1998	18.6	2003	2006+
1997	17.6	2002	2005
1995	18.3	2003	2007
1994	18.2	2002	2006
1993	16.5	2001	2005
1992	16.0	2000	2004
1991	18.2	1996	1999
1990	16.7	1995	1998
1989	16.0	1990	1991

SEMILLON RESERVE

Lower Hunter Valley $$$$

1997	18.9	2009	2017
1996	18.7	2008	2016
1995	18.1	2003	2007+

**Region: NE Victoria Winemaker: Rob Scapin
Viticulturist: Jim Baxendale Chief Executive: John G. Brown**

Brown Brothers is an enigmatic and enormous family-owned winemaking empire founded at Milawa in Victoria's northeast. It specialises in diversity, making wines from virtually every winegrape introduced to Australia. Occasionally its wines can be spectacular, but sadly these are the wines that catch you by surprise, since the vast majority, while being perfectly sound and free of fault, simply lack the stuffing and flavour to excite the imagination. Of its recent releases, the 1997 Pinot Chardonnay Brut is first-rate, but frustratingly so.

FAMILY RESERVE
CABERNET SAUVIGNON

NE Victoria $$$$

1994	17.0	2006	2014
1992	15.0	2000	2004
1991	18.1	2003	2011
1988	14.0	2000	2008
1987	15.0	1992	1995
1986	18.2	1994	1998
1978	17.6	1990	1998

KING VALLEY
GEWURZTRAMINER

King Valley $$

1999	16.4	2001	2004
1998	16.0	2003	2006
1997	15.6	1999	2002
1996	17.0	1998	2001
1995	17.5	1997	2000
1994	16.8	1996	1999

KING VALLEY RIESLING

King Valley $$

1999	16.0	2001	2004
1997	16.0	1999	2002
1996	15.7	1998	2001
1995	15.5	2000	2003
1994	15.5	1999	2002
1993	17.5	1998	2001
1992	17.3	1997	2000
1991	17.5	1993	1996
1990	17.0	1992	1995

NOBLE RIESLING

NE Victoria $$$$

1997	15.3	1999	2002
1996	14.8	1998	2001
1994	15.0	1999	2002
1993	17.8	1998	2001
1992	17.0	1997	2000
1988	15.3	1990	1995
1986	16.7	1994	1998
1985	16.7	1993	1997
1984	17.7	1989	1992

PINOT NOIR CHARDONNAY BRUT

NE Victoria $$$$

1995	18.7	2000	2003+
1994	16.7	1999	2002
1993	14.3	1995	1998
1992	16.5	1997	2000
1991	18.4	1996	1999
1990	17.3	1995	1998
1989	16.8	1991	1994

SHIRAZ MONDEUSE & CABERNET

NE Victoria $$$

1995	17.5		2007+
1992	17.9	2004	2012
1990	17.5		2002+
1989	17.2	2001	2009
1988	17.0	2000	2005
1987	17.0	1999	2004
1986	17.5		2006+
1985	17.5		2015+
1984	15.5	1992	1996
1983	17.5		2003+
1980	18.3		2010+

VICTORIA CABERNET SAUVIGNON

Victoria $$$

1998	15.6	2000	2003
1997	16.4	2002	2005
1996	17.3	2001	2004
1994	16.9	2002	2006
1993	17.3		2005+
1992	17.9	2000	2004
1991	17.3	1999	2003
1990	16.5	1995	1998
1989	16.5	1994	1997
1988	16.8	1993	1996
1987	15.2	1992	1995
1986	17.5	1994	1998

VICTORIA CHARDONNAY (FORMERLY KING VALLEY)

King Valley $$

1998	14.5	1999	2000
1997	16.6	1999	2002
1996	17.4	1998	2001
1995	16.0	1997	2000
1994	14.2	1995	1996

VICTORIA SHIRAZ

Victoria $$$

1998	16.5	2000	2003
1997	15.3	1999	2002
1996	16.3	1998	2001
1995	15.8	2000	2003
1994	14.9	1999	2002
1992	17.4		2004+
1990	15.5	1995	1998

VINTAGE PORT

NE Victoria $$$

1992	18.0		2004+
1991	17.8		2003+
1988	16.5	2000	2005
1987	16.5		2007+
1986	18.5		2016+
1985	17.0		2005+
1984	15.0	1996	2001
1983	17.0		2003+
1982	16.5		2002+
1981	16.0	2001	2011
1980	18.5		2010+

Region: NE Victoria Winemaker: Colin Campbell
Viticulturist: Malcolm Campbell Chief Executives: Colin & Malcolm Campbell

With its two very approachable regional specials in The Barkly Durif and the Bobbie Burns Shiraz, Campbells is helping to return the red table wines of Rutherglen to their traditional popularity and status. Its Riesling can develop some toasty complexity with age and while its Chardonnay is ripe and approachable, Campbells also boasts one of the most extensive ranges of premium fortified wines in Australia.

BARKLY DURIF

NE Victoria $$$$

1997	16.9	2002	2005
1995	16.7	2000	2003
1994	18.1	2002	2006
1993	16.6	2001	2005
1992	18.3		2004+
1991	17.0	1999	2003
1990	17.5		2002+

BOBBIE BURNS SHIRAZ

NE Victoria $$$

1999	17.5	2007	2011
1998	16.9	2006	2010
1997	16.8	2002	2005
1996	16.8	2004	2008+
1995	16.7	2000	2003
1994	17.5	2002	2006
1993	16.7	2001	2005
1992	17.1	2004	2012
1991	14.5	1996	1999
1990	17.5	1995	1998

CHARDONNAY

NE Victoria $$

1998	16.3	1999	2000
1997	17.0	1999	2002
1996	16.8	1998	2001
1995	16.1	1997	2000

RIESLING

NE Victoria $$

1999	16.0	2004	2007
1998	15.8	2003	2006
1997	15.2	2002	2005
1996	16.5	2001	2004
1994	15.2	1996	1999
1993	16.8	2001	2005
1992	15.7	1997	2000+
1991	17.0	1999	2003
1990	15.8	1995	1998

VINTAGE PORT

NE Victoria $$$

1993	17.8		2005+
1991	16.2	1999	2003
1990	18.2		2002+
1988	17.5	2000	2005
1986	18.4	1998	2003
1983	18.3	1995	2000

Region: Margaret River Winemaker: Peter Stark
Viticulturist:: Brian Martin Chief Executive: William Martin

Its new owners haven't yet had the time to put into bottle and release the sorts of wines they wish Cape Clairault to be known for, so it's a little premature to make sweeping statements about its future direction. That said, the legacy of fine red and white wines made from Bordeaux varieties and left by the Lewises provides a huge headstart.

JUPITER SEMILLON SAUVIGNON BLANC

Margaret River $$$

1998	17.1	2000	2003
1997	18.5	1999	2002+
1996	18.2	1998	2001
1995	16.9	1997	2000
1994	18.3	1999	2002

THE CLAIRAULT (FORMERLY CABERNET SAUVIGNON)

Margaret River $$$$

1997	14.7	2002	2005
1996	16.3	2001	2004+
1995	18.5	2003	2007
1994	18.3		2006+
1993	16.4	2001	2005
1991	18.7		2003+
1990	18.1		2002+
1989	17.4	1997	2001
1988	17.6	1996	2000
1987	16.2	1995	1999
1986	18.0	1998	2006

THE CLAIRAULT SAUVIGNON BLANC

Margaret River $$$

1999	15.3	2000	2001
1998	16.7	1999	2000
1997	17.9	1999	2002
1996	18.6	1998	2001
1995	18.3	2000	2003
1994	18.5	1996	1999
1993	18.2	1995	1998
1992	17.8	1994	1997

Cape Clairault

Henry Road
Willyabrup WA 6280
Tel: (08) 9755 6225
Fax: (08) 9755 6229

Cape Mentelle

Lot 722 Wallcliffe Road
Margaret River WA 6285
Tel: (08) 9757 3266
Fax: (08) 9757 3233

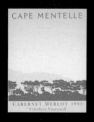

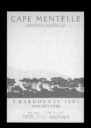

Region: Margaret River Winemaker: John Durham
Viticulturist: Brenton Air Chief Executive: David Hohnen

Cape Mentelle has steadily evolved its red wines into highly complex and briary, meaty expressions of their varieties which are distinctively different from those of their neighbours. Special credit is due to the team for its spectacular 1998 Chardonnay.

CABERNET MERLOT (TRINDERS)

Margaret River $$$

1998	15.7	2000	2003
1997	15.2	1999	2002+
1996	17.0	2004	2008
1995	17.3	2003	2007
1994	17.2	1999	2002
1993	17.1	2001	2005
1992	18.0	1997	2000
1991	17.3	1999	2003

CABERNET SAUVIGNON

Margaret River $$$$$

1996	17.9	2004	2008+
1995	16.6	2003	2007
1994	18.2		2014+
1993	18.3	2005	2013
1992	18.4		2004+
1991	16.0	2003	2011
1990	18.4	1998	2002
1989	18.3	1997	2001
1988	17.8	2000	2008
1987	18.5		2007+
1986	17.5	1998	2006
1985	17.0	1993	1997
1984	18.0	1996	2001
1983	17.2	1995	2003
1982	18.0	1994	1999

CHARDONNAY

Margaret River $$$$

1998	18.7	2003	2006+
1997	17.0	2002	2005
1996	18.6	2001	2004
1995	18.4	2000	2003
1994	18.5	2002	2006
1993	18.5	1998	2001
1992	17.2	1997	2000
1991	17.8	1996	1999
1990	18.4	1995	1998

SEMILLON SAUVIGNON

Margaret River $$$

1999	16.6	1999	2000
1998	18.6	2000	2003
1997	18.1	1997	1998
1996	18.3	1997	1998
1995	17.2	1997	2000
1994	16.6	1996	1999
1993	18.2	1995	1998
1992	18.0	1994	1997

SHIRAZ

Margaret River $$$

1998	16.7	2006	2010
1997	16.7	2005	2009
1996	17.9		2008+
1995	16.8	2003	2007+
1994	18.6	2002	2006
1993	16.8	2001	2005
1992	18.2	2000	2004
1991	18.4		2003+
1990	18.2	1998	2002
1989	16.9	1994	1997
1988	18.6	2000	2005
1987	16.6	1992	1995

ZINFANDEL

Margaret River $$$

1998	18.6	2006	2010+
1997	18.5	2005	2009+
1996	16.0	2001	2004
1995	18.3	2003	2007
1994	16.8	2002	2006
1993	16.5	1998	2001
1992	18.0	1997	2000
1991	18.0		2003+
1990	18.2	1998	2002
1989	17.0	1997	2001
1988	18.3	1996	2000
1987	17.0	1995	1999
1986	17.0	1994	1998
1985	14.5	1993	1997
1984	16.5	1992	1996
1983	18.0		2003+
1982	17.0	1990	1994
1981	18.2	2001	2011

Capel Vale

Lot 5 Capel
North West Road
Stirling Estate
Capel WA 6271
Tel: (08) 9727 1986
Fax: (08) 9791 2452

Region: Geographe Winemaker: Krister Jonsson
Viticulturist: Peter Pratten Chief Executive: Peter Pratten

It's a concern that Capel Vale's wines consistently under-perform in my tastings, yet they continually show clear evidence of poor viticulture and winemaking. Even the reserve wines, whose packaging rivals those of any in Australia, cannot be excused from these remarks. Something needs to happen here.

CABERNET SAUVIGNON

Various, WA $$$

1998	14.8	1999	2003
1997	14.8	1999	2002
1996	16.1	1998	2001
1995	18.0	2003	2007
1994	17.8	2002	2006
1993	14.4	1995	1998
1991	17.5	1999	2003
1990	16.8	1998	2002
1989	17.5	1997	2001
1988	17.7	1996	2000

FREDERICK CHARDONNAY

Various, WA $$$$

1997	15.0	1999	2002
1996	18.5	1998	2001
1995	17.6	1997	2000
1994	18.5	1999	2002
1993	16.6	1995	1998
1992	18.2	1997	2000

RIESLING

Various, WA $$

1999	14.0	2000	2001
1998	16.0	2000	2003
1997	14.5		1998
1996	16.0	2001	2004
1995	16.9	2003	2007
1994	17.0	1999	2002
1993	18.3	2001	2005
1992	16.1	1997	2000
1991	15.0	1993	1996
1990	15.3	1995	1998
1989	16.8	1997	2001
1988	17.0	1996	2000
1986	18.6	1998	2006
1983	18.8	1995	2003

SHIRAZ

Various, WA $$$

1997	16.4	2002	2005
1996	17.9	2001	2004
1995	18.1	2003	2007
1993	16.3	1998	2001+
1992	16.8	1997	2000
1991	15.0	1999	2003
1990	16.8	1998	2002
1989	18.3	1997	2001
1988	18.0	1996	2000
1987	15.5	1992	1995
1986	18.0	1998	2003

WHISPERING HILL RIESLING

Great Southern $$$

1998	16.0	2000	2003+
1997	18.2	2002	2005
1996	18.5	2004	2008

Region: Hastings River Winemaker: John Cassegrain
Viticulturist: Phil Burns Chief Executive: Anthony Mullot

Cassegrain is effectively operating two separate wineries now that wines like its Reserve Chambourcin are made in biodynamic fashion. Cassegrain has pioneered the use of this hybrid variety in Australia and their efforts are now paying off with some distinctive wines which you will either enjoy or find not to your taste at all.

CHAMBOURCIN

Hastings River $$

1998	15.7	2000	2003
1997	14.8	1999	2002
1996	17.0	1998	2001
1995	15.7	1996	1997
1994	14.8	1996	1999
1993	15.2	1995	1998
1992	16.1	1994	1997
1991	15.5	1993	1996
1990	16.0	1992	1995

CHARDONNAY

Hastings River $$$

1997	16.7	1999	2002
1996	16.2	1998	2001
1995	16.0	1997	2000
1994	17.6	1999	2002
1993	17.8	1998	2001
1992	18.1	1997	2000
1991	17.7	1996	1999
1990	16.5	1992	1995

FROMENTEAU VINEYARD CHARDONNAY

Hastings River $$$$

1996	16.6	1998	2001
1995	17.6	2000	2003
1993	16.5	1998	2001
1991	18.4	1996	1999
1990	16.2	1995	1998

SEMILLON

Hastings River $$$

1998	16.6	2000	2003
1997	16.0	2002	2005
1996	16.5	2001	2004
1993	17.2	2001	2005
1992	16.3	1997	2000
1991	18.0	1999	2003
1990	16.0	1992	1995
1989	15.0	1994	1997

Region: Great Southern Winemaker: Michael Staniford
Viticulturist: Angelo Diletti Chief Executive: Angelo Diletti

Castle Rock is a small vineyard in the Porongorup Ranges found to
the south of WA's Great Southern region. Its Riesling can present
as a fragrant and spotlessly clean, steely cellaring style, while its
Chardonnay is forward, juicy and relatively fast to develop.

CHARDONNAY

Great Southern $$$$

1999	15.6	2001	2004
1998	14.0	1999	2000
1997	16.2	1998	1999
1996	15.0	1997	1998

Region: McLaren Vale Winemakers: Pamela Dunsford, Angela Meaney
Viticulturist: Richard Schultz Chief Executive: Robert Gerard

Chapel Hill's excellent performance with red wines from the difficult 1997 vintage, well above the mean in McLaren Vale, reinforces its place amongst the leading lights in this rejuvenated wine area. The Shiraz is lighter than Pam Dunsford would usually release, but is beautifully balanced, dark and harmonious.

Chapel Hill

Chapel Hill Road
McLaren Vale SA 5171
Tel: (08) 8323 8429
Fax: (08) 8323 9245

CABERNET SAUVIGNON

McLaren Vale, Coonawarra $$$

1998	15.1	2003	2006
1997	18.1	2005	2009
1996	18.1	2004	2008+
1995	16.7	2000	2003
1994	17.8	2002	2006
1993	18.0	2001	2005
1992	17.7	1997	2000
1991	17.7	1999	2003
1990	18.5	2002	2010
1989	18.0	1997	2001

McLAREN VALE SHIRAZ

McLaren Vale $$$

1997	18.5	2005	2009
1995	17.7	2000	2003
1994	18.1	1999	2002
1993	18.5	2001	2005
1992	18.0	2000	2004
1991	18.3	1999	2003
1990	17.5	2002	2010
1989	17.5	1997	2001

RESERVE CHARDONNAY

McLaren Vale $$$$

1998	16.7	2000	2003+
1997	16.7	1999	2002
1996	18.2	2001	2004
1995	17.8	2000	2003
1994	18.7	2002	2006
1993	18.6	1998	2001
1992	18.2	1997	2000
1991	17.6	1996	1999
1990	18.0	1998	2002

THE VICAR
McLaren Vale $$$

1996	18.3	2004	2008+
1994	17.9	2002	2006
1993	16.8	1998	2001

UNWOODED CHARDONNAY
Padthaway $$

1999	16.6	2000	2001
1998	16.3	1999	2000
1997	15.7	1998	1999
1996	16.0	1997	1998

Charles Melton

Krondorf Road
Tanunda SA 5352
Tel: (08) 8563 3606
Fax: (08) 8563 3422

Region: Barossa Valley Winemaker: Charlie Melton
Chief Executive: Charlie Melton

Charles Melton is one of the Barossa Valley's most sought-after wine labels. While its style is consistently ripe, generous and approachable, its best wine is the provocatively titled Nine Popes, a particularly flavoursome and surprisingly sophisticated grenache blend of considerable longevity and character. The 1998 vintage is sensational, but keep your hands off it!

NINE POPES
Barossa Valley $$$$

1998	17.8	2006	2010
1997	16.5	1999	2002
1996	18.8	2004	2008
1995	18.3	2003	2007+
1994	16.8	1999	2002
1993	16.0	2001	2005
1990	17.9	1998	2002

Chateau Leamon

140 km post
Calder Highway
Bendigo Vic 3550
Tel: (03) 5447 7995
Fax: (03) 5447 0855

Region: Bendigo Winemaker: Ian Leamon
Viticulturist: Ian Leamon Chief Executive: Alma Leamon

Chateau Leamon is a small vineyard and winery near Bendigo in central Victoria with access to mature cabernet sauvignon, shiraz and riesling vines. Its best fruit and best oak come together in the Reserve Shiraz, which enjoyed an excellent year in 1997.

CABERNET MERLOT

Bendigo $$$

1998	16.7	2006	2010
1997	17.0	2005	2009+
1995	16.2	2003	2007
1994	17.2	2002	2006
1993	15.4	1998	2001
1992	17.5	2000	2004
1991	17.4		2003+
1990	16.4		2002+
1989	16.5	1997	2001
1988	17.6	2000	2005
1987	17.0	1999	2004
1986	17.5	1998	2003

SHIRAZ

Bendigo $$$

1997	15.3	2002	2005
1996	13.8	1997	1998
1995	15.7	2000	2003
1994	17.0	2002	2006
1992	17.3		2004+
1990	17.2		2002+

**Region: McLaren Vale Winemakers: Stephen Pannell, Tom Newton
Viticulturist: Brenton Baker Chief Executive: Stephen Millar**

Chateau Reynella's surviving label is its Vintage Port, the guardian of the 'Australian style' of vintage port. It's typically deep, dark, smooth and brambly, powerfully constructed and built to last. From an unusually hot season, the 1997 edition is almost too porty!

VINTAGE PORT

NE Victoria $$

1997	17.2	2009	2017
1996	18.1	2008	2016
1994	18.9		2014+
1993	18.3		2013+
1990	18.6		2010+
1987	18.9		2007+
1983	18.1		2003+
1982	17.0		2002+
1981	18.0		2001+
1980	17.3	2000	2005
1979	18.2		2009+
1978	18.0	1998	2003
1977	16.7	1997	2002
1976	17.8	1996	2001
1975	19.3		2005+
1972	18.3		2002+

Chateau Reynella

Reynell Road
Reynella SA 5161
Tel: (08) 8392 2222
Fax: (08) 8392 2202

Chateau Tahbilk

Off Goulburn Valley Highway
Tabilk Vic 3608
Tel: (03) 5794 2555
Fax: (03) 5794 2360

Region: Nagambie Lakes - Goulburn Valley
Winemakers: Alister Purbrick, Neil Larson, Tony Carapetis
Viticulturist: Ian Hendy Chief Executive: Alister Purbrick

Alister Purbrick is determined that Chateau Tahbilk remains true to its generations of winemaking traditions, choosing to use the large old oak casks which have resided in Tahbilk's cellars for many decades ahead of the small oak preferred by most contemporary makers and indeed by Purbrick himself for his Dalfarras brand. My favourite Tahbilk wine remains its Marsanne, which acquires delicious honeysuckle-like complexity after about eight years in the bottle. It's best to keep the reds for even longer, much longer!

1860 VINES SHIRAZ (FORMERLY CLARET)

Nagambie Lakes - Goulburn Valley $$$$

1995	17.9		2015+
1994	17.2	2002	2006
1992	16.6	1997	2000
1991	16.8		2003+
1990	17.3		2010+
1989	15.0	2001	2011
1988	16.4	2000	2010
1987	17.8		2007+
1986	18.5		2006+

CABERNET SAUVIGNON

Nagambie Lakes - Goulburn Valley $$

1997	15.8	2005	2009
1996	15.2	2001	2004
1995	17.9		2015+
1994	17.3		2006+
1993	17.6		2005+
1992	18.0		2004+
1991	18.2		2011+
1990	18.1		2010+
1989	15.3	1997	2001
1988	18.4	2000	2005
1987	16.5	1995	1999
1986	18.5		2006+
1985	18.3		2005+
1984	18.2		2004+
1983	18.2		2013+
1982	17.0		2012+
1981	17.6	2001	2011
1980	17.3		2000+
1979	16.5	1999	2009
1978	17.0	1990	1998
1977	16.0	1989	1994
1976	16.5	1988	1996

CHARDONNAY

Nagambie Lakes - Goulburn Valley $$

Year	Rating		
1998	15.2	2000	2003
1997	15.6	1999	2002
1996	15.8	1998	2001
1995	16.6	2000	2003
1994	16.2	1999	2002
1993	16.8	1998	2001
1992	16.6	1994	1997

Château Tahbilk
CHARDONNAY

MARSANNE

Nagambie Lakes - Goulburn Valley $$

Year	Rating		
1998	16.6	2003	2006+
1997	18.0	2005	2009
1996	18.0	2004	2008
1995	17.0		2007+
1994	17.8		2006+
1993	16.0	1998	2001
1992	16.8	1997	2000+
1991	17.0	1999	2003
1990	17.0	1998	2002
1989	17.3	1994	1997
1988	18.1	2000	2008
1987	17.1	1999	2007
1986	17.0	1998	2002

Château Tahbilk
MARSANNE

RESERVE RED (FORMERLY SPECIAL BIN)

Nagambie Lakes - Goulburn Valley $$$$

Year	Rating		
1993	16.0	2001	2005
1992	16.7		2004+
1991	17.3		2011+
1986	18.1	1998	2003
1985	17.5		2005+
1984	16.4	1996	2001
1983	17.0		2003+
1982	17.3		2002+
1981	18.3	2001	2011
1980	17.9	1992	1997
1979	16.0	1999	2009
1978	17.4		2008+
1977	16.6	1989	1994
1976	17.0		2006+
1975	17.3		2005+
1974	16.5	1986	1992
1973	18.2	1993	2003
1972	18.0	1984	1990
1971	18.2	1991	1996

CHÂTEAU TAHBILK
VICTORIA, AUSTRALIA
CABERNET SAUVIGNON

RIESLING

Nagambie Lakes - Goulburn Valley $$

1998	15.0	2003	2006+
1997	18.1	2005	2009
1996	17.7	2004	2008
1995	17.0	2003	2007
1994	17.6	2002	2006
1993	17.2	2001	2005
1992	17.7	1997	2000
1991	17.9		2003+
1990	17.5	1998	2002

SHIRAZ

Nagambie Lakes - Goulburn Valley $$

1997	16.0	2005	2009
1996	15.0	2001	2004
1995	16.9		2007+
1994	17.3		2014+
1993	15.8	1998	2001
1992	18.0		2004+
1991	17.7		2011+
1990	16.8		2002+
1989	16.5	2001	2009
1988	18.0	2000	2008
1987	16.6	1995	1999
1986	18.4		2006+

Region: Margaret River Winemaker: Jurg Muggli
Viticulturist: Leonard Russell Chief Executive: Conor Lagan

Chateau Xanadu is an assertive Margaret River brand whose wines can be inconsistent, but rarely lack character. Its reds tend to be very evolved and spicy by time of release, while its whites are typically fresh, clean and very stylish. The Secession is Chateau Xanadu's popular bistro blend of white grapes.

CABERNET RESERVE

Margaret River $$$$$

1997	15.7	2005	2009
1996	16.1		2008+
1995	17.0	2003	2007+
1994	17.0	2006	2014
1993	18.2		2005+
1992	18.7		2004+
1991	18.6	2003	2011+
1990	18.3		2006+
1989	16.9	1997	2001

CABERNET SAUVIGNON

Margaret River $$$$

1998	15.2	2003	2006
1997	16.3	2002	2005
1996	17.6	2004	2008
1995	18.4	2007	2014
1994	17.6	1999	2002
1993	18.5		2005+
1992	18.4	2000	2004
1991	17.5		2003+
1990	16.0	1992	1995
1989	16.5	1997	2001

CHARDONNAY

Margaret River $$$

1998	18.3	2003	2006
1997	17.2	2002	2005
1996	18.4	2004	2008
1995	17.4	1997	2000
1994	18.4	2002	2006
1993	17.8	1998	2001
1992	16.8	1997	2000
1991	16.8	1996	1999
1990	16.5	1992	1995

SECESSION

Margaret River $$

1999	16.7	2000	2001+
1998	17.0	1999	2000
1997	18.2	1998	1999
1996	17.3	1997	1998
1995	15.0	1996	1997
1994	16.8	1996	1999

SEMILLON

Margaret River $$$

1998	18.0	2003	2006
1997	18.0	2002	2005
1996	18.5	2001	2004
1995	16.3	1996	1997
1994	17.2	2002	2006
1993	17.1	1995	1998
1992	18.4	1997	2000
1991	18.0	1996	1999
1990	16.0	1995	1998
1989	15.0	1994	1997

Chatsfield

O'Neill Road
Mount Barker WA 6324
Tel: (08) 9851 1704
Fax: (08) 9851 1704

Region: Mount Barker Winemakers: Rob Lees, John Wade
Viticulturist: Ronan Lynch Chief Executive: Ken Lynch

Recent vintages have been a little erratic at Chatsfield, whose vineyard is undoubtedly capable of producing some highly aromatic Riesling and Gewurztraminer, plus some very elegant and spicy fine-grained Shiraz. With John Wade back in a consultancy role, I expect Chatsfield to return to its usual form.

CABERNET FRANC
Great Southern $$

1999	16.5	2000	2001
1998	16.5	1999	2000
1997	16.9	1997	1998
1996	16.0	1997	1998
1995	16.6	1997	2000
1994	16.8	1996	1999
1992	15.5	1994	1997

CHARDONNAY
Great Southern $$$

1997	15.8	1999	2002
1996	16.2	1997	1998
1995	16.0	1996	1997
1994	18.0	1999	2002
1993	18.2	1998	2001

RIESLING
Great Southern $$

1999	14.5	2000	2001
1998	17.2	2003	2006+
1997	16.5	1999	2002
1996	17.5	1998	2001
1995	16.4	2000	2003
1994	18.4	2002	2006
1993	18.6	1998	2001
1992	17.4	1997	2000
1990	17.5	1992	1995

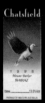

SHIRAZ
Great Southern $$

1998	15.3	2000	2003
1997	15.8	1999	2002
1996	17.2	2001	2004
1995	15.0	1997	2000
1994	18.3	2002	2006
1993	17.4	1998	2001
1992	16.5	1997	2000
1991	17.6	1999	2003
1990	18.0	1998	2002

Region: McLaren Vale Winemaker: Roman Bratasiuk
Viticulturist: Various Chief Executive: Roman Bratasiuk

Clarendon Hills

Brookmans Road
Blewitt Springs SA 5171
Tel: (08) 8364 1484
Fax: (08) 8364 1484

Its plethora of individual vineyard labels makes it harder to keep track of Clarendon Hills, which boasts an extraordinary number of different labels for a relatively small crush. Its style remains relatively consistent, however, as Roman Bratasiuk seeks concentration and density in his reds. His wines are also considerably more evolved at an early age than they used to be, reflecting what would appear to be a hands-off winemaking approach.

ASTRALIS

McLaren Vale $$$$$

1998	18.1		2010+
1997	18.2	2009	2017
1996	18.6	2008	2016
1995	18.9	2007	2015
1994	18.4	2006	2014

OLD VINES GRENACHE BLEWITT SPRINGS

McLaren Vale $$$$

1998	17.7	2003	2006
1997	17.0	2002	2005
1995	18.6	2003	2007+
1994	17.5	2002	2006
1993	17.3	1998	2001

OLD VINES GRENACHE CLARENDON VINEYARD

McLaren Vale $$$$

1998	17.9	2003	2006
1997	14.5	1999	2002
1996	15.6	2004	2008
1995	18.6	2000	2003

Clonakilla

Crisps Lane
Murrumbateman
NSW 2582
Tel: (02) 6227 5877
Fax: (02) 6227 5871

Region: Canberra Winemaker: Tim Kirk
Viticulturist: Michael Lahiff Chief Executive: John Kirk

Clonakilla has quickly established itself as one of the most important shiraz/viognier vineyards in this country with a remarkably consistent sequence of luxuriant and long-living wines obviously inspired by Côte-Rôtie. Its Riesling can also be exceptional, while it enjoyed its best Cabernet Merlot year in 1998.

CABERNET MERLOT

Canberra $$$

1998	18.1	2003	2006+
1997	16.5	2005	2009+
1996	15.4	1998	2001
1995	16.5	2003	2007
1994	17.8	2002	2006
1993	15.7	1998	2001
1992	16.4	1997	2000

RIESLING

Canberra $$

1999	18.6	2004	2007+
1998	18.3	2003	2006+
1997	18.6	2005	2009
1996	18.4	2001	2004
1995	17.8	2003	2007
1994	15.0	1996	1999
1993	18.4	2001	2005

SHIRAZ

Canberra $$$$$

1999	17.6	2007	2011
1998	19.0	2010	2018
1997	19.1	2005	2009
1996	16.6	2001	2004
1995	18.2	2003	2007+
1994	18.9	2006	2014+
1993	16.8	1998	2001
1992	18.3	2000	2004
1991	16.5	1999	2003

Clover Hill

60 Clover Hill Road
Lebrina Tas 7254
Tel: (03) 6395 6115
Fax: (03) 6395 6257
Website:
www.taltarni.com.au
E-mail:
taltarni@netconnect.
com.au

Region: Pipers River Winemakers: Shane Clohesy, Philippe Bru
Viticulturist: Chris Smith Chief Executive: Chris Markell

Taltarni's sparkling wine project is one of the most popular and most consistent of premium Australian fizzes, although I find some releases just that little bit too herbal for my taste. It's a creamy, crackly wine with bright, almost tropical fruit and typically bracing Tasmanian acidity.

METHODE CHAMPENOISE

Pipers River $$$$

1996	17.8	2001	2004
1995	17.5	1997	2000
1994	18.3	1999	2002
1993	18.2	1998	2001
1992	17.0	1997	2000
1991	15.0	1996	1999

Region: Various Winemakers: Neil McGuigan, Phil Ryan
Viticulturist: Evan Powell Chief Executive: David Clarke

Cockfighter's Ghost

331 Milbrodale Road
Broke NSW 2330
Tel: (02) 9667 1622
Fax: (02) 9667 1442

Cockfighter's Ghost is one of the most successful of all Australian bistro wine labels and it's easy to see why. Its wines are typically clean and well made, and ready to drink at time of release.

CHARDONNAY

Hunter Valley $$

1998	16.8	2000	2003
1997	15.1	1998	1999
1996	14.8	1997	1998

SEMILLON

Hunter Valley $$

1998	16.2	2000	2003+
1997	16.0	1999	2002
1996	16.5	1998	2001+

UNWOODED CHARDONNAY

Hunter Valley $$

1999	16.2	2000	2001
1998	16.0	1999	2000
1997	14.5	1998	1999

As Southcorp's Yarra Valley headquarters, Coldstream Hills is today a considerable operation. Significantly, it hasn't lost its focus as a dedicated maker of fine pinot noir and chardonnay, with occasionally excellent releases of Reserve Cabernet Sauvignon and Merlot to boot. Under James Halliday, who remains a consultant to the brand, its Reserve Pinot style is heavily focused towards barrel fermentation, resulting in a distinctive wine of typically high quality. While it may take a few years to deliver on its promises, the Reserve Chardonnay can evolve into a wine very reminiscent of excellent Puligny.

BRIARSTON

Yarra Valley $$$

1998	15.2	2000	2003
1997	15.2	1998	1999
1996	16.0	1998	2001
1995	15.4	1997	2000
1994	16.5	1999	2002
1993	15.6	1998	2001
1992	18.3	1997	2000
1991	16.7	1996	1999

CHARDONNAY

Yarra Valley $$$

1999	15.8	2000	2001
1998	16.8	2000	2003
1997	17.6	1999	2002
1996	17.5	1998	2001
1995	17.4	1997	2000
1994	17.6	1996	1999

PINOT NOIR

Yarra Valley $$$

1999	18.0	2001	2004
1998	16.9	2000	2003
1997	17.5	2002	2005
1996	17.8	1998	2001
1995	15.0	1996	1997
1994	17.0	1999	2002
1993	17.3	1995	1998
1992	16.7	1994	1997
1991	16.5	1993	1996

RESERVE CABERNET SAUVIGNON

Yarra Valley $$$$

1997	16.0	2002	2005
1995	17.0	2000	2003
1994	17.5	2002	2006
1993	18.0	1998	2002
1992	19.0	2004	2012+
1991	18.2	1999	2003
1990	18.0	1995	1998

RESERVE CHARDONNAY

Yarra Valley $$$$

1998	18.5	2003	2006
1997	17.5	2002	2005
1996	18.1	2001	2004+
1995	18.5	2000	2003
1994	18.7	1999	2002
1993	17.0	1995	1998
1992	19.0	2000	2004
1991	18.2	1993	1996
1990	18.3	1995	1998

RESERVE PINOT NOIR

Yarra Valley $$$$

1998	18.3	2003	2006+
1997	18.5	2004	2008
1996	17.9	1998	2001
1995	17.3	1997	2000
1994	18.5	1999	2002
1993	16.5	1995	1998
1992	18.5	1997	2000
1991	16.5	1993	1996
1990	16.0	1991	1992

SAUVIGNON BLANC

Yarra Valley $$$

1999	16.7	2000	2001
1998	15.4	1998	1999
1997	16.7	1998	1999

Coriole is well known for both its spicy, earthy Shiraz and sumptuous Lloyd Shiraz, but is making wonderful progress with its Sangiovese, a wine acquiring fine, drying astringency to partner its sour-edged fruit. A recent tasting of every Lloyd Shiraz released confirmed its status amongst Australia's best and the 1998 vintage as its finest yet. Coriole's range of white wines includes one of the nation's more attractive and drinkable examples of Chenin Blanc.

CHENIN BLANC

McLaren Vale $$

2000	16.5	2000	2001
1999	16.8	2001	2004
1998	16.0	1999	2000
1997	16.6	1999	2002
1996	16.7	1998	2001
1995	15.5	1996	1997
1994	17.2	1999	2002
1993	16.0	1998	2001

LLOYD SHIRAZ

McLaren Vale $$$$

1998	19.1	2010	2018+
1997	16.7	2002	2005
1996	18.8	2008	2016
1995	18.6	2007	2015
1994	18.4	2006	2012
1993	16.7	2001	2005
1992	18.8	2004	2012
1991	18.3	2003	2011+
1990	17.6	2002	2010
1989	18.1	2001	2009

MARY KATHLEEN

McLaren Vale $$$$

1997	16.8	2005	2009
1996	18.1	2004	2008+
1995	17.1	2003	2007
1994	16.7	2002	2006
1992	15.7	1994	1997

REDSTONE SHIRAZ CABERNET GRENACHE

McLaren Vale $$

1998	16.7	2003	2006+
1997	16.3	2002	2005
1996	16.0	2004	2008
1995	16.8	2001	2004
1994	17.6	2002	2006
1993	15.9	1998	2001
1992	16.7	2000	2004

SANGIOVESE

McLaren Vale $$

1998	15.8	2000	2003
1997	17.2	2002	2005
1996	17.0	2001	2004
1995	17.2	2003	2007
1994	16.8	1999	2002
1993	16.5	2001	2005
1992	15.3	1997	2000

SHIRAZ

McLaren Vale $$$

1998	16.7	2006	2010
1997	16.7	2002	2005
1996	17.7	2001	2004
1995	18.2	2002	2007
1994	16.8	2002	2006
1993	17.5	2001	2005
1992	18.2	1997	2000
1990	18.0	1995	1998
1989	17.5	1994	1997

Region: Sunbury Winemaker: Patrick Carmody
Viticulturist: Patrick Carmody Chief Executive: Patrick Carmody

Against the modern trend, Pat Carmody chooses not to use a high percentage of new oak to mature his Craiglee Shiraz, which he crafts into an elegant, spicy and occasionally very peppery wine with sweet cherry/plum flavours and fine tannins. As the excellent 1997 vintage shows, it's a proven cellar style and acquires even more spiciness with age. Craiglee's Chardonnay is typically long, savoury and minerally, with tangy citrus flavours.

CHARDONNAY

Sunbury $$$

1998	14.5	1999	2000
1997	17.0	2002	2005
1996	17.5	2001	2004
1995	17.5	2000	2003
1994	18.2	1999	2002
1993	17.7	1998	2001
1992	18.0	1997	2000
1991	18.5	1993	1996
1990	18.0	1995	1998
1989	16.0	1990	1991

SHIRAZ

Sunbury $$$

1998	16.7	2006	2010
1997	18.8	2005	2009
1996	17.8	2004	2008
1995	17.6	2003	2007
1994	18.8	2002	2012+
1993	18.6	2001	2005
1992	16.8	1997	2000
1991	17.5	1999	2003
1990	18.0	2002	2010
1989	17.5	1991	1994
1988	18.5	1996	2000

Region: Mudgee Winemaker: Brett McKinnon
Viticulturist: Stephen Guilbaud-Oulton Chief Executive: Christian

Craigmoor is one of Orlando Wyndham's Mudgee-based brands which is presently undergoing some changes. Its successful Chardonnay is to be retained, but we will have to wait and see whose company it will keep.

CHARDONNAY

Mudgee $$

1999	17.6	2001	2004
1998	16.5	2000	2003
1997	16.8	1999	2002
1996	18.2	2001	2004
1995	17.0	1997	2000
1994	17.0	1996	1999
1993	16.8	1997	2001
1991	17.3	1999	2003
1990	17.8	1998	2002

Region: Riverina Winemaker: Tim Pearce
Viticulturist: Andrew Schulz Chief Executive: Graham Cranswick Smith

Cranswick Estate's Autumn Gold is a first-class dessert wine made using late-harvest semillon from Griffith. Picked earlier than the De Bortoli Noble One with a lesser degree of botrytis infection, it is clearly less luscious, but reveals intense honeycomb and citrusy flavours.

AUTUMN GOLD

Riverina $$$$$

1996	18.7	2001	2004+
1995	18.2	2000	2003
1994	18.3	1996	1999
1993	18.5	2001	2005

Region: WA, Winemaker: Larry Cherubino
Viticulturist: Ron Page Chief Executive: Stephen Millar

BRL Hardy's Crofters label is simply one of the hottest prospects around for value. The Cabernet Merlot, which has a habit of doing very well in wine shows, is a terrific multi-regional WA red based around ripe, small berry fruit and some pretty smart oak.

CABERNET MERLOT

Various, WA $$$

1998	16.1	2003	2006
1997	18.0	2002	2005+
1996	17.2	2001	2004
1995	17.3	2000	2003
1994	16.7	1999	2002

Region: Margaret River Winemakers: Vanya Cullen, Trevor Kent
Viticulturist: Dick Marcus Chief Executive: Diana Cullen

There's a restless drive apparent at Cullen and an underlying
determination to further improve this already first class breed by
paying even more attention to detail in the vineyard. The results
can be seen in new-found refinement and elegance in the
Chardonnay, a brightness, length and lustre in the Sauvignon Blanc
Semillon and even in a step up in the elegance and poise of the
now very aristocratic Cabernet Sauvignon Merlot. Full marks to
Vanya Cullen, *Wine Magazine's* Winemaker of the Year in 2000,
and maker of the OnWine Wine of the Year for 2000, the 1998
Cullen Cabernet Sauvignon Merlot.

CABERNET SAUVIGNON MERLOT

Margaret River $$$$$

1998	19.0		2010+
1997	18.2	2005	2009+
1996	18.1		2008+
1995	19.2	2007	2015+
1994	18.7		2006+
1993	17.9	2001	2005
1992	18.7		2004+
1991	18.2		2003+
1990	18.5		2002+
1989	15.0	2001	2009
1988	17.0	2000	2005
1987	16.5		2007+
1986	19.0	1998	2003
1985	17.0	1997	2002
1984	17.7	1996	2001
1983	16.5		2003+
1982	17.5	1994	1999
1981	16.5		2001+
1980	18.0	2000	2005

CHARDONNAY

Margaret River $$$$$

1999	18.6	2007	2011
1998	18.2	2006	2010
1997	16.0	2002	2005
1996	19.2	2004	2008
1995	18.3	2000	2003
1994	18.6	2002	2006
1993	18.4	1998	2001
1992	18.6	1997	2000
1990	18.6	1995	1998
1989	16.0	1994	1997

PINOT NOIR

Margaret River $$$$

1999	16.8	2001	2004+
1998	17.8	2000	2003
1997	15.9	1998	1999
1996	16.8	1998	2001
1995	15.8	1997	2000
1994	16.5	1999	2003
1993	18.0	2001	2005
1992	16.6	2000	2004
1991	16.5	1999	2003

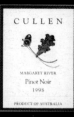

SAUVIGNON BLANC SEMILLON

Margaret River $$$$

1999	19.0	2007	2011
1998	18.6	2006	2010
1997	18.4	2005	2009
1995	17.6	2000	2003
1994	18.2	1996	1999
1993	18.7	1998	2001
1992	16.8	2000	2004
1991	17.0	1996	1999

Region: McLaren Vale, Fleurieu Peninsula
Winemakers: Chester Osborn, Philip Dean
Viticulturists: Phil Williams, Mark Needle Chief Executive: d'Arry Osborn

d'Arenberg is one of McLaren Vale's larger producers whose steadily increasing portfolio of robust reds and generous white wines is characterised by its consistent quality, the definite article and some of the wordiest back labels in Christendom. While wines like The Other Side Chardonnay are a little hard to understand, most are generous, firm and long-living.

d'Arenberg

Osborn Road
McLaren Vale SA 5171
Tel: (08) 8323 8206
Fax: (08) 8323 8423
E-mail:
winery@darenberg.com.au

d'ARRY'S ORIGINAL SHIRAZ GRENACHE

McLaren Vale $$

1998	17.2	2006	2010+
1997	16.8	2002	2005+
1996	16.8	2004	2008
1995	17.7	2003	2007
1994	17.8	2002	2006
1993	16.8	2001	2005
1992	17.4	2000	2004
1991	16.5	1999	2003
1990	17.4	1998	2002
1989	16.0	1997	2001
1988	18.0	2000	2008
1987	16.4	1997	1999
1986	17.0	1996	1998

THE COPPERMINE ROAD CABERNET SAUVIGNON

McLaren Vale $$$$

1998	18.3	2010	2018+
1997	17.2	2005	2009+
1996	16.8		2008+

THE CUSTODIAN GRENACHE

McLaren Vale $$$

1998	16.3	2003	2006
1997	17.8	2002	2005
1996	17.6	2004	2008
1995	18.2	2003	2007
1994	16.8	1999	2002

THE DEAD ARM SHIRAZ

McLaren Vale $$$$$

1998	18.0		2010+
1997	17.8	2005	2009
1996	18.8		2008+
1995	18.5		2007+
1994	18.2		2006+
1993	16.8	2001	2005

THE DRY DAM RIESLING

McLaren Vale $$

1999	17.9	2004	2007
1997	16.2	2002	2005
1996	16.0	2001	2004
1995	17.8	2003	2007
1994	17.6	2002	2006
1993	16.8	1998	2001
1992	16.0	2000	2004
1990	17.0	1998	2002

THE FOOTBOLT
OLD VINE SHIRAZ

McLaren Vale $$$

1998	17.3	2006	2010
1997	16.2	2002	2005+
1996	17.2	2004	2008
1995	17.3	2003	2007
1994	17.5		2006+
1993	17.0	2001	2005
1992	17.0		2004+
1991	18.0		2003+
1990	17.0	1998	2002

THE HIGH TRELLIS
CABERNET SAUVIGNON

McLaren Vale $$$

1997	16.5	2002	2005+
1995	17.8	2003	2007
1994	16.6	1999	2002
1993	16.3	2001	2005
1992	16.3	1997	2000
1991	17.7	2003	2011
1990	17.9	2002	2010

THE IRONSTONE
PRESSINGS

McLaren Vale $$$$

1998	16.8		2010+
1997	17.5	2005	2009
1996	18.4		2008+
1995	18.1		2007+
1994	16.8		2006+
1993	17.6		2005+
1992	18.6	2000	2004
1991	17.6		2003+
1990	17.0		2002+
1989	16.8	2001	2009

THE NOBLE RIESLING

McLaren Vale $$$$$

1999	16.0	2001	2004
1998	15.3	2000	2003
1997	17.0	2002	2005
1996	16.1	1998	2001
1995	17.1	2000	2003
1994	18.2	2002	2006
1993	16.8	1995	1998
1992	18.4	1997	2000
1991	17.0	1996	1999

THE OLIVE GROVE CHARDONNAY

McLaren Vale $$

1999	17.7	2001	2004+
1998	17.8	2003	2006
1997	16.6	1999	2002
1996	16.1	1997	1998
1995	16.7	1997	2000
1994	16.8	1996	1999

THE OTHER SIDE CHARDONNAY

McLaren Vale $$$$

1999	16.4	2001	2004
1998	16.0	1999	2000
1997	15.0		1998
1996	16.7	1998	2001

THE PEPPERMINT PADDOCK CHAMBOURCIN

McLaren Vale $$$

1998	16.6	2003	2006
1997	15.8	2002	2005
1996	16.9	2001	2004
1995	16.4	2000	2003
1994	16.0	1999	2002
1993	16.6	1998	2001

THE TWENTYEIGHTH ROAD MOURVEDRE

McLaren Vale $$$

1998	16.7	2003	2006+
1997	16.3	2002	2005
1996	17.9	2004	2008+
1995	16.8	2003	2007

VINTAGE FORTIFIED SHIRAZ

NE Victoria $$$

1998	18.0		2010+
1997	18.1	2005	2009+
1995	18.3		2007+
1993	18.2		2005+
1987	18.5		2007+
1978	17.0	1998	2008
1976	18.0	1996	2006
1975	18.2	1995	2005
1973	18.6	1993	2003

Regions: Nagambie Lakes - Goulburn Valley, Coonawarra, McLaren Vale
Winemaker: Alister Purbrick
Viticulturist: Ian Hendy Chief Executive: Alister Purbrick

Dalfarras

Goulburn Valley Highway
Nagambie Vic 3608
Tel: (03) 5794 2637
Fax: (03) 5794 2360

With a brand new winery complex on the other side of Nagambie, Dalfarras now has a new home outside its parent, Chateau Tahbilk. These wines give Alister Purbrick and his team more of a chance to try their hand with contemporary styles of softer and more approachable red wines like the 1998 Shiraz.

CABERNET SAUVIGNON

Coonawarra (Formerly Goulburn River) $$

1997	16.8	2005	2009+
1996	15.6		2008+
1995	16.6	2003	2007
1993	15.0	2001	2005
1992	16.2		2004+
1991	17.8		2011+
1990	16.0	2002	2010

MARSANNE

Nagambie Lakes - Goulburn Valley $$

1997	16.0	1999	2002
1996	15.2	1998	2001
1995	15.0	1997	2000
1994	14.5	1995	1996

SAUVIGNON BLANC

Nagambie Lakes - Goulburn Valley $$

1999	16.0	2000	2001
1998	16.8	1999	2000
1997	14.0		1998
1996	15.5	1997	1998
1995	15.0	1996	1997

SHIRAZ

Nagambie Lakes - Goulburn Valley $$

1998	16.0	2003	2006
1997	16.2	2002	2005
1996	17.6	2004	2008+
1995	17.8	2003	2007+
1994	16.8	2006	2014
1993	15.3	2001	2005
1992	16.6	2000	2004
1991	17.8	1999	2003
1990	16.4	1998	2002

Dalwhinnie

RMB 4378 Taltarni Road
Moonambel Vic 3478
Tel: (03) 5467 2388
Fax: (03) 5467 2237

Region: Pyrenees Winemaker: David Jones
Viticulturist: David Jones Chief Executive: David Jones

The 1997 Eagle Series Shiraz, a small-production wine of exceptional quality made in small open fermenters on site at Dalwhinnie, has entirely altered my expectations of what is and what is not possible at this vineyard, now clearly one of the best shiraz sites in Australia. Meantime, the 'standard' wines continue their very impressive form and longevity.

CHARDONNAY

Pyrenees $$$$

1998	18.8	2006	2010
1997	18.3	2002	2005
1996	18.2	2001	2004+
1995	18.3	2000	2003
1994	18.5	2002	2006
1993	18.6	1998	2001
1992	18.2	2000	2004
1991	18.0	1999	2003
1990	18.5	1998	2002

MOONAMBEL CABERNET

Pyrenees $$$$

1998	17.8		2010+
1997	17.1		2009+
1996	17.8		2008+
1995	18.3	2003	2007
1994	16.2	1999	2002
1993	17.5		2005+
1992	17.3		2004+
1991	17.8		2003+
1990	16.6		2010+

MOONAMBEL SHIRAZ

Pyrenees $$$$

1998	18.6	2006	2010+
1997	19.1	2005	2009+
1996	18.4	2008	2016
1995	18.1		2007+
1994	17.7		2006+
1993	18.2	2001	2005
1992	19.0		2004+
1991	18.4		2011+
1990	18.5	2002	2010
1989	16.0	1997	2001
1988	18.5	2000	2008
1987	16.5	1995	1999
1986	17.0	1994	1998
1985	16.5	1993	1997

The best David Traeger Cabernet for several years, another fine spicy Shiraz and a zesty, tangy Verdelho complete an excellent trio of new releases from this specialist central Victorian maker. Traeger's reds are acquiring more flesh and mouthfeel, the result of extensive work in both young and old vine vineyards.

CABERNET
Goulburn Valley $$$

1998	17.2		2010+
1997	15.7	2005	2009
1996	16.8	2004	2008
1995	16.5	2003	2007
1993	17.6	2001	2005
1992	18.4		2004+
1990	18.2		2002+
1989	17.8	1997	2001
1988	16.5	1996	2000

SHIRAZ
Goulburn Valley $$$

1998	17.8	2006	2010+
1997	18.0	2005	2009+
1996	17.8	2004	2008
1995	17.0	2003	2007
1993	15.5	1998	2001
1992	16.4	2000	2004
1990	16.8	1998	2002
1988	18.1	1996	2000

VERDELHO
Goulburn Valley $$

1999	18.0	2004	2007
1998	17.6	2003	2006
1997	16.5	1999	2002
1996	16.8	1998	2001
1995	16.7	1997	2000
1994	17.5	1999	2002
1993	17.0	1998	2001
1992	15.2	1994	1997
1991	16.8	1996	1999
1990	15.7	1995	1998

Region: Eden Valley Winemakers: Adam Wynn, Andrew Ewart
Viticulturist: Adam Wynn Chief Executive: Adam Wynn

David Wynn is generally a brand of easy, early-drinking table wines of no great complexity or claim to attention, but the Patriarch Shiraz is made into a more sumptuous, fleshy, firmly structured and often statuesque wine of considerable merit.

PATRIARCH SHIRAZ

Eden Valley $$$$

1998	17.9	2006	2010
1997	16.4	2002	2005
1996	18.7	2003	2008
1995	18.4	2003	2007
1994	17.8	1999	2002
1993	17.8	2001	2005
1992	17.6	2002	2004
1991	18.4	1999	2003
1990	17.9	1998	2002

Region: Riverina Winemaker: Darren De Bortoli
Viticulturist: Kevin De Bortoli Chief Executive: Deen De Bortoli

Australia's premier dessert wine is the luscious, complex and concentrated Noble One from De Bortoli in Griffith. It has inspired a new generation of late-harvest dessert wines from Griffith and typically matures for a decade and more, developing complex savoury, citrusy and pastry-like flavours.

NOBLE ONE

Riverina $$$$$

1998	18.8	2010	2018
1997	16.9	2002	2005
1996	18.8	2004	2008
1995	18.6	2003	2007
1994	19.0	2002	2006
1993	18.2	1998	2001
1992	18.4	1997	2000
1991	18.7		2003+
1990	18.7	1998	2002
1988	17.8	1996	2000
1987	18.0	1995	1999
1986	16.0	1991	1994
1985	17.7	1993	1997
1984	18.2	1992	1996
1983	16.5	1995	2000
1982	18.3	1990	1994

Its excellent recent string of vintages confirms De Bortoli's arrival amongst the best of the Yarra Valley's wineries. It boasts some of the Valley's more consistent cabernet vineyards, while its Chardonnay and Pinot Noir are developing more finesse and power.

CABERNET SAUVIGNON
Yarra Valley $$$$

1997	16.4	2002	2005
1996	17.5	2001	2004
1995	18.8		2007+
1994	16.7	1999	2002
1993	17.2	2001	2005
1992	18.2	2000	2004
1991	16.8	1999	2003
1990	17.4	1995	1998

CHARDONNAY
Yarra Valley $$$

1999	17.0	2001	2004
1998	18.0	2003	2006
1997	17.8	2002	2005
1996	18.5	2001	2004+
1995	16.8	1997	2000
1994	16.0	1996	1999
1993	16.0	1995	1998
1992	17.6	1997	2000
1991	18.1	1996	1999
1990	18.2	1995	1998

MELBA BARREL SELECT
Yarra Valley $$$$$

1995	16.6	2000	2003+
1994	16.6	2002	2006
1993	17.2	1998	2001+
1992	16.2	1997	2000

PINOT NOIR
Yarra Valley $$$$

1998	16.8	2000	2003
1997	18.3	2002	2005
1996	18.6	2001	2004
1995	15.0	1996	1997
1994	17.5	1999	2002
1992	16.7	1994	1997
1991	17.3	1993	1996

De Bortoli
Yarra Valley
**Pinnacle Lane
Dixon's Creek Vic 3775
Tel: (03) 5965 2271
Fax: (03) 5965 2442
Website:
www.debortoli.com.au
E-mail:
dbw@debortoli.com.au**

Deakin Estate

Kulkyne Way
Iraak via Red Cliffs
Vic 3496
Tel: (03) 5029 1666
Fax: (03) 5024 3316

Delatite

cnr Stoney's &
Pollard's Roads
Mansfield Vic 3722
Tel: (03) 5775 2922
Fax: (03) 5775 2911

SHIRAZ
Yarra Valley $$$$

1998	16.8	2003	2006+
1997	18.2	2002	2005+
1996	18.1	2001	2004
1995	18.2	2003	2007
1994	18.1	1999	2002
1993	17.2	1998	2001
1992	18.0	2000	2004

Region: Murray Darling Winemakers: Graham Dixon, Linda Jakubans
Viticulturist: Jeff Milne Chief Executive: David Yunghanns

Deakin Estate is a highly rated maker of inexpensive but flavoursome table wines from the warm river regions of Victoria. Its Merlot is one of the leading cheaper examples of this popular variety.

MERLOT
Murray Darling $$

1999	16.2	2000	2001+
1998	15.0	1999	2000
1997	15.5	1998	1999

Region: Mansfield Winemaker: Rosalind Ritchie
Viticulturist: David Ritchie Chief Executives: Robert & Vivienne Ritchie

Some of Australia's finest riesling comes from Delatite, a substantial vineyard near Mansfield in Victoria's high country. The superb VS Riesling from 1999 is one of the best for some years and a finalist in the OnWine Wine of the Year. Delatite's collection of reds are distinctive, minty and individual.

CHARDONNAY
Mansfield $$$

1998	15.3	2000	2003
1997	15.0	1998	1999
1996	17.2	2001	2004
1995	16.2	1997	2000
1994	18.2	1999	2002
1993	18.3	1998	2001
1992	17.4	2000	2004
1991	16.8	1996	1999
1990	16.5	1995	1998
1989	16.0	1994	1997

DEAD MAN'S HILL GEWURZTRAMINER

Mansfield $$$

1999	18.0	2004	2009
1998	16.5	2003	2006
1997	18.4	2005	2009
1996	18.5	2004	2008
1995	18.0	2000	2003
1994	18.0	2002	2006
1992	18.2	2000	2004
1991	18.0	1996	1999
1990	16.5	1992	1995
1989	17.5	1994	1997

DEMELZA

Mansfield $$$$

1994-95	18.2	1999	2002+
1987/88	16.2	1995	1997
1991	15.3	1996	1999

DEVILS RIVER

Mansfield $$$

1998	15.2	2003	2006
1997	15.1	2002	2005
1996	15.4	2001	2004
1995	16.7	2000	2003
1994	16.5		2006+
1993	17.6		2005+
1992	18.0	2000	2004
1991	17.0	1999	2003
1990	17.0	1998	2002

PINOT NOIR

Mansfield $$$

1998	14.0		1998
1997	17.6	2002	2005
1996	16.7	2001	2004
1995	15.5	2000	2003
1994	15.4	1999	2003
1992	16.8	1997	2000
1990	17.0	1998	2002
1989	17.5	1994	1997

Mansfield $$$

1999	17.9	2007	2011
1998	18.5	2006	2010
1997	16.5	2005	2009
1996	18.2	2004	2008
1995	18.0	2000	2003
1994	18.5	2002	2005
1993	18.8	2001	2005
1992	18.6	2000	2004
1991	18.0	1999	2003
1990	18.5	1998	2002
1989	17.5	1997	2001
1988	17.0	2000	2008
1987	17.5	1995	1999
1986	18.5	1994	1998

SAUVIGNON BLANC

Mansfield $$$

1999	16.7	2000	2001+
1998	16.5	1999	2002+
1997	17.8	1999	2002
1996	16.0	1997	1998
1995	18.5	1996	1997

SHIRAZ

Mansfield $$$

1998	15.8	2000	2003
1997	16.8	2002	2005+
1996	15.7	1998	2001
1994	15.0	1996	1999
1993	15.2	1998	2001
1992	16.7	1997	2000
1991	15.0	1996	1999
1990	17.6	1998	2002

Region: Margaret River Winemaker: Janice McDonald
Viticulturist: Simon Robertson Chief Executive: Tom Park

One can't help the feeling that with its extraordinary vineyard and winery resource in the southern reaches of Margaret River that Devil's Lair still dwells on unfulfilled potential. The exceptional quality of the 1999 Chardonnay and 1998 Devil's Lair red (a cabernet blend) by departing winemaker Janice McDonald supports that view. Have Southcorp's other winemakers lost interest in Western Australia?

Devil's Lair

Rocky Road
via Margaret River
WA 6285
Tel: (08) 9757 7573
Fax: (08) 9757 7533

CHARDONNAY

Margaret River $$$$

1999	18.8	2004	2007+
1998	16.8	2000	2003+
1997	18.6	2002	2005
1996	16.6	1998	2001
1995	18.0	2000	2003
1994	18.4	1996	1999
1993	17.2	1995	1998
1992	17.5	1994	1997

MARGARET RIVER (FORMERLY CABERNET SAUVIGNON)

Margaret River $$$$

1998	18.5	2006	2010
1997	16.7	2002	2005+
1996	18.7	2004	2008
1995	18.3	2003	2007
1994	18.2	2002	2006
1993	18.4	2001	2005
1992	18.0		2004+
1991	17.4	1999	2003
1990	18.4		2002+

**Region: Yarra Valley Winemakers: David Lance, James Lance
Viticulturist: David Lance Chief Executive: David Lance**

Diamond Valley's two principal pinots, the Estate Pinot Noir and the Close-Planted Pinot Noir, continue to re-establish this significant vineyard at the cutting edge of Australian pinot noir. The present winemaking combination of David Lance's experience and James Lance's travel-inspired enthusiasm is certainly working well.

BLUE LABEL CHARDONNAY

Yarra Valley $$$

1998	16.5	2000	2003
1997	17.5	1999	2000
1996	16.8	1998	2001
1995	16.0	1996	1997
1994	15.6	1996	1999
1993	16.8	1993	1998
1992	17.9	1997	2000

BLUE LABEL PINOT NOIR

Yarra Valley $$$

1999	17.0	2001	2004
1998	17.0	2000	2003
1997	18.3	1998	2001
1996	17.5	1998	2001
1994	15.6	1996	1999
1993	15.0	1998	2001
1992	15.6	1994	1997
1991	18.0	1993	1996

CLOSE-PLANTED PINOT NOIR

Yarra Valley $$$$

1997	18.4	1999	2002
1996	18.5	2001	2004
1995	18.1	1997	2000

ESTATE CABERNET MERLOT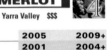

Yarra Valley $$$

1997	17.0	2005	2009+
1996	16.6	2001	2004+
1994	17.2	2002	2006+
1992	15.6	2000	2004
1991	15.6	1999	2003
1990	18.1	1998	2002
1989	16.3	1997	2001
1988	17.0	1996	2000

ESTATE CHARDONNAY

Yarra Valley $$$$

1998	16.7	2000	2003
1997	16.6	1999	2002
1996	16.3	1998	2001
1995	17.8	2000	2003
1994	18.2	2002	2006
1993	16.6	1998	2001
1992	18.1	1997	2000
1991	16.3	1996	1999
1990	18.0	1995	1998

ESTATE PINOT NOIR

Yarra Valley $$$$

1998	18.3	2003	2006
1997	19.0	2002	2005+
1996	18.7	2001	2004
1995	17.1	2000	2003
1994	16.4	1996	1999
1993	17.6	1998	2001
1992	16.4	1994	1997
1991	18.0	1996	1999
1990	16.8	1992	1995

Region: Coal River Valley Winemaker: Peter Althaus
Viticulturist: Peter Althaus Chief Executive: Peter Althaus

Another excellent Pinot Noir from 1998 and an elegant, albeit rather leafy Cabernet Sauvignon from 1997 reinforces my view that Domaine A is one of the vineyards to watch for. Peter Althaus declassifies its wine to the 'Stoney Vineyard' label in lesser years.

CABERNET SAUVIGNON

Coal Creek Valley $$$$$

1997	16.0	2005	2009
1995	18.4	2007	2015
1994	18.0	2006	2014
1993	16.8	2005	2013
1992	17.3	2004	2012
1991	18.8	2003	2011
1990	16.3	1995	1998

PINOT NOIR

Coal Creek Valley $$$$$

1998	18.7	2003	2006+
1997	18.3	2005	2009
1995	16.8	1997	2000
1994	18.7	1999	2002+
1992	18.3	1997	2000+
1991	18.0	1996	1999
1990	16.6	1995	1998

Region: Yarra Valley Winemakers: Wayne Donaldson, Neville Rowe, James Gosper
Viticulturist: Bernie Wood Chief Executive: Chris Lynch

A typically complete and elegant Vintage Brut from 1997 is clearly the pick of an otherwise underwhelming series of current releases from Domaine Chandon, which has successfully redefined the premium Australian sparkling wine market over the last decade. The company sources fruit from a significant number of vineyards in the cooler and more southerly regions from several states. Its first Non-Vintage release is a fast-maturing wine made from inferior fruit when compared to what we are used to witnessing under this label.

VINTAGE BLANC DE BLANCS

Southern Australia $$$$

1996	17.9	2001	2004
1995	18.2	1997	2000+
1993	18.4	1998	2001
1992	18.8	2000	2004
1991	18.7	1999	2003
1990	18.1	1995	1998
1989	17.7	1994	1997
1986	18.6	1994	1998

VINTAGE BLANC DE NOIRS

Southern Australia $$$$

1996	16.7	2001	2004
1994	18.5	1996	1999
1993	18.4	1998	2001
1992	18.7	1997	2000
1991	17.8	1996	1999
1990	18.3	1992	1995

VINTAGE BRUT

Southern Australia $$$$

1997	18.2	1999	2002
1996	15.6	1998	2001
1995	17.5	1997	2000
1994	18.5	1996	1999
1993	18.6	1995	1998
1992	18.5	1994	1997
1991	18.7	1996	1999
1990	18.4	1992	1995

VINTAGE BRUT ROSÉ

Southern Australia $$$$

1997	15.0	1999	2002
1996	16.0	1998	2001
1995	18.1	1997	2000
1994	18.3	1996	1999
1993	18.3	1998	2001
1992	17.4	1994	1997
1989	18.3	1994	1997

**Region: Mornington Peninsula Winemaker: Garry Crittenden
Viticulturist: Garry Crittenden Chief Executive: Garry Crittenden**

Recently announced expansion plans in conjunction with the substantial Mornington Vineyards development and a major funds raising operation reveals Dromana Estate's intention to become a larger player in Victorian wine. From the quality perspective, the 'standard' Chardonnay from 1999 is a delicious young wine, while the Reserve Chardonnay and spicy Reserve Pinot Noir maintain their consistent quality.

CABERNET MERLOT

Mornington Peninsula $$$$

1998	15.3	2000	2003
1997	17.0	2002	2005+
1996	16.0	1998	2001
1995	16.4	2000	2003
1994	17.8	2002	2006
1993	17.6	2001	2005
1992	17.2	2000	2004
1991	16.8	1996	1999
1990	18.0	1998	2002

CHARDONNAY

Mornington Peninsula $$$$

1999	18.1	2001	2004
1998	17.2	2000	2003
1997	16.1	1999	2002
1996	16.5	1998	2001
1995	17.0	1997	2000
1994	18.6	1999	2002
1993	18.0	1998	2001
1992	18.0	1997	2000
1991	18.5	1996	1999
1990	17.0	1995	1998

PINOT NOIR

Mornington Peninsula $$$$

1999	16.3	2001	2004
1998	16.5	1999	2000
1997	17.6	2002	2005
1996	18.0	2001	2004
1995	18.2	1997	2000
1994	18.1	1999	2002
1993	18.0	1998	2001

RESERVE CHARDONNAY

Mornington Peninsula $$$$

1998	17.5	2003	2006
1997	18.7	2002	2005
1996	17.6	2001	2004
1995	17.9	1997	2000
1994	18.4	1996	1999

RESERVE PINOT NOIR

Mornington Peninsula $$$$

1998	17.6	2000	2003
1997	18.8	2002	2005+
1996	18.3	2001	2005+
1995	18.0	2000	2003+
1994	15.0	1996	1999

Region: Clare Valley Winemakers: Wendy Stuckey, John Glaetzer
Viticulturist: Peter Pawelski Chief Executive: Terry Davis

Eaglehawk began its life as a second Wolf Blass label based at the old Quelltaler winery in the Clare Valley. Its modern wines are fairly open, honest and straightforward, but won't set you on fire.

glehawk

ara Vineyards
t Highway
ootpa SA 5355
(08) 8562 1955
(08) 8562 4127

RIESLING

Clare Valley $$

1999	16.3	2000	2001+
1998	16.6	1999	2000
1997	16.5	2002	2005
1996	16.7	2001	2004

SHIRAZ MERLOT CABERNET SAUVIGNON

Clare Valley $$

1998	15.7	2000	2003
1997	16.0	1999	2002
1996	15.0	1998	2001

Region: McLaren Vale Winemaker: Fiona Donald
Viticulturist: Brian Hill Chief Executive: Tom Park

Traditionalists mightn't like it, but Seaview is virtually no more, since most of its wines have been re-branded under the Edwards & Chaffey tag. There are doubtless sound reasons for dispensing with another historic Australian label, but I think I detect the work of a product manager determined to justify a job. Either way, the wines are very good, just like those from Seaview used to be...

CABERNET SAUVIGNON

McLaren Vale $$$

1998	16.8	2003	2006+
1996	15.0	2001	2004
1995	16.4	2000	2003
1994	16.4	1999	2002
1993	16.8	2001	2005
1992	16.9	2000	2004
1991	16.8		2003+
1990	16.4	1995	1998

CHARDONNAY

McLaren Vale $

1999	16.0	2000	2001
1998	16.6	2000	2003
1997	15.4	1998	1999
1996	16.3	1998	2001
1995	15.0	1996	1997
1994	16.0	1996	1999

PINOT NOIR CHARDONNAY

South Australia $$$$

1995	18.4	1997	2000+
1993	16.7	1995	1998
1992	18.7	1997	2000
1991	17.5	1993	1996
1990	18.3	1995	1998
1989	18.5	1991	1994

SECTION 353 CABERNET SAUVIGNON

McLaren Vale $$$$

1998	17.2	2003	2006
1997	16.2	1999	2002+
1996	18.6	2004	2008+
1994	17.8	2002	2006+
1992	18.0	2000	2004

SECTION 353 CHARDONNAY

McLaren Vale $$$$

1997	17.3	1999	2002+
1996	17.0	1998	2001
1995	18.0	1997	2000
1994	17.2	1996	1999

SECTION 353 SHIRAZ

McLaren Vale $$$$

1998	18.5	2006	2010
1997	16.6	2002	2005
1996	18.0	2001	2004+
1995	16.8	1997	2000
1994	18.0	2002	2006

SHIRAZ

McLaren Vale $$

1998	17.2	2003	2006
1997	16.7	2002	2005+
1996	16.2	2001	2004
1995	16.0	2000	2003
1994	16.7	2002	2006
1993	16.2	1998	2001
1992	16.7	1997	2000

Region: Barossa Valley Winemaker: James Irvine
Viticulturist: David Young Chief Executive: Lorraine Ashmead

With the exception of the Command Shiraz, a more powerfully structured wine matured in oak for more than two years, Elderton's collection of red wines presents an early-drinking smorgasbord of ripe Barossa flavours, creamy oaky textures and supple, soft tannins. It's little wonder they're so popular.

CABERNET SAUVIGNON

Barossa Valley $$$

1998	17.5	2003	2006
1997	16.0	1999	2002+
1996	16.8	2001	2004
1995	16.5	2000	2003
1994	18.0	1999	2002
1993	17.4	1998	2001
1992	16.6	1997	2000
1991	17.5	1996	1999
1990	17.3	1995	1998
1989	15.5	1994	1997
1988	17.0	1990	1993

COMMAND SHIRAZ
Barossa Valley $$$$$

1996	17.2	2004	2008
1995	17.6	2003	2007
1994	18.4	2002	2006
1993	16.8	2001	2005
1992	18.6	1997	2000
1990	17.8	1995	1998
1988	18.3	1996	2001
1987	18.5	1999	2004
1986	17.7	1998	2003

EDEN VALLEY RIESLING
Eden Valley $$

1999	15.8	2000	2001
1998	15.0	2000	2003
1997	13.5	1998	1999
1994	16.7	1999	2002
1993	18.2	1998	2001
1992	16.3	1994	1997
1991	18.0	1999	2003

SHIRAZ
Barossa Valley $$$

1998	17.1	2003	2006
1997	16.3	1999	2002
1996	16.2	1998	2003+
1995	17.2	2000	2003
1994	16.8	1999	2002
1993	17.0	1995	1998
1992	16.4	2000	2004
1991	17.0	1999	2003
1990	16.8	1998	2002

Region: Mornington Peninsula
Winemakers: Tod Dexter, Kevin McCarthy, Michael Cope-Williams
Viticulturist: Lawrence Tedesco Chief Executive: Baillieu Myer

Elgee Park was one of the first vineyards in the Mornington
Peninsula and developed an early following for its Chardonnay and
Cabernet Sauvignon. Today it is perhaps best known
for its Viognier and Riesling.

CUVÉE BRUT

Mornington Peninsula $$$$

1996	16.6	2001	2004
1995	16.5	1997	2000
1994	17.2	1999	2002
1993	16.0	1995	1998
1992	17.6	1994	1997

FAMILY RESERVE CHARDONNAY

Mornington Peninsula $$$

1998	16.0	2000	2003
1997	15.3	1999	2002
1995	16.5	1996	1997
1994	16.1	1996	1999
1993	18.7	1998	2001
1992	18.3	1997	2000
1991	17.4	1996	1999
1990	17.5	1995	1998

FAMILY RESERVE PINOT NOIR

Mornington Peninsula $$$$

1998	14.7	2000	2003
1997	16.7	1999	2002
1996	16.2	1998	2001+
1995	15.6	1997	2000

FAMILY RESERVE VIOGNIER

Mornington Peninsula $$

1998	14.5	1999	2000
1997	17.0	1999	2002
1996	17.2	1998	2001
1995	17.2	1997	2000
1994	15.0	1996	1999
1992	15.2	1993	1994

Region: Southern Tasmania Winemakers: Andrew Hood, Steve Lubiana
Viticulturist: Eric Phillips Chief Executives: Eric & Jette Phillips

Elsewhere Vineyard is undergoing some changes in sourcing, but one hopes it will be able to maintain the occasionally excellent standard it has set as one of Tasmania's leading pinot makers.

PINOT NOIR
Southern Tasmania $$$$

1998	16.5	2000	2003+
1995	16.8	1997	2000+
1994	17.8	1999	2002

Elsewhere Vineyard

40 Dillons Hill Road
Glaziers Bay Tas 7109
Tel: (03) 6295 1509
Fax: (03) 6295 1509

Region: Lower Hunter Valley Winemaker: Keith Tulloch
Viticulturist: Alan Townley Chief Executive: Len Evans

Len Evans' own chardonnay is a boots-and-all affair dished up with considerable pomp, style and circumstance – a little like lunch with the man himself. Typical of most Hunter chardonnays, it drinks best at around five years of age.

CHARDONNAY
Lower Hunter Valley $$$$

1998	17.6	2003	2006
1997	15.6	2002	2005
1996	18.6	2001	2004
1995	18.5	2003	2007
1994	16.8	1999	2002
1993	18.1	1998	2001
1990	17.5	1992	1995

Evans Family

Pokolbin NSW 2321
Tel: (02) 4998 7333
Fax: (02) 4998 7798

Region: Margaret River Winemaker: Brian Fletcher
Viticulturist: Murray Edmonds Chief Executive: Franklin Tate

Evans & Tate has made a major winery and vineyard development near Jindong, to the north and east of the established Margaret River vineyards. It's not alone in this respect and at this time is confident that it can maintain and improve on its quality.

GNANGARA SHIRAZ
Swan Valley $$

1998	16.6	2000	2003+
1997	14.6	1999	2002
1996	16.7	1998	2001
1995	16.9	1997	2000
1994	15.0	1996	1999
1993	16.7	1998	2001
1992	15.6	1994	1997
1991	16.8	1993	1996

Evans & Tate

cnr Caves & Metricup Rds
Willyabrup WA 6280
Tel: (08) 9755 6244
Fax: (08) 9755 6346

MARGARET RIVER CABERNET SAUVIGNON

Margaret River $$$$

1998	18.1	2006	2010
1997	16.0	2002	2005
1996	17.2	2004	2008
1995	15.9	2003	2007
1994	18.3	2002	2006
1993	18.2	2001	2005
1992	18.4	2000	2004
1991	18.0	1999	2003
1990	15.0	1995	1998
1989	15.0	1991	1994

MARGARET RIVER CHARDONNAY

Margaret River $$$$

1996	16.0	2001	2004
1995	15.3	1996	1997
1994	16.5	1999	2002
1993	18.1	1995	1998
1991	14.8	1992	1993
1990	16.2	1995	1998

MARGARET RIVER CLASSIC

Margaret River $$$

2000	16.7		2000
1999	14.7	1999	2000
1998	17.5	1998	1999
1997	16.8	1997	1998
1996	16.5	1996	1997
1995	18.0	1996	1997
1994	18.0	1996	1999

MARGARET RIVER MERLOT

Margaret River $$$$

1998	17.6	2003	2006
1996	17.5	2004	2010
1995	16.8	2000	2003
1994	16.7	1999	2002
1993	17.0	2001	2005
1992	17.3	1997	2000
1991	18.3	1999	2003
1990	18.0	1998	2002
1989	17.8	1994	1997
1988	16.5	1993	1996

MARGARET RIVER SAUVIGNON BLANC SEMILLON (FORMERLY SEMILLON)

Margaret River $$$

1999	17.2	2000	2001
1998	17.2	1999	2000
1997	18.4	2002	2005+
1996	17.5	1998	2001
1995	18.5	2000	2003
1994	18.2	1999	2002
1993	18.5	1998	2001
1991	17.5	1996	1999
1990	16.0	1998	2002
1989	18.0	1994	1997
1988	16.5	1996	2000

MARGARET RIVER SHIRAZ

Margaret River $$$$

1998	16.1	2003	2006
1997	17.6	2005	2009
1996	17.2	2004	2008
1995	17.8		2007+
1994	18.3	2002	2006
1993	15.8	2001	2005
1992	18.0	2000	2004
1991	18.0	1999	2003
1990	18.4	1995	1998
1989	15.5	1991	1994

TWO VINEYARDS CHARDONNAY

Margaret River $$$

1999	16.8	2001	2004
1998	16.8	2000	2003
1997	15.0	1998	1999
1996	17.1	1998	2001
1995	16.7	1997	2000
1994	17.6	1996	1999
1993	15.3	1994	1995

Fox Creek is a dynamic new McLaren Vale vineyard which burst
onto the scene with its sumptuous 1994 Reserve Shiraz, a wine
quick to join the ranks of the serious 'Grange Pretenders'. Since
then it has constantly repeated its good form with shiraz and has
launched a rich, sumptuous Reserve Cabernet Sauvignon label,
plus a flinty, mineral Verdelho. It recently lost its energetic
founding winemaker, Sparky Marquis.

JSM SHIRAZ CABERNET FRANC

McLaren Vale $$$$

1998	16.8	2003	2006
1997	16.1	1999	2002
1996	15.3	1998	2001+

RESERVE CABERNET SAUVIGNON

McLaren Vale $$$$

1998	16.8	2006	2010
1997	17.0	2005	2009+
1996	17.9	2004	2008+
1995	16.5	2000	2003

RESERVE SHIRAZ

McLaren Vale $$$$

1998	17.9	2003	2006
1997	18.4	2005	2009
1996	18.6		2008+
1995	18.1	2003	2005
1994	18.4		2006+

VERDELHO

McLaren Vale $$

1999	15.7	2001	2004
1998	16.7	2000	2003
1997	15.2	1998	1999
1996	16.6	1998	2001

It's been a little erratic in recent vintages, but Frankland Estate has undoubted potential as a maker of fine wine from both shiraz and the red Bordeaux varieties, plus riesling. It's found well towards the north of the large Great Southern region and can list amongst its achievements the excellent Olmo's Reward blend of 1995.

ISOLATION RIDGE CABERNET SAUVIGNON

Great Southern $$$

1998	14.8	2003	2006
1997	16.7	2002	2005
1996	17.5		2008+
1995	16.2		2007+
1994	16.0	1999	2002
1993	17.6		2005+
1992	16.6	1997	2000
1991	16.6	1996	1999

ISOLATION RIDGE CHARDONNAY

Great Southern $$$

1998	15.8	1999	2000
1997	16.2	2002	2005
1996	16.0	2001	2004
1994	18.5	1992	2002
1993	15.5	1998	2001
1992	16.4	1994	1997

ISOLATION RIDGE RIESLING

Great Southern $$

1999	16.6	2004	2007+
1998	18.2	2006	2010
1997	16.5	2002	2005
1996	17.4	2001	2004
1995	17.6	2000	2003
1994	16.6	1999	2002
1993	16.0	1995	1998
1992	16.7	1997	2000
1991	17.2	1993	1996

ISOLATION RIDGE SHIRAZ

Great Southern $$

1998	16.3	2003	2006+
1997	15.3	2002	2005
1996	16.9	2001	2004
1995	17.1	2000	2003
1994	17.4	1999	2002
1993	16.3	2001	2005
1992	16.5	2000	2004

OLMO'S REWARD

Great Southern $$$

1997	15.0	2002	2005
1996	16.0	2001	2004
1995	18.7		2007+
1994	16.5	2002	2006
1993	17.5	1998	2001
1992	17.3	1997	2000

Region: East Coastal Tasmania Winemakers: Claude Radenti & Lindy Bull
Viticulturist: Geoff Bull Chief Executive: Geoff Bull

Freycinet's heat trap-like site on Tasmania's east coast gives it a brilliant advantage when it comes to ripening grapes and a real headstart with its best varieties of pinot noir and chardonnay. The Pinot Noirs from 1999 and 1998 are dark, ripe and charming, bursting with spicy berry fruit wound around fine tannins.

CABERNET MERLOT

East Coastal Tasmania $$$$

1998	16.7	2000	2003+
1997	15.0	1999	2002
1995	16.2	2000	2003
1994	18.3	2002	2006
1992	15.8	2000	2004
1991	18.0	2003	2011
1990	16.0	1998	2002

CHARDONNAY

East Coastal Tasmania $$$$

1999	18.1	2004	2007
1998	17.0	2000	2003+
1997	15.1	1998	1999
1996	16.7	1998	2001
1995	18.6	2003	2007
1994	18.2	2002	2006
1992	16.6	1994	1999
1991	16.3	1993	1996

PINOT NOIR

East Coastal Tasmania $$$$

1999	17.9	2004	2007
1998	17.2	2000	2003+
1997	16.0	1999	2002
1996	17.0	2001	2004
1995	18.5	2000	2003
1994	16.0	1996	1999
1993	14.9	1998	2001
1992	15.7	1997	2000
1991	18.7	1996	1999
1990	16.2	1995	1998

Region: Clare Valley Winemaker: Stephen George
Chief Executive: Stephen George

Stephen George makes a blockbusting, dark, peppery and minty shiraz with an astringent, savoury finish which is built for genuinely long term cellaring from old-vine Clare Valley fruit. He also creates his own version of the traditional cabernet-malbec Clare blend, a wine of similar dimensions, power and longevity.

SHIRAZ

Clare Valley $$$

1998	16.7	2006	2010+
1997	17.8		2009+
1996	16.2	2001	2004
1995	18.0		2007+
1994	18.1	2002	2006
1993	15.6	1998	2001
1992	17.9		2004+
1991	17.5	1999	2003
1990	17.6	2002	2010
1989	16.0	1997	2001

rry
ttenden 'i'

son's Road
ana Vic 3936
(03) 5987 3800
(03) 5981 0714

GARRY CRITTENDEN

SANGIOVESE

mbrook Hill

ching Place Road
brook Vic 3783
(03) 5968 1622
(03) 5968 1699

GEMBROOK HILL
1995
YARRA VALLEY
CHARDONNAY
PRODUCT OF AUSTRALIA 750 ml

GEMBROOK HILL
1995
YARRA VALLEY
PINOT NOIR
PRODUCT OF AUSTRALIA 750 ml

GEMBROOK HILL
1997
YARRA VALLEY
SAUVIGNON BLANC
PRODUCT OF AUSTRALIA 750 ml

Region: Alpine Valleys Winemaker: Garry Crittenden
Viticulturist: Garry Crittenden Chief Executive: Garry Crittenden

Garry Crittenden's 'i' label burst onto the scene around three years ago and has since established itself as Australia's leading collection of table wines made from Italian varieties. The Sangiovese is always a charmer, with dark, savoury fruit and tight-knit tannins. The range includes a Nebbiolo, Barbera and Riserva blend.

'i' SANGIOVESE
Alpine Valleys $$$$

1999	18.2	2001	2004
1998	16.6	2000	2003
1997	17.9	1998	2002+

Region: Yarra Valley Winemakers: Ian Marks, Helen Smythe, Martin Williams
Viticulturist: Ian Marks Chief Executive: Ian Marks

It's located in a cooler, higher portion of the Yarra Valley, so its wines, Pinot Noir and Chardonnay especially, offer fragrance and intensity instead of the richness of some grown on the valley floor. Gembrook Hill makes an enticing and racy Sauvignon Blanc.

CHARDONNAY
Yarra Valley $$$$

1997	15.8	1999	2002
1995	17.6	2000	2003
1994	16.9	1999	2002
1993	17.9	1998	2001

PINOT NOIR
Yarra Valley $$$$

1998	17.5	2003	2006
1997	16.8	1999	2002
1996	15.8	1997	1998
1995	16.0	1996	1997
1994	16.0	1996	1999
1993	17.9	1998	2001
1992	16.8	1994	1997

SAUVIGNON BLANC
Yarra Valley $$$$

1999	15.8	2000	2001
1998	18.5	2000	2003
1997	18.0	1998	1999
1996	17.0	1998	2001
1994	16.0	1996	1999

The best of Geoff Merrill's present wines is the Reserve Cabernet Sauvignon 1995, which recently made the grade on Qantas First Class. Generally, Merrill's style remains fine and relatively light.

CABERNET MERLOT (FORMERLY MOUNT HURTLE)

McLaren Vale, Goulburn Valley, Coonawarra $$$

1997	15.1	1997	1998
1996	15.8	1998	2001
1995	16.7	2003	2007
1994	16.5	1996	1999
1993	16.6	1995	1998
1992	16.2	1997	2000
1991	16.7	1996	1999
1990	17.9	1998	2002

CABERNET SAUVIGNON RESERVE (FORMERLY CABERNET SAUVIGNON)

Coonawarra, McLaren Vale, Goulburn Valley $$$$

1995	17.2	2003	2007
1994	16.6	1999	2002
1993	17.0		2005+
1992	16.3	2000	2004
1991	15.0	1999	2003
1990	16.6	1998	2002
1989	18.0	1997	2001
1988	17.5	1996	2000
1987	17.0	1995	1999
1986	17.5	1994	1998

CHARDONNAY

South-Eastern Australia $$$$

1997	15.6	1998	1999
1996	16.8	1998	2001
1995	15.8	1996	1997

CHARDONNAY RESERVE

South-Eastern Australia $$$$

1996	15.5	1997	1998
1995	15.8	1997	2000
1994	16.4	1996	1999
1993	15.2	1995	1998
1992	16.5	1997	2000
1991	17.9	1996	1999
1990	18.0	1998	2002

SAUVIGNON BLANC (FORMERLY MOUNT HURTLE)

McLaren Vale $$

1999	14.5		2000
1998	16.6	1999	2000
1997	14.6		1998
1996	16.7	1996	1997
1995	16.8	1996	1997
1994	17.9	1996	1999

SHIRAZ (FORMERLY MOUNT HURTLE)

McLaren Vale $$$$

1997	16.3	2002	2005
1996	16.7	2001	2004
1995	16.1	2000	2003
1994	17.0	1999	2002
1992	16.7	1998	2001
1991	16.4	1997	2000

Region: Adelaide Hills Winemaker: Geoff Weaver
Viticulturist: Geoff Weaver Chief Executive: Geoff Weaver

Each of Geoff Weaver's quartet of table wines from Lenswood in the Adelaide Hills reflects his preference for restrained, elegant and complex wine that gradually unravels itself in the glass before you. His Riesling, Sauvignon Blanc and Chardonnay are each pristine and spotless, while the suppleness, tightness and poise of the Cabernet Merlot unashamedly flies directly against the modern trend in Australian red wine.

CABERNET SAUVIGNON MERLOT

Adelaide Hills $$$$

1997	15.8		2009+
1994	17.9	2002	2006
1993	18.1	2001	2005
1991	16.2	1999	2003
1990	18.3	1998	2002

CHARDONNAY

Adelaide Hills $$$

1998	16.6	2003	2006
1997	18.5	2002	2005+
1996	17.8	1998	2001
1995	18.4	2000	2003+
1994	17.0	1999	2002
1993	18.3	2001	2005
1992	17.3	1997	2000
1991	18.5	1996	1999
1990	16.5	1995	1998

RIESLING

Adelaide Hills $$

1999	17.8	2007	2011
1998	18.1	2003	2006
1997	18.5	2005	2009
1996	16.0	1998	2001
1995	17.8	2003	2007
1994	14.0	1995	1996
1993	18.4	2001	2005
1991	18.4	1999	2003
1990	17.2	1995	1998

SAUVIGNON BLANC

Adelaide Hills $$$

1999	15.4	2000	2001
1998	18.5	2000	2003
1997	18.3	1999	2002
1996	18.1	1998	2001
1995	16.6	1997	2000
1994	18.6	1996	1999
1993	18.8	1995	1998
1992	18.5	1994	1999

One of Australia's most sought-after labels, Giaconda has established itself at the sharp end of our chardonnay production and sits amongst the leading group of pinot makers. Its cabernet is underrated and its first Shirazes from 1997 are 1998 are stupendous.

CABERNET SAUVIGNON/MERLOT/ CABERNET FRANC

Alpine Valleys $$$$

1998	18.8	2006	2010+
1997	18.6	2005	2009+
1996	18.3	2004	2008+
1995	18.3	2003	2007
1994	18.1	2002	2006
1993	18.0	1998	2001
1992	18.6		2004+
1991	18.9	1999	2003
1990	17.9	1998	2002
1988	18.4	1996	2000
1987	15.0	1995	1999
1986	16.7	1994	1998

CHARDONNAY

Alpine Valleys $$$$$

1999	19.4	2007	2011
1998	19.0	2003	2006+
1997	19.2	2005	2009
1996	18.9	2004	2008
1995	17.8	2003	2007
1994	18.8	2002	2006
1993	18.8	2001	2005
1992	19.0	1997	2000
1991	18.4	1995	1999
1990	18.6	1998	2002
1989	17.8	1991	1994

PINOT NOIR

Alpine Valleys $$$$$

1999	19.2	2004	2007+
1998	18.4	2006	2010
1997	18.8	2002	2005+
1996	16.8	2001	2004+
1995	14.7	2000	2003
1994	18.2	1999	2002
1993	17.9	1998	2001
1992	19.0	1997	2000
1991	18.5	1996	1999
1990	17.5	1995	1998
1989	18.7	1994	1997

Region: Sunbury Winemaker: John Barnier
Viticulturist: John Barnier Chief Executive: John Barnier

Goona Warra

Sunbury Road
Sunbury Vic 3429
Tel: (03) 9740 7766
Fax: (03) 9744 7648

In almost total contrast to the scale and magnificence of its restaurant housed above the century-old bluestone winery at Sunbury, Goona Warra's output is restricted to small amounts of red and white table wines, including Bordeaux-like blends of Cabernet Sauvignon and Cabernet Franc, plus Semillon and Sauvignon Blanc.

CABERNETS (FORMERLY CABERNET FRANC)

Sunbury $$$

1998	15.8	2000	2003+
1997	14.8	1999	2002
1996	17.8	2001	2004
1995	15.0	1997	2000
1994	16.0	1996	1999
1993	17.3	1998	2001
1992	17.3	1997	2000
1991	16.5	1993	1996

SEMILLON SAUVIGNON BLANC (FORM. SEMILLON)

Sunbury $$$

2000	16.8	2002	2005
1997	17.9	2002	2005
1996	17.6	2001	2004
1995	18.2	2000	2003
1994	17.7	1999	2002
1993	17.2	1998	2001
1992	16.5	1997	2000
1991	18.0	1996	1999

Goundrey

Muir Highway
Mount Barker WA 6324
Tel: (08) 9851 1777
Fax: (08) 9851 1997

Region: Great Southern Winemaker: Keith Bown
Viticulturist: Cate Finlay Chief Executive: Ted Avery

Goundrey's future looks bright under its new ownership and the efforts presently being made to fulfill the potential of its excellent large vineyard. While there's little doubt that the company's best wines are still ahead of it, present releases continue to disappoint perhaps rather more than they should. A fine exception is the ripe, almost jammy 1996 Reserve Cabernet Sauvignon.

RESERVE CABERNET SAUVIGNON

Great Southern $$$

1996	17.0	2002	2008
1995	17.0	2003	2007
1993	16.0	2001	2005
1992	15.6	1997	2000
1991	18.1		2003+
1990	15.5	1998	2002
1989	17.0	1997	2001
1988	15.5	1996	2000
1987	16.0	1995	1999
1986	14.5	1994	1998
1985	17.6	1993	1997

RESERVE CHARDONNAY

Great Southern $$$

1999	14.8	2000	2001
1998	15.6	2000	2003
1997	16.4	1999	2002
1995	16.2	1997	2000
1994	18.0	1999	2002
1993	16.3	1995	1998
1992	17.4	1997	2000
1991	18.0	1996	1999

RESERVE RIESLING

Great Southern $$

1999	15.2	2001	2004
1998	16.5	2000	2003
1997	17.0	2002	2005
1996	18.1	2004	2008
1995	16.0	2003	2007
1994	18.4	2002	2006
1993	18.7	1998	2001
1991	17.5	1996	1999
1990	17.0	1995	1998
1989	16.5	1994	1997

Region: Barossa Valley Winemaker: Philip Laffer
Viticulturist: Joy Dick Chief Executive: Christian Porta

Gramp's is an exclusively Barossa region label of Orlando Wyndham whose wines are generous, ripe and relatively early to mature and easy to understand. The Botrytis Semillon often makes a pleasant surprise.

BOTRYTIS SEMILLON

Barossa Valley $$$$

1997	16.7	1999	2002
1996	16.8	1998	2001
1994	15.0	1995	1996

CABERNET MERLOT

Barossa Valley $$

1997	16.8	2002	2005
1996	15.8	1998	2001
1995	15.6	1997	2000
1994	15.0	1999	2002
1993	13.5	1995	1998

CHARDONNAY

Barossa Valley $$

1999	16.3	2001	2004
1998	15.0	1999	2000
1997	16.7	1999	2002
1996	16.0	1998	2001
1995	14.5	1996	1997

GRENACHE

Barossa Valley $$

1998	16.3	2000	2003
1997	16.6	1999	2002
1996	15.4	1997	1998
1995	15.9	1997	2000
1994	15.3	1996	1999

t Burge

Valley Way
Creek
SA 5352
) 8563 3700
) 8563 2807
www.grantburge
m.au

bwines.com.au

Region: Barossa Valley Winemaker: Grant Burge
Viticulturist: Michael Schrapel Chief Executive: Grant Burge

Grant Burge has recently acquired the old Krondorf winery (but not the brand, which still belongs to Mildara Blass), which he will develop into his white wine making headquarters. Led by a string of excellent shirazes under the Filsell and prestigious Meshach labels, Burge has created a strong regional brand of ripe, flavoursome wines which effectively trap the Barossa in a bottle.

CAMERON VALE CABERNET SAUVIGNON

Barossa Valley $$$

1998	16.6	2006	2010
1997	16.0	2002	2005
1996	17.6	2004	2008
1995	17.4	2003	2007
1994	16.7	2002	2006
1993	16.6	2001	2005

FILSELL SHIRAZ

Barossa Valley $$$$

1998	18.0	2003	2006+
1997	18.3	2005	2009
1996	18.6	2008	2016
1995	18.5	2007	2015
1994	18.2	2002	2006
1993	16.8	2001	2005
1992	16.6	2000	2004
1991	18.5	2003	2011
1990	18.2	2002	2010

HILLCOT MERLOT

Barossa Valley $$$$

1998	16.7	2000	2003+
1997	15.8	1999	2002
1996	16.3	1998	2001
1995	16.5	2000	2003
1994	16.8	1999	2002

KRAFT SAUVIGNON BLANC

Eden Valley $$

1999	15.4		2000
1998	17.3	1999	2000
1997	15.5	1997	1998

MESHACH

Barossa Valley $$$$$

1996	18.8		2008+
1995	19.0		2007+
1994	18.6		2006+
1993	18.1	2001	2005
1992	18.2	2000	2004
1991	19.2	2003	2011
1990	18.2	1998	2002+
1988	18.3	1996	2000

THE HOLY TRINITY

Barossa Valley $$$

1997	16.7	1999	2002
1996	16.7	1998	2001
1995	15.8	1997	2000

THORN RIESLING

Eden Valley $$

1999	16.6	2001	2004+
1998	18.0	2003	2006
1997	16.1	1999	2002
1996	16.8	1998	2001+
1995	15.1	1996	1997

ZERK SEMILLON

Barossa Valley $$$

1999	17.8	2001	2004+
1998	16.6	2000	2003
1997	16.8	2002	2005
1996	15.0	1997	1998
1995	16.0	1996	1997

Green Point

Green Point
Maroondah Highway
Coldstream Vic 3770
Tel: (03) 9739 1110
Fax: (03) 9739 1095

Region: Yarra Valley
Winemakers: Wayne Donaldson, Neville Rowe, James Gosper
Viticulturist: Bernie Wood Chief Executive: Chris Lynch

Domaine Chandon markets its still table wines under the same label it sells its sparkling wine overseas: Green Point. The Reserve Chardonnay is a rich, complex and heavily worked wine with genuine potential, while releases to-date of Reserve Pinot Noir have yet to develop comparable sweetness of fruit and intensity.

YARRA VALLEY CHARDONNAY

Yarra Valley $$$

1998	16.9	2003	2006
1996	15.0	1996	1997
1995	18.2	2000	2003
1994	17.8	1999	2002
1993	16.7	1998	2001
1992	17.9	1997	2000

Grosset

King Street
Auburn SA 5451
Tel: (08) 8849 2175
Fax: (08) 8849 2292
E-mail:
grosset@capri.net.au

Region: Clare Valley Winemaker: Jeffrey Grosset
Viticulturist: Jeffrey Grosset Chief Executive: Jeffrey Grosset

With a string of excellent wines under the Polish Hill and Watervale labels, Jeffrey Grossett has established himself at the head of the riesling revival in Australia. His Adelaide Hills wines offer suppleness and charm, while recent releases of the increasingly beefed-up Gaia blend of red Bordeaux varieties offer long-term potential in the cellar. Grossett was also recently commissioned by Qantas to produce a riesling exclusively for the airline.

GAIA (CABERNET BLEND)

Clare Valley $$$$

1998	18.8		2010+
1996	17.5	2004	2008
1995	18.0		2007+
1994	18.5		2006+
1993	18.3		2005+
1992	18.6		2004+
1991	16.6	1996	1999
1990	16.8	2002	2010
1989	16.6	1994	1997
1988	15.6	1990	1993
1987	16.5	1992	1995
1986	18.0	1994	1998

NOBLE RIESLING

Clare Valley $$$$

1999	17.6	2001	2004
1998	16.7	2000	2003
1997	18.7	2002	2005
1996	18.2	1998	2001
1995	18.5	2000	2003
1994	18.5	1999	2002
1993	17.2	1995	1998
1992	17.6	1994	1997

PICCADILLY (CHARDONNAY)

Piccadilly Valley (Largely Clare until 1993) $$$$

1999	18.7	2004	2007+
1998	17.3	2003	2006
1997	18.3	2002	2005
1996	18.7	2001	2004
1995	18.4	2000	2003
1994	18.4	2002	2006
1993	18.1	1998	2001
1992	16.8	1997	2000
1991	17.7	1996	1999

PINOT NOIR

Adelaide Hills $$$$

1998	18.2	2003	2006
1997	18.6	2002	2005+
1996	18.5	2004	2008
1995	17.5	1997	2000
1994	18.1	1999	2002
1993	17.0	1998	2001

POLISH HILL

Clare Valley $$$

1999	18.5	2007	2011+
1998	18.8	2010	2018
1997	19.0	2005	2009
1996	18.5	2004	2008
1995	19.0		2007+
1994	18.6	2002	2006
1993	18.7	2001	2005
1992	18.3	2000	2004
1991	16.5	1996	1999
1990	18.4		2002+
1989	15.0	1991	1994
1988	17.5	1993	1996
1987	18.0	1999	2004
1986	17.7	1994	1998
1985	18.8	1997	2005

SEMILLON SAUVIGNON BLANC

Clare Valley (with Adelaide Hills from 1992) $$$

1999	17.0	2004	2007
1998	18.0	2003	2006
1997	17.0	1998	1999
1996	18.1	1998	2001
1995	18.3	1997	2000
1994	18.5	1999	2003
1993	18.3	2001	2005
1992	17.5	1997	2000
1991	18.0	1996	1999
1990	17.5	1998	2002

WATERVALE RIESLING

Clare Valley $$

1999	18.7	2007	2011+
1998	18.3	2006	2010+
1997	18.3	2002	2005
1996	17.2	2001	2004
1995	18.5	2000	2003
1994	18.4	2002	2006
1993	18.5	2001	2005
1992	17.8	1997	2000
1991	17.7	1996	1999
1990	18.5		2002+

Gulf Station

Pinnacle Lane
Dixon's Creek Vic 3775
Tel: (03) 5965 2271
Fax: (03) 5965 2442

Region: Yarra Valley Winemakers: Stephen Webber, David Slingsby-Smith, David Bicknell
Viticulturist: Philip Lobley Chief Executive: Darren De Bortoli

Gulf Station is a fast-growing De Bortoli brand of attractive early-drinking white wines made from Yarra Valley fruit. The Chardonnay is deliberately made with modest oak treatment, but presents generous, vibrant ripe grapefruit and peachy flavours.

CHARDONNAY

Yarra Valley $$

1999	17.0	2000	2001
1998	17.3	1999	2002
1997	16.9	1999	2002
1996	16.5	1997	1998
1995	17.0	1996	1997

RIESLING

Yarra Valley $$

1999	15.2	2001	2004
1998	17.6	2003	2006
1997	16.0	2002	2005
1996	15.0	1998	2001
1994	15.8	1994	1999

Region: McLaren Vale Winemaker: Phillipa Treadwell
Viticulturist: Dean Whiteman Chief Executive: Dr Richard Hamilton

I'm delighted with the ripeness, richness and restraint of the Centurion Shiraz 1998 and the Hut Block 1998, genuine McLaren Vale reds with distinctive poise and class. Hamilton's wines are typically more reserved and elegant than most from this region.

BURTON'S VINEYARD

McLaren Vale $$

1997	15.9	2005	2009
1996	16.9	2001	2004
1995	18.1	2003	2007
1994	16.6	1999	2002
1992	15.7	1998	2001

CENTURION SHIRAZ

McLaren Vale $$$

1998	18.2	2006	2010+
1996	16.4	2001	2004+
1995	18.3	2003	2007
1994	17.5	2002	2006
1992	16.0	2000	2004

CHARDONNAY

McLaren Vale $$

1999	16.8	2001	2004
1998	16.0	2000	2003
1997	16.0	1999	2000
1996	16.7	1998	2001
1995	16.5	1997	2000
1994	16.8	1996	1999
1993	16.8	1995	1998
1992	16.0	1994	1997

HUT BLOCK CABERNETS

McLaren Vale $$

Year	Score		
1998	18.3	2006	2010
1997	16.5	2002	2005
1996	15.4	2004	2008
1995	17.6	2003	2007
1994	16.8	1999	2002
1993	16.3	1998	2001
1992	17.1	2000	2004
1991	18.5	1999	2003

Region: Macedon Winemaker: John Ellis
Viticulturist: John Ellis Chief Executive: John Ellis

With another fine Heathcote Shiraz on the market and some excellent sparkling Macedon in the bottle, John Ellis' premium wines are returning to top form. Ellis' style of sparkling wine is considerably more oxidative and complex in nature than the norm in Australia, while the Heathcote Shiraz is typically black and spicy.

HEATHCOTE SHIRAZ

Heathcote $$$$$

Year	Score		
1998	18.3	2006	2010
1997	17.0	2002	2005+
1992	18.4		2004+
1991	18.0		2011+
1990	18.7		2002+
1989	16.0	1997	2001
1988	16.8	1993	1996
1987	18.4		2007+

MACEDON

Macedon $$$$

Cuvée	Score		
Cuvée VII	17.0	2001	2005
Cuvée VI	18.6	2000	2002
Cuvée V	16.0	1997	2000
Cuvée IV	18.4	1996	1999
Cuvée III	17.6	1995	1999

"THE JIM JIM" (SAUVIGNON BLANC)

Macedon $$$

Year	Score		
1999	17.8	2000	2001
1998	16.6	1999	2000
1997	16.6		1998
1996	15.1	1997	1998

VICTORIA CABERNET SAUVIGNON & MERLOT

Victoria $$$

1998	14.3	2000	2003
1997	15.3	2002	2005+
1996	16.4	2001	2004
1995	16.6	2003	2007
1994	15.7	2002	2006

VICTORIA SHIRAZ

Victoria $$$

1998	15.7	2000	2003
1997	17.5	2002	2005
1996	16.8	2001	2004
1995	15.1	2000	2003

Region: McLaren Vale Winemakers: Peter Dawson, Stephen Pannell (red), Tom Newton (white), Ed Carr (sparkling). Viticulturist: Brenton Baker Chief Executive: Stephen Millar

Hardys continues to lay down the red wine challenges to Southcorp and has gradually returned the focus of its premier reds back to the McLaren Vale. It will become the exclusive source of shiraz for the Eileen Hardy label as well as the Tintara and Reynell brands. The less-publicised of Hardys' premium reds is the Thomas Hardy Cabernet Sauvignon, a Coonawarra red which enjoyed another successful season in 1996.

EILEEN HARDY CHARDONNAY

Padthaway, McLaren Vale $$$$

1998	18.5	2003	2006
1997	18.3	2002	2005
1996	18.5	2001	2004
1995	18.1	2000	2003
1994	17.4	1996	1999
1993	17.2	1998	2001
1992	15.6	1997	2000
1991	17.8	1996	1999
1990	18.1	1995	1998

EILEEN HARDY SHIRAZ

McLaren Vale, Padthaway $$$$$

1997	17.6	2009	2017
1996	18.1	2004	2008+
1995	18.8	2007	2015
1994	18.0	2002	2006
1993	18.0		2005+
1992	18.0	2000	2004
1991	17.9		2003+
1990	18.5		2002+
1989	17.0	1997	2001
1988	17.0	1996	2000
1987	17.5	1995	1999
1986	16.5	1994	1998
1976	18.2	1988	1996
1970	18.9	1990	1995

NOTTAGE HILL CABERNET SHIRAZ

South Australia $

1999	14.5	2000	2001
1998	16.4	2000	2003+
1996	15.0	2001	2004
1995	15.2	1997	2000
1994	15.5	1996	1999

SIEGERSDORF RHINE RIESLING

Padthaway $

1999	14.5	2004	2007
1998	16.7	2003	2006+
1997	16.7	2002	2005
1996	16.5	2001	2004
1995	15.8	1996	1997
1994	17.2	2002	2006
1993	16.1	1995	1998
1992	18.2	2000	2004
1991	17.9	1996	1999

THOMAS HARDY CABERNET SAUVIGNON

McLaren Vale, Coonawarra $$$$

1996	18.3		2008+
1995	17.7	2003	2007+
1994	18.0		2006+
1993	17.3	2001	2005
1992	18.2	2000	2004
1991	18.5		2003+
1990	18.6		2002+
1989	18.3	2001	2009

TINTARA GRENACHE

McLaren Vale $$$$

1998	16.0	2000	2003
1997	17.4	2002	2005+
1996	18.2	2001	2004+
1995	18.1	2000	2003

TINTARA SHIRAZ

McLaren Vale $$$$

1998	18.2	2006	2010
1997	18.6	2005	2009
1996	18.3	2004	2008
1995	18.7	2000	2003+

Region: Great Southern Winemaker: Michael Kerrigan
Viticulturist: Keith Graham Chief Executives: Keith & Margie Graham

Harewood Estate is a pristine small vineyard in the Great Southern which sells substantial amounts of its fruit to Howard Park and Domaine Chandon. An ever-increasing allocation finds its way under the property's own brand, which produced an excellent wine in 1998 after several promising early vintages aged quickly.

Harewood Estate

Scotsdale Road
Denmark WA 6333
Tel: (08) 9840 9078
Fax: (08) 9840 9053

CHARDONNAY

Great Southern $$$$

1998	18.3	2003	2006
1997	15.3	1998	1999
1996	14.5	1997	1998

Region: Heathcote Winemaker: Mark Kelly
Viticulturist: Andrew Mepham Chief Executive: Steve Wilkins

The Heathcote Winery is a small quality operation whose energies are directed to creating a series of shirazes of varying depth and concentration. Second tier from the top is the Mail Coach Shiraz, a wine that other wineries might be happy to call their flagship.

Heathcote Winery

183 High Street
Heathcote Vic 3523
Tel: (03) 5433 2595
Fax: (03) 5433 3081

CHARDONNAY

Heathcote $$$

1998	16.6	2000	2003+
1997	14.7	1998	1999
1996	16.8	1998	2001
1994	14.5	1995	1996

Heggies
Vineyard

Heggies Range Road
Eden Valley SA 5353
Tel: (08) 8561 3200
Fax: (08) 8561 3393

MAIL COACH SHIRAZ

Heathcote $$$

1998	18.3	2006	2010+
1997	18.0	2002	2005+
1995	15.6	1997	2000
1994	17.6	1999	2002

Region: Eden Valley Winemaker: Hugh Reimers
Viticulturist: Robin Nettelbeck Chief Executive: Robert Hill Smith

It's a reflection of the sheer quality of its recent Rieslings, Merlots and Viognier that Heggies' Pinot Noir and Chardonnay are in danger of looking second rate. That's meant as a compliment to this thoroughly revitalised vineyard whose riesling has long been considered an Eden Valley classic, but, without doubt the greatest achievement at Heggies has been to create a Merlot that will surely help define this grape variety in Australia.

BOTRYTIS RIESLING

Eden Valley $$$$

1999	18.7	2004	2007
1998	18.0	2002	2006
1997	17.1	2002	2005
1996	18.0	2001	2004
1995	16.0	1997	2000
1994	17.7	1999	2002
1992	18.4	1997	2000
1991	18.0	1996	1999
1990	17.5	1992	1995

CHARDONNAY

Eden Valley $$$

1998	16.7	2000	2003+
1997	16.0	1999	2002
1996	16.3	1998	2001
1995	17.5	2000	2003
1994	16.5	1996	1999
1993	16.7	1995	1998
1992	17.0	1994	1997
1991	18.0	1996	1999

MERLOT (FORMERLY CABERNET BLEND)

Eden Valley $$$$

1996	18.7	2004	2010+
1995	18.0	2000	2003+
1994	18.2	2002	2006
1993	18.3	2001	2005
1992	16.0	2000	2004
1991	16.6	1996	1999
1990	17.4	1998	2002
1989	16.6	1994	1997
1988	17.5	1996	2000
1987	16.1	1989	1992

PINOT NOIR

Eden Valley $$$$

1998	15.8	2000	2003
1997	17.8	2002	2005
1996	16.0	2001	2004
1994	14.5	1995	1996
1993	14.0	1994	1995

PINOT NOIR
1994

RIESLING

Eden Valley $$

1999	18.6	2007	2011
1998	19.0	2006	2010+
1997	16.9	2002	2005
1996	16.5	2003	2007
1995	18.3	2003	2007
1994	14.0	1996	1999
1993	18.5		2005+
1992	18.2	1997	2000
1991	15.2	1993	1996
1990	15.5	1995	1998

RIESLING
1995

VIOGNIER

Eden Valley $$

1999	15.4	2001	2004
1998	18.0	2000	2003
1997	17.9	1999	2002
1996	15.7	1997	1998
1995	14.5	1996	1997
1994	17.0	1999	2002
1993	17.5	1998	2001
1992	16.5	1997	2000

VIOGNIER
1995

Region: Eden Valley Winemaker: Stephen Henschke
Viticulturist: Prue Henschke Chief Executive: Stephen Henschke

It is an incredible achievement for a winery as small as Henschke to have created from vineyards old and new a twin set of wine ranges, each of which is considered to be at the forefront of its kind. It's a measure of Steve Henschke's ability that while the Eden Valley and Lenswood wines have many distinct and clear differences, his stamp as a winemaker shines strongly through, with precise berry fruit qualities and assertive, but balanced oak influences. The 1999 whites and 1997 reds have clearly been affected by the difficulties associated with each season.

ABBOTTS PRAYER

Adelaide Hills $$$$$

1997	17.9	2002	2005+
1996	18.8	2004	2008+
1995	18.5	2003	2007
1994	18.7		2006+
1993	18.5		2005+
1992	17.7	2000	2004
1991	18.0		2003+
1990	19.0	2002	2010
1989	16.9	1994	1997

CRANES EDEN VALLEY CHARDONNAY (FORMERLY BAROSSA RANGES CHARDONNAY)

Eden Valley $$$

1999	15.0	2000	2001
1998	17.9	2003	2006
1997	17.0	2002	2005
1996	18.2	2001	2004
1995	17.3	1997	2000
1994	18.2	1999	2002
1993	17.5	1995	1998
1992	17.7	1997	2000
1991	18.5	1996	1999
1990	18.7	1998	2002

CROFT CHARDONNAY

Adelaide Hills $$$$

1999	15.3	2001	2004
1998	18.3	2003	2006+
1997	16.0	2002	2005
1996	18.4	2001	2004
1995	17.3	1997	2000
1994	18.4	1999	2003
1993	16.8	1995	1998
1990	18.3	1995	1998

CYRIL HENSCHKE CABERNET SAUVIGNON

Eden Valley $$$$

1997	16.5	2005	2009
1996	18.6	2008	2016+
1995	17.6	2003	2007
1994	17.2	2002	2006+
1993	18.7		2005+
1992	18.3		2004+
1991	18.7		2003+
1990	18.8		2002+
1989	17.4	2001	2009
1988	19.0	1996	2000
1987	16.0	1992	1995
1986	17.8	1998	2003
1985	18.1	1997	2002
1984	18.8	1992	1996
1983	17.0	1995	2000
1982	16.0	1987	1990
1981	18.5	1993	1998
1980	17.3	1992	1997
1979	16.0	1987	1991
1978	17.6	1990	2000

GILES PINOT NOIR

Adelaide Hills $$$

1998	15.4	2003	2006+
1997	17.3	2002	2005
1996	17.3	2001	2004
1994	16.8	1999	2002
1993	17.0	1998	2002
1992	15.3	1994	1997
1991	18.3	1996	1999
1989	17.3	1994	1997

GREEN'S HILL RIESLING

Adelaide Hills $$

1999	17.1	2001	2004
1998	18.1	2003	2006+
1997	18.3	2005	2009
1996	18.6	2004	2008
1995	18.0	2003	2007
1994	18.0	2002	2006
1993	18.3	1998	2001

HILL OF GRACE

Eden Valley $$$$$

Year	Score		
1998	19.0		2018+
1997	18.7		2017+
1996	18.5	2008	2016
1995	18.2		2015+
1994	18.5	2006	2014+
1993	17.6		2013+
1992	18.8		2012+
1991	18.6		2011+
1990	19.0		2010+
1989	16.0	1994	1997
1988	18.9		2008+
1987	16.6	1999	2007+
1986	19.2		2006+
1985	17.4	2005	2015
1984	16.6	1996	2004
1983	15.4	1991	1995
1982	16.8	1994	2002
1981	15.3	1986	1989
1980	16.7	1992	2000
1979	17.3	1991	1999
1978	18.8	1998	2008
1977	17.2	1989	1997+
1976	18.4		1996+
1975	16.0	1983	1987
1973	18.6		1993+
1971	18.3		1991+
1970	18.2		1990+
1969	15.7	1981	1989
1968	19.0		1988+
1967	18.2		1987+
1966	19.0	1986	1996+
1965	16.5	1973	1979+
1964	16.7	1976	1984+
1963	16.4	1975	1983
1962	19.5	1982	1992+
1961	18.8	1973	1981+
1959	18.0	1979	1989
1958	18.8	1978	1988+

JULIUS RIESLING

Eden Valley $$

1999	18.0	2004	2007
1998	17.5	2006	2010
1997	18.5	2005	2009
1996	18.5	2004	2008
1995	17.5	1997	2000
1994	18.6		2006+
1993	18.6	2000	2005
1992	18.4	2000	2004
1991	17.0	1999	2003
1990	18.7	1995	1998
1989	16.0	1994	1997
1988	16.5	1993	1996
1987	18.5	1999	2004
1986	17.0	1991	1994

KEYNETON ESTATE

Eden Valley $$$$

1997	16.2	2002	2005
1996	18.2	2004	2008+
1994	18.1	2002	2006
1993	18.3		2005+
1992	18.0	1997	2000
1991	17.8	1999	2003
1990	16.5	1995	1998
1989	16.0	1994	1997
1988	18.1	1996	2000
1987	15.5	1992	1995
1986	18.5	1998	2003
1985	16.0	1997	2002
1984	18.2	1992	1996
1983	14.5	1991	1995
1982	17.0	1994	1999

LOUIS EDEN VALLEY SEMILLON

Eden Valley $$$

1999	15.1	2001	2004
1998	16.6	2003	2006
1997	17.0	2002	2005
1996	15.8	1998	2003
1995	18.3	2000	2003
1994	18.0	2002	2006
1993	18.7	1998	2001
1992	17.9	1997	2000
1991	18.4	1996	1999
1990	18.0	1998	2002
1989	16.7	1994	1997

MOUNT EDELSTONE

Eden Valley $$$$$

Year	Score		
1998	18.0	2006	2010
1997	16.6	2005	2009
1996	18.4	2004	2008+
1995	18.1		2007+
1994	18.9		2006+
1993	18.6		2005+
1992	18.5		2004+
1991	18.8		2003+
1990	18.6		2002+
1989	16.8	1997	2003
1988	18.5	2000	2005
1987	16.0	1995	2001
1986	18.2	1998	2003
1985	16.0		2005+
1984	16.5	1996	2001
1983	17.0	1995	2000
1982	17.0	1994	1999
1981	15.0	1993	1998
1980	17.0	2000	2005
1979	15.0	1991	1996
1978	18.0	1990	1995
1977	16.0	1989	1994
1976	15.0	1988	1993
1975	16.0	1987	1992
1974	14.0	1982	1986
1973	15.0	1985	1990
1972	18.8	1992	1997

Highbank Vineyards

Riddoch Highway
Coonawarra SA 5263
Tel: (08) 8736 3311
Fax: (08) 8736 3122

Region: Coonawarra Winemakers: Dennis Vice, Trevor Mast
Viticulturist: Dennis Vice Chief Executive: Dennis Vice

Highbank is an exciting new entrant in the famous Coonawarra region which has adopted a totally organic vineyard system under the energetic and enthusiastic management of Dennis Vice. The vineyard's principal wine is a joyous blend of Bordeaux varieties made at Mount Langi Ghiran with another proponent of organic viticulture, Trevor Mast.

COONAWARRA

Coonawarra $$$$

Year	Score		
1998	16.8	2006	2010
1997	18.7	2005	2009
1994	18.6	2002	2006
1993	18.1	1998	2001
1992	18.4	2000	2004

Region: Eden Valley Winemaker: Hugh Reimers
Viticulturist: Robin Nettlebeck Chief Executive: Robert Hill Smith

The Hill-Smith Estate's Chardonnay and Sauvignon Blanc are consistently generous, flavoursome, well-made and true to type. The Chardonnay is more forward and brassy, while the Sauvignon Blanc will suit those who enjoy the herbaceous aspect of this variety's character.

CHARDONNAY

Eden Valley $$

1998	16.6	2000	2003+
1997	16.2	1999	2002
1996	16.5	1998	2001
1995	17.4	2000	2003
1994	14.3	1996	1999
1993	17.0	1995	1998

SAUVIGNON BLANC

Eden Valley $$

1999	17.8	2000	2001
1998	18.2	1999	2000
1997	16.5	1998	1999
1996	17.2	1998	2001
1995	17.2	1996	1997

Region: Coonawarra Winemakers: Ian Hollick, David Norman
Viticulturist: Ian Hollick Chief Executive: Ian Hollick

Recent vintages of Hollick wines don't quite capture the magic of the early 1990s, but offer easy and early drinking, lighter expressions of Coonawarra reds and whites which aren't going to need long in the cellar to look at their best.

CABERNET SAUVIGNON MERLOT

Coonawarra $$$

1998	16.5	2000	2003+
1997	15.0	1999	2002
1996	14.5	1997	1998
1995	16.1	1997	2000
1994	17.5	1999	2002
1993	17.0	1998	2001
1992	16.7	1997	2000
1991	17.4	1996	1999
1990	18.0	1995	1998

RAVENSWOOD (CABERNET SAUVIGNON)

Coonawarra $$$$$

1996	16.0	2001	2004
1994	16.9	2002	2006+
1993	17.8	2001	2005
1992	18.0	2000	2004
1991	18.7		2003+
1990	18.4		2002+
1989	17.9	2001	2009
1988	18.2	2000	2005

RESERVE CHARDONNAY

Coonawarra $$$

1998	15.2	2000	2003
1997	15.0	1998	1999
1996	16.0	1998	2001
1995	15.2	2000	2003
1994	17.7	1999	2002
1993	17.1	1995	1998
1992	16.8	1994	1997
1991	18.0	1996	1999
1990	17.0	1995	1998

RIESLING

Coonawarra $$

1999	15.8	2001	2004
1998	15.5	2000	2003
1997	15.1	1999	2002
1995	16.5	2000	2003
1994	16.6	1999	2002
1992	18.4	1997	2000
1991	17.5	1993	1996

WILGHA SHIRAZ

Coonawarra $$$$

1997	15.7	1999	2002
1996	15.0	1998	2001
1994	17.5	1996	1999
1993	17.3	1998	2001
1992	16.8	1997	2000
1991	17.8	1996	1999
1990	17.5	1995	1998
1989	16.5	1991	1994
1988	17.0	1993	1996

Region: Various WA Winemaker: Larry Cherubino
Viticulturist: Ron Page Chief Executive: Stephen Millar

While I can't help thinking that the benchmark White Burgundy has rather gone off the boil in recent years, Houghton's red wines are moving from strength to strength. The premium Jack Mann wine has set a very high standard with its first three vintages, but none was made from the difficult 1997 season.

JACK MANN RED

Great Southern $$$$$

1996	18.7	2004	2008+
1995	18.2	2003	2007+
1994	17.8	2002	2005

WHITE BURGUNDY

Swan Valley $

1999	16.0	2001	2004
1998	16.0	2000	2003
1997	16.0	1999	2002
1996	15.7	1998	2001
1995	15.5	1997	2000
1994	16.0	1999	2002
1993	16.8	1998	2001

Regions: Great Southern, Margaret River Winemaker: Michael Kerrigan
Chief Executive: Jeff Burch

Just prior to the 2000 vintage Howard Park commissioned its red wine processing and cellar door facility at Margaret River. Aside from the 1998 Chardonnay, an excellent wine with a terrific future, the 1997 cabernet blend and 1999 riesling, both from difficult years, fail to live up to the standards of the past decade.

CABERNET SAUVIGNON MERLOT

Great Southern $$$$$

1997	15.4	2005	2009
1996	19.0		2008+
1995	15.0	2000	2003
1994	19.2		2006+
1993	18.1	2001	2005
1992	19.4		2004+
1991	18.4		2003+
1990	17.5	2002	2010
1989	18.7	2001	2009
1988	17.0	2000	2008
1987	18.4	1999	2004
1986	18.5		2006+

CHARDONNAY

Great Southern $$$$

1998	18.7	2003	2006+
1997	16.0	1999	2002
1996	17.5	1998	2001
1995	18.5	2000	2003
1994	18.5	1999	2002
1993	18.0	1998	2001

RIESLING

Great Southern $$$

1999	15.7	2004	2007
1998	18.1	2006	2010
1997	17.7	2002	2005
1996	18.4		2008+
1995	18.7		2007+
1994	18.5		2006+
1993	18.4	2001	2005
1992	18.2	2000	2004
1991	18.5		2003+
1990	18.0	1998	2002
1989	17.8	1994	1997
1988	18.5	2000	2005
1987	16.2	1995	1999
1986	18.8	1998	2003

Region: McLaren Vale Winemaker: John Hugo
Viticulturist: John Hugo Chief Executive: John Hugo

A small McLaren Vale maker with a lower profile than its quality warrants, Hugo is as reliable a brand as you can find. The 1998 reds are especially drinkable wines based around deeply flavoured and fully ripened fruit with carefully married sweet and savoury oak influences.

CABERNET SAUVIGNON

McLaren Vale $$$

1998	17.6	2006	2010
1997	15.0	2002	2005+
1996	17.0	2001	2004
1995	16.8	2000	2003
1994	16.5	1992	2002
1993	17.5	2001	2005
1992	18.2	1997	2000

CHARDONNAY

McLaren Vale $$

1999	16.8	2001	2004
1998	15.8	1999	2000
1997	17.2	2002	2005
1996	16.0	1999	2001
1994	17.3	1999	2002
1993	18.0	2001	2005
1992	16.6	1994	1997

SHIRAZ

McLaren Vale $$$

1998	17.0	2003	2006
1997	16.2	1999	2002+
1996	17.6	2001	2004
1995	17.3	2000	2003
1994	17.2	1999	2002
1993	17.2	2001	2005
1992	17.7	1997	2000
1991	17.0	1996	1999
1990	18.3	1995	1998

Region: Mudgee Winemaker: Susan Roberts
Viticulturist: Robert Welch Chief Executive: Bob Roberts

It's a constant source of amazement that more people are not familiar with the exceptional value presented by Huntington Estate's richly textured cellaring styles of red wine, which include a creamy Shiraz, a sumptuously firm Cabernet Merlot and generously flavoured Cabernet Sauvignon.

CABERNET SAUVIGNON

Mudgee $$

1997	15.5	2002	2005+
1995	16.4	2003	2007
1994	16.6	2002	2006
1993	16.8	2001	2005
1992	18.2	2004	2012
1991	17.0	1996	1999
1990	16.5	1995	1998
1989	18.0	1994	1997
1988	15.0	1993	1996

SEMILLON
Mudgee $$

1999	15.3	2001	2004
1998	15.7	2000	2003
1997	17.0	2002	2005
1996	18.1	2001	2004
1995	17.7	2000	2003
1994	16.0	1999	2003
1993	16.7	1998	2001
1992	15.0	1994	1997
1991	17.5	1996	1999

SHIRAZ
Mudgee $$

1997	17.0	2005	2009
1995	16.7	2003	2007+
1994	15.7	1999	2002
1993	18.6		2005+
1992	16.7	1997	2000
1991	17.6	1999	2003
1990	16.7	1998	2002
1989	16.5	1994	1997
1988	16.5	1993	1996

Region: McLaren Vale Winemaker: Charles Hargrave
Viticulturist: Guy Rayner Chief Executive: Terry Davis

Another arm of Mildara Blass' push into McLaren Vale, Ingoldby
has produced some generously flavoured reds from 1998 which,
while being a small improvement on recent years, still fall short of
the Ingoldby of old. They still lack the punch and penetration of
others doing similar things at McLaren Vale.

CABERNET SAUVIGNON
McLaren Vale $$

1998	15.6	2003	2006
1997	14.9	1999	2002+
1996	15.0	1998	2001
1995	16.9	2000	2003
1994	17.0	1999	2002
1993	16.8	2000	2005
1992	18.1	2000	2004
1991	18.7		2003+
1990	17.0		2002+

SHIRAZ

McLaren Vale $$

1998	16.6	2000	2003+
1997	16.4	2002	2005
1996	16.0	1998	2001
1995	17.2	2000	2003
1994	16.1	1996	1999
1993	17.5	1999	2001
1991	18.6	1999	2003
1990	18.0	1998	2002

Region: Eden Valley Winemaker: James Irvine
Viticulturist: James Irvine Chief Executive: Marjorie Irvine

James Irvine has been a specialist in merlot for a decade and a half at his Eden Valley base. The Grand Merlot is his flagship, a robust and sumptuous long-living wine constructed around very ripe and low-yielding fruit which then sees a considerable time in small oak. Parts of the batch are even given bubbles!

James Irvine

Roeslers Road
Eden Valley SA 5235
Tel: (08) 8564 1046
Fax: (08) 8546 1314

GRAND MERLOT

Eden Valley $$$$

1996	16.8	2004	2008
1995	17.8	2003	2007
1994	18.8		2006+
1993	18.6		2005+
1992	16.9	2000	2004
1991	18.4	1999	2003
1990	18.2		2002+
1989	17.2	1994	1997
1988	18.2	1996	2000
1987	16.2	1992	1995
1986	18.1	1994	1998

Jamiesons Run

Riddoch Highway
Coonawarra SA 5263
Tel: (08) 8736 3380
Fax: (08) 8736 3307

Region: Coonawarra Winemaker: David O'Leary
Viticulturist: Vic Patrick Chief Executive: Terry Davis

Jamieson's Run is a brand created by Mildara Blass around a popular Coonawarra wine, which remains its best individual component. The debut of a new Merlot is quite encouraging, but I'd be happy to stick with the 'original' red.

JAMIESON'S RUN RED

Coonawarra $$

1997	16.6	2002	2005
1996	16.4	2001	2004
1995	17.0	2000	2003
1994	18.2	2002	2006
1993	17.9	2001	2005
1992	16.5	2000	2004
1991	16.4	1999	2003
1990	16.6	1998	2002
1989	16.7	1993	1996
1988	17.9	1996	2000

Jansz

1216 Pipers Brook Road
Pipers Brook Tas 7254
Tel: (03) 6382 7122
Fax: (03) 6382 7225

Region: Pipers River Winemaker: Tony Davis
Viticulturist: Ben Wagner Chief Executive: Robert Hill Smith

Originally the long-awaited Heemskerk sparkling wine developed with Champagne Louis Roederer, Jansz is today owned by S. Smith & Son (owners of Yalumba), which views it as an opportunity to partner the successful 'D' brand with another distinctively different sparkling wine, this time from Tasmania. The wines are typically fine and elegant, and finish with occasionally bracing acidity.

BRUT CUVÉE

Pipers River $$$$

1995	16.8	2000	2003
1994	17.6	1999	2002
1993	18.5	1998	2001
1992	18.5	1997	2000
1991	16.8	1993	1996

Jasper Hill

Drummonds Lane
Heathcote Vic 3523
Tel: (03) 5433 2528
Fax: (03) 5433 3143

Region: Heathcote Winemaker: Ron Laughton
Viticulturist: Ron Laughton Chief Executive: Ron Laughton

Jasper Hill sits amongst the premier shiraz vineyards in Australia. Sited on some of the best soils of the Heathcote region, which is rapidly becoming synonymous with first-rate dark and peppery shiraz, Jasper Hill's wines have followed a recent trend towards extreme ripeness and alcoholic strengths. Its modern wines have little in common with the long-living classics of a decade ago and we will simply have to wait and see how they develop.

EMILY'S PADDOCK SHIRAZ/CABERNET FRANC

Heathcote $$$$$

1998	17.5	2006	2010
1997	18.5		2009+
1996	16.9	2004	2008
1995	16.2	2000	2003
1994	18.4	2002	2006
1993	15.9		2005+
1992	16.7		2012+
1991	18.6		2011+
1990	18.4		2002+
1989	14.8	1994	1997
1988	18.7	2000	2008+

GEORGIA'S PADDOCK RIESLING

Heathcote $$$

1998	17.2	2003	2006
1997	18.0	2005	2009
1996	16.0	1998	2001
1994	17.2	1999	2002
1993	14.5	1994	1995
1992	16.8	1997	2000
1991	18.5	1999	2003
1990	16.7	1998	2002
1989	17.0	1994	1997+
1988	18.3	1996	2000
1987	15.6	1992	1995
1986	15.2	1991	1994
1985	17.8	1993	1997

GEORGIA'S PADDOCK SHIRAZ

Heathcote $$$$$

1998	16.6	2006	2010
1997	18.0		2008+
1996	18.5		2008+
1995	18.9		2007+
1994	18.7	2002	2006+
1993	19.0		2005+
1992	18.8		2004+
1991	17.7	1999	2003+
1990	18.5		2002+
1989	15.7	1997	2001
1988	18.6		2008+
1987	15.8	1999	2007
1986	18.1		2006+
1985	18.7		2005+

Jim Barry

Main North Road
Clare SA 5453
Tel: (08) 8842 2261
Fax: (08) 8842 3752

Region: Clare Valley Winemaker: Mark Barry
Viticulturist: Peter Barry Chief Executive: Peter Barry

Jim Barry's leading red wine, The Armagh, is aimed both stylistically and fiscally at those who'd like to buy Grange but can only afford half a bottle. Like most of its predecessors, the 1997 again justifies its lofty reputation, while the excellent and cheaper McCrae Wood red wines offer closely related style and quality.

CABERNET BLEND ▮

Clare Valley $$

1997	15.1	1999	2002
1996	15.4	1997	1998
1995	15.9	2000	2003
1994	16.8	1996	1999
1993	17.0	1998	2001
1992	16.8	1997	2000

CABERNET SAUVIGNON ▮

Clare Valley $$

1997	15.3	2002	2005
1996	15.4	2001	2004
1995	17.9	2003	2007
1994	16.4	1999	2002
1993	16.5	1998	2001
1992	17.4	2000	2004
1990	16.5	1995	1998
1989	16.7	1994	1997
1988	18.5	1996	2000

McCRAE WOOD CABERNET MALBEC ▮

Clare Valley $$

1997	16.8		2009+
1996	17.1	2004	2008+
1995	16.2	2000	2003
1994	17.0	2002	2006+

McCRAE WOOD SHIRAZ ▮

Clare Valley $$$

1996	18.0	2004	2008
1995	17.5	2000	2003
1994	18.3	2002	2006
1993	16.2	1995	1998
1992	18.1	2000	2004

THE ARMAGH SHIRAZ

Clare Valley $$$$$

1997	18.6	2005	2009+
1996	18.8	2004	2008
1995	18.6	2003	2007+
1994	18.0	2002	2006
1993	18.7		2005+
1992	18.8		2004+
1991	18.0		2003+
1990	18.6		2010+
1989	18.3		2009+
1988	18.2	2000	2005
1987	18.1		2007+
1985	16.0	1997	2002

WATERVALE RIESLING

Clare Valley $$

1999	18.6	2004	2007
1998	18.1	2003	2006+
1997	18.0	2005	2009
1996	16.7	2004	2008
1995	17.5	2003	2007+
1994	16.4	1999	2002
1993	17.5	2001	2005

**Region: Porongorup Winemakers: Stephen Pester, John Wade
Viticulturists: Geoff Clarke & Barry Coad Chief Executive: Shelley Coad**

Its fine and fragrant riesling from 1999 suggests a bright future for Jingalla, a small vineyard in the Porongorup Ranges of WA's Great Southern district, which has moved into a new shared winemaking facility with other local producers.

CABERNET SAUVIGNON

Great Southern $$$

1997	14.7	1999	2002
1996	16.8	2004	2008
1995	15.0	2000	2003+
1994	16.5	1999	2002
1993	14.2	1998	2001
1991	16.7	1999	2003
1989	17.0	1994	1997
1988	17.0	1996	2000
1987	16.5	1999	2004
1986	15.0	1991	1994

Jingalla

**RMB 1316 Bolganup Dam Rd
Porongorup WA 6324
Tel: (08) 9853 1023
Fax: (08) 9853 1102**

Katnook Estate

Riddoch Highway
Coonawarra SA 5263
Tel: (08) 8737 2394
Fax: (08) 8737 2397

RIESLING

Great Southern $$

1999	16.8	2004	2007
1998	15.5	1999	2000
1996	17.5	2001	2004
1995	16.0	1997	2000
1994	17.6	1999	2002
1993	18.0	1998	2001
1990	17.2	1992	1995

VERDELHO

Great Southern $$

1998	14.7	1999	2000
1997	16.0	1999	2002
1996	18.3	2001	2004
1995	17.6	2000	2003
1994	16.8	1996	1999
1993	15.8	1994	1995

Region: Coonawarra Winemaker: Wayne Stehbens
Viticulturist: Leon Oborne Chief Executive: David Yunghanns

Katnook Estate continues to cement its place amongst the best makers of Coonawarra red wines. It enjoyed the great 1998 vintage with spectacular results. While the 'regular' Cabernet Sauvignon moves from strength to strength, the Odyssey label is gaining respect as a showcase red. The debut Prodigy Shiraz 1997, winner of the 1998 Jimmy Watson Trophy, is a powerfully concentrated and statuesque wine in a Wynns Michael-like style.

CABERNET SAUVIGNON

Coonawarra $$$$

1998	18.7		2010+
1997	17.7	2002	2005+
1996	18.6	2008	2016
1995	16.5	2000	2003
1994	18.5	2002	2006
1993	18.4		2005+
1992	16.0	2004	2012
1991	18.6		2003+
1990	17.8		2002+
1988	16.2	1996	2000
1987	16.5	1991	1995
1986	18.3	1998	2003
1985	16.5	1993	1997
1984	16.5	1988	1992
1983	16.0	1991	1995
1982	16.0	1990	1994
1981	17.0	1989	1993
1980	18.0	1992	1997

CHARDONNAY

Coonawarra $$$$

1998	15.8	2000	2003
1997	16.8	1999	2002
1996	18.2	2001	2004
1995	18.4	2000	2003
1994	18.3	1999	2002
1993	18.4	1998	2001
1992	18.2	1997	2000
1991	16.8	1996	1999
1990	17.8	1998	2002
1989	18.2	1997	2001

CHARDONNAY BRUT

Coonawarra $$$

1996	16.2	2001	2004
1995	17.2	2000	2003
1994	15.0	1996	1999
1993	17.1	1995	1998
1990	18.4	1995	1998

MERLOT

Coonawarra $$$$

1998	18.4	2006	2010
1997	18.2	2002	2005+
1996	18.5	2004	2008
1995	16.0	1997	2000
1994	18.3	1999	2002
1993	18.3	1998	2001
1992	18.2	1997	2000
1991	16.0	1996	1999
1990	16.8	1995	1998

ODYSSEY

Coonawarra $$$$$

1996	18.8	2004	2008+
1994	18.7	2002	2006+
1992	16.9	1997	2000
1991	18.7	2003	2011

Kay's Amery

Kays Road
McLaren Vale SA 5171
Tel: (08) 8323 8211
Fax: (08) 8323 9199

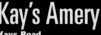

RIESLING

Coonawarra $$

1999	15.0	2001	2004
1998	17.6	2003	2006+
1997	17.0	2002	2005
1996	16.0	2001	2004
1995	15.0	2000	2003
1994	16.8	1999	2002

SAUVIGNON BLANC

Coonawarra $$$

1999	15.0		2000
1998	16.6		1999
1997	17.6	1999	2002
1996	18.3	1998	2001
1995	18.5	1997	2000
1994	17.5	1995	1996

Region: McLaren Vale Winemaker: Colin Kay
Viticulturist: Colin Kay Chief Executive: Colin Kay

Kays' red wines are reaping the rewards of a renewed emphasis on the vineyard and quality of oak. The Block 6 is, for the time being at least, one of the true bargains in premium Australian red wine, and given the exceptional quality of the 1998 Shiraz, one should perhaps be placing orders for the 1998 Block 6 right now.

BLOCK 6 SHIRAZ

McLaren Vale $$$$

1997	16.4	2002	2005
1996	18.7	2004	2008+
1995	18.2	2003	2007+
1994	18.4		2005+
1993	18.2		2005+
1992	18.5		2004+
1991	18.2	1999	2003
1990	18.1		2002+
1989	17.2	1994	1997
1988	15.6	1993	1996
1987	14.5	1989	1992

CABERNET SAUVIGNON

McLaren Vale $$$

1998	16.8	2006	2010+
1997	17.2	2005	2009
1996	17.8	2004	2008
1995	16.8	2003	2007
1994	17.0		2006+
1993	16.0	2001	2005
1992	16.7	2000	2004
1989	16.7	1995	1997
1985	16.0	1990	1993

SHIRAZ

McLaren Vale $$$

1998	18.4	2006	2010
1997	16.5	2002	2005+
1996	18.4	2004	2008
1995	17.5		2006+
1994	17.1		2006+
1993	16.2	2001	2005
1992	16.7	2000	2004

Region: Geographe Winemaker: Paul Boulden
Viticulturist: Paul Boulden Chief Executive: Ben Killerby

Killerby is an energetic wine company established in 1973 by Dr
Barry Killerby. The 1998 Shiraz is a welcome return to the Rhône-
ish Shirazes of previous years, but the wines from other
varieties are still not showing Killerby at its best.

Killerby

Lakes Road
Capel WA 6230
Tel: 1-800 655 722
Fax: 1-800 679 578
Website:
www.killerby.com.au
E-mail:
killerby@killerby.com.au

CABERNET SAUVIGNON

Geographe $$$

1998	15.7	2003	2006+
1997	15.8	2002	2005
1996	15.2	2004	2008
1995	16.0	2003	2007
1994	15.0	1999	2002
1993	18.2		2005+
1992	18.5	2000	2004
1991	16.0		2003+
1989	18.5	2001	2009

CHARDONNAY

Geographe $$$

1999	14.5		2000
1998	15.8	2000	2003+
1997	16.0	1998	1999
1996	18.1	2001	2004
1995	18.0	2000	2003
1994	18.2	1999	2002
1993	17.9	1998	2001
1992	18.2	1994	1997
1991	18.5	1999	2003

SEMILLON

Geographe $$$

1998	15.3	2000	2003
1997	17.0	2002	2005
1996	18.2	2001	2004
1995	18.3	2000	2003
1994	17.6	2002	2006
1993	17.0	1998	2001
1992	17.5	1997	2000
1991	17.5	1999	2003
1990	16.0	1995	1998
1989	17.5	1997	2001
1988	16.5	1993	1996

SHIRAZ

Geographe $$$

1998	17.8	2006	2010
1997	15.7	2002	2005
1996	16.7	2001	2004
1995	18.3	2003	2007
1994	18.3	2002	2006
1993	18.1	2001	2005
1992	15.0	1997	2000
1991	18.4	1999	2003
1989	16.8	1997	2001

Subject to considerable recent controversy concerning the use of a
non-permitted additive to its wine, Kingston Estate has
nevertheless championed the cause of the Riverlands as a
consistent producer of affordable and flavoursome table wines.

MERLOT ■

Riverlands $$

1999	16.0	2000	2001
1998	15.3	2000	2003
1997	15.7	1999	2002
1996	15.0	1997	1998

Andrew Hardy's team at Knappstein are on a roll. From the top-
drawer Enterprise Shiraz and Cabernet Sauvignon reds to the
established classics of Riesling and Gewurztraminer, this winery
isn't missing a skip. Furthermore, the cheaper Cabernet Merlot
and Shiraz reds offer plenty of flavour and some class.

CABERNET MERLOT ■

Clare Valley $$$

1998	17.0	2003	2006
1997	16.8	2002	2005
1996	17.4	2001	2004
1995	16.8	2000	2003
1994	16.8	2002	2006
1993	16.0	1998	2001
1992	16.5	1997	2000
1991	17.5	1999	2003
1990	17.0	1992	1995

CHARDONNAY ■

Clare Valley, Lenswood $$$

1998	15.2	1999	2000
1996	16.4	1998	2001
1995	17.0	2000	2003
1994	15.0	1996	1999
1993	18.2	1995	1998
1992	18.0	1997	2000
1991	18.0	1993	1996
1990	17.0	1995	1998

ENTERPRISE CABERNET SAUVIGNON

Clare Valley $$$$$

1997	18.0	2005	2009+
1996	17.5	2004	2008+
1995	17.0	2003	2007+
1994	18.3	2002	2006
1993	17.6	2001	2005
1990	18.5	1998	2002
1989	18.0	1997	2001
1988	17.8	1993	1996
1987	16.4	1989	1992
1986	18.0	1994	1998

ENTERPRISE SHIRAZ

Clare Valley $$$$$

1997	18.5	2005	2009+
1996	18.2	2004	2008
1995	18.1	2003	2007

GEWÜRZTRAMINER

Clare Valley $$

1999	16.7	2004	2007
1998	18.2	2003	2006
1997	18.4	2002	2005
1996	18.2	2001	2004
1995	16.8	2000	2003
1994	17.5	2002	2006
1993	18.5	1998	2001
1992	17.0	1994	1997
1991	18.0	1993	1996

RIESLING

Clare Valley $$

1999	18.0	2004	2007
1998	18.7	2006	2010
1997	18.5	2005	2009
1996	18.3	2004	2008
1995	17.8	2003	2007
1994	18.3		2006+
1993	18.6	2001	2005
1992	17.5	1997	2000
1991	17.0	1996	1999
1990	18.0	1998	2002
1989	17.0	1991	1994

SEMILLON SAUVIGNON BLANC

Clare Valley $$$

1998	15.9	2000	2003
1997	16.0	1999	2002
1996	17.7	2001	2004
1995	18.0	1997	2000
1994	16.8	1999	2002
1993	18.4	1995	1998
1992	18.0	1997	2000
1991	17.0	1993	1996

SHIRAZ

Clare Valley $$$

1998	17.8	2003	2006+
1997	16.6	2002	2005
1996	15.2	1998	2001

**Region: Macedon Winemaker: Llew Knight
Viticulturist: Llew Knight Chief Executive: Llew Knight**

One of mainland Australia's coolest and latest vineyards, Knights tends to perform best and most consistently with its Riesling, and Chardonnay. In warmer years the Cabernet Sauvignon and Shiraz develop attractive berry flavours and cool minty complexity.

CABERNET SAUVIGNON

Macedon $$$

1998	17.0	2006	2010
1997	15.7	2002	2005
1996	15.4	2001	2004
1995	16.8	2003	2007
1992	15.8	1997	2000
1991	16.2		2003+
1989	15.8	1991	1994
1988	15.0	1996	2000

CHARDONNAY

Macedon $$$

1997	15.2	1999	2002
1996	17.2	2001	2004
1995	18.0	2003	2007
1994	15.2	1996	1999
1993	17.8	1998	2001
1992	18.0	2000	2004
1991	18.0	1996	1999
1990	18.5	1995	1998
1989	16.0	1991	1994

Knights Granite Hills

**1481 Burke & Wills Track
Baynton
Kyneton Vic 3444
Tel: (03) 5423 7264
Fax: (03) 5423 7288**

Lake's Folly
Broke Road
Pokolbin NSW 2320
Tel: (02) 4998 7507
Fax: (02) 4998 7322
Website:
www.lakesfolly.com.au
E-mail:
folly@ozemail.com.au

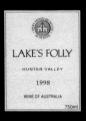

RIESLING
Macedon $$$

Year	Score		
1999	17.8	2007	2011
1998	17.6	2003	2006+
1997	18.5		2009+
1995	18.0	2003	2007
1994	16.8	2002	2006
1993	15.6	1998	2001
1992	18.4	2000	2004
1991	16.5	1996	1999
1990	18.0	1995	1998
1989	15.0	1991	1994

Region: Lower Hunter Valley Winemaker: Stephen Lake
Viticulturist: Bob Davies Chief Executive: Peter Fogarty

Australia's first 'boutique' or 'weekend' winery and vineyard has changed hands, but the winemaker over the last two decades, Stephen Lake, is staying on to continue his fine work.

CABERNETS
Lower Hunter Valley $$$$

Year	Score		
1998	18.1	2006	2010
1997	16.3	2005	2009
1996	16.2	2001	2004
1995	17.2		2007+
1994	18.7		2006+
1993	18.8		2005+
1992	17.6	2000	2004
1991	17.5		2003+
1990	16.0	1998	2002
1989	17.8	2001	2009
1988	16.0	1996	2000
1987	17.0	1995	1999
1986	16.0	1994	1998
1985	17.4	1997	2005

CHARDONNAY
Lower Hunter Valley $$$$

Year	Score		
1998	18.5	2006	2010
1997	17.0	2002	2005
1996	18.3	2001	2004
1995	18.7	2003	2007
1994	17.8	2002	2006
1993	18.7	2001	2005
1992	17.8	2000	2004
1991	17.8	1999	2003
1990	16.5	1995	1998
1989	18.0	1997	2001
1988	16.5	1993	1996
1987	18.0	1992	1995
1986	18.2	1998	2003

From its Classic Clare range to the excellent and traditionally
labelled Bin series of wines, Bin 56 and Bin 61 especially,
Leasingham has entirely and successfully refocused its approach
towards all aspects of red wine making from the vineyard upwards.

BIN 7 RIESLING

Clare Valley $$

1999	16.9	2004	2007
1998	17.8	2006	2010
1997	15.6	2002	2005
1996	17.0	2001	2004+

BIN 56 CABERNET MALBEC

Clare Valley $$

1997	15.8	2002	2005+
1996	17.0	2004	2008
1995	17.0	2000	2003
1994	17.1	1999	2002
1993	16.7	2001	2005
1992	18.0	2000	2004
1991	16.0	1997	2000
1990	17.0	1998	2002
1989	15.8	1994	1997
1988	17.0	1993	1996

BIN 61 SHIRAZ

Clare Valley $$

1998	18.5	2003	2006+
1997	17.6	2005	2009
1996	17.2	2001	2004
1995	18.0	2003	2007
1994	18.2	1999	2002
1993	16.8	2001	2005
1992	16.3	1997	2000

CLASSIC CLARE CABERNET SAUVIGNON

Clare Valley $$$$

1998	17.8	2006	2010+
1997	15.7	2002	2005
1996	17.5	2004	2008
1995	16.0	2000	2003
1994	17.5	2002	2006
1993	18.0	2001	2005
1992	18.5		2004+
1991	18.4	1996	1999

CLASSIC CLARE RIESLING

Clare Valley $$

1998	16.5	2000	2003
1996	18.2	2004	2008
1995	18.4	2003	2007
1994	18.6	2002	2006+

CLASSIC CLARE SHIRAZ

Clare Valley $$$$

1998	18.8	2006	2010+
1997	??		
1996	18.7	2001	2004+
1995	17.9	2003	2007
1994	18.5	1999	2002
1993	18.3	2001	2005
1992	16.5	1997	2000
1991	18.5		2003+

**Region: Coonawarra Winemaker: Phillipa Treadwell
Viticulturist: Dean Whiteman Chief Executive: Dr Richard Hamilton**

Leconfield's red wines are a reserved, tight-knit group, whose sweet berry fruits are usually backed by herbaceous notes and sweet oak. They're given every change to develop earthy and spicy complexity by their time of release, and I consider them to be more suited to short to medium-term cellaring than stayers for the haul.

CABERNETS

Coonawarra $$$

1998	16.8	2003	2006
1997	15.8	1999	2002
1996	16.0	2001	2004
1995	15.0	2000	2003
1994	16.8	1999	2002
1993	14.8	2001	2005
1992	17.3	1997	2000
1991	17.5	1999	2003
1990	17.0	1998	2002

CHARDONNAY

Coonawarra $$$

1999	15.3	2000	2001
1998	17.0	2000	2003
1997	14.5	1998	1999
1996	16.4	1998	2001
1995	15.0	1996	1997

MERLOT

Coonawarra $$$$

1998	17.0	2003	2006
1997	17.8	2002	2005
1996	18.7	2004	2008

OLD VINES RIESLING

Coonawarra $$$

1999	14.0	2000	2001
1998	16.9	2003	2006+
1997	17.3	2002	2005
1996	16.0	2001	2004
1995	17.5	2000	2003
1994	16.0	2002	2006
1993	17.7	1998	2001
1992	16.0	1994	1997

SHIRAZ

Coonawarra $$$

1998	16.6	2003	2006
1997	17.8	2002	2005
1996	17.8	1998	2001
1995	18.1	2003	2007
1994	17.7	1999	2002
1993	18.2	2001	2005
1992	18.0	1997	2000
1990	18.7	1998	2002

Region: Margaret River Winemaker: Bob Cartwright
Viticulturist: John Brocksopp Chief Executive: Denis Horgan

With yet another spectacular Art Series Chardonnay from 1997, Leeuwin Estate again stamps its authority as a world-class chardonnay producer. Its new Siblings Sauvignon Blanc Semillon blend could also herald a new speciality for this top-rated estate.

Leeuwin Estate

Stevens Road
Witchcliffe WA 6286
Tel: (08) 9757 6253
Fax: (08) 9757 6364

CABERNET SAUVIGNON

Margaret River $$$$

1996	15.2	2001	2004
1995	14.5	2003	2007
1994	16.8		2006+
1993	16.5	2001	2005
1992	18.7	2000	2004
1991	18.7	2003	2011+
1990	18.7	2002	2010
1989	18.6	2001	2009
1988	18.4	1996	2000
1987	16.0	1999	2004

CHARDONNAY

Margaret River $$$$$

1997	19.3	2005	2009
1996	18.7	2004	2008
1995	19.4	2003	2007+
1994	18.4	2002	2006
1993	18.3	2001	2005
1992	18.2	1998	2001
1991	18.1	1999	2003
1990	18.7	2002	2010
1989	18.3	1997	2001
1988	18.2	1996	2000
1987	19.4	1999	2007
1986	19.2	1998	2006
1985	18.3	1993	1997+
1984	17.5	1992	1996+
1983	18.6	1995	2003
1982	18.6	1990	1994+
1981	18.3	1989	1993+
1980	18.1	1988	1992

PRELUDE CABERNET SAUVIGNON

Margaret River $$$

1997	15.0	1999	2002+
1996	16.6	2001	2004
1994	15.7	2002	2006
1993	15.6	1998	2001
1991	16.8	1999	2003
1990	17.3		2002+
1989	18.1	2001	2009
1988	17.0	2000	2008

PRELUDE CHARDONNAY

Margaret River $$$

1999	17.2	2001	2004+
1998	17.9	2000	2003+
1997	16.0	1999	2002
1996	15.0	1997	1998
1994	17.8	1999	2002
1993	18.2	1998	2001
1992	16.8	1997	2000

RIESLING

Margaret River $$

1999	16.0	2001	2004
1998	15.2	1999	2000
1997	16.0	2002	2005
1996	17.0	2001	2004
1995	16.8	2000	2003
1994	16.0	1999	2002
1993	16.5	1998	2001
1992	16.7	1997	2000

SAUVIGNON BLANC

Margaret River $$$$

1999	17.5	2000	2001+
1998	18.0	1999	2000
1997	18.5	1999	2002
1996	18.6	1998	2001
1995	18.3	1997	2000
1994	18.3	1996	1999
1993	18.0	1995	1998
1992	18.1	1994	1997

Region: Lenswood Winemaker: Tim Knappstein
Viticulturists: Tim Knappstein, Paul Smith Chief Executive: Annie Knappstein

Tim Knappstein's move from Clare to Lenswood in the Adelaide
Hills continues to pay dividends. While much of his passion is
directed towards Lenswood's Pinot Noir, which is constantly being
refined towards a tight-knit Pommard style, he's also established
an excellent lineage of Chardonnay and Sauvignon Blanc,
while also sneaking out small volumes of an
old favourite, Gewurztraminer.

CHARDONNAY

Adelaide Hills $$$$

1998	18.2	2003	2006
1997	17.2	1999	2002
1996	17.8	2001	2004
1995	18.8	2000	2003+
1994	17.5	1999	2002
1993	17.8	1998	2001
1992	18.4	1997	2000
1991	18.1	1996	1999+

PINTON BRAE

es Road
abrup Valley
aret River WA 6295
(08) 9755 6255
(08) 9755 6268

PINOT NOIR

Adelaide Hills $$$$

1998	18.7	2003	2006+
1997	18.3	2002	2005+
1996	17.5	2004	2008
1995	16.6	2000	2003+
1994	18.2	1999	2002+
1993	17.5	1998	2001
1992	15.0	1994	1997
1991	18.3	1996	1999

SAUVIGNON BLANC

Adelaide Hills $$$

1999	18.4	2001	2004
1998	18.3	1999	2000
1997	17.6	1998	1999
1996	18.0	1997	1998
1995	18.6	1997	2000
1994	17.5	1995	1996

Region: Margaret River Winemaker: Edward Tomlinson
Viticulturist: Bruce Tomlinson Chief Executive: Bruce Tomlinson

Lenton Brae is an emerging Margaret River winery of real class.
Its leading wines are its Cabernet Sauvignon, now labelled as
'Margaret River' while its white wines, featuring a Chardonnay,
Sauvignon Blanc and Semillon Sauvignon Blanc, are consistently
finely directed, stylish and flavoursome.

CABERNET MERLOT

Margaret River $$$$

1998	16.1	2000	2003
1997	15.0	1998	1999
1996	16.0	2001	2004
1995	16.8	2000	2003
1993	15.0	1995	1998

MARGARET RIVER (FORMERLY CABERNET SAUVIGNON)

Margaret River $$$$

1998	17.6	2006	2010+
1997	16.1	2002	2005
1996	18.6	2004	2008+
1995	18.2	2003	2007
1994	17.8	2006	2014
1993	15.0	1995	1998
1992	16.7	2000	2004

CHARDONNAY

Margaret River $$$

1999	18.0	2004	2007
1998	17.9	2000	2003
1997	16.8	1999	2002+
1996	16.8	2001	2004
1995	15.7	1996	1997
1994	17.6	1996	1999

SAUVIGNON BLANC

Margaret River $$$

1999	16.7	2000	2001
1998	17.4	1999	2000
1997	17.3	1999	2002
1996	18.3	1998	2001
1995	17.3	1997	2000

SEMILLON SAUVIGNON BLANC

Margaret River $$$

1999	16.8		2000
1998	15.7	2000	2003
1997	16.4	1999	2002
1996	18.1	2001	2004
1995	17.5	1997	2000

Region: Barossa Valley Winemaker: Geoff Henriks
Viticulturist: John Matz Chief Executive: Tom Park

Still a benchmark in Australian riesling, Leo Buring shows time and again that riesling is one of our best cellaring wines, although the company style has developed considerably since the classic wines made by John Vickery in the 1960s and 1970s. The Leonay Eden Valley Riesling from 1995 is simply awesome, a near-perfect essay in the limey, long and steely expression of this grape. The Clare Riesling from 1999 makes an attractive and very affordable alternative.

Leo Buring

Tanunda Road
Nuriootpa SA 5355
Tel: (08) 8560 9389
Fax: (08) 8562 1669

CLARE VALLEY CHARDONNAY

Clare Valley $$

1999	14.5		2000
1997	16.4	1999	2002
1996	14.5	1997	1998
1994	16.3	1996	1999
1993	16.0	1995	1998
1992	16.0	1993	1996

CLARE VALLEY RIESLING

Clare Valley $$

1999	18.0	2007	2011
1998	16.7	2000	2003
1997	17.5	2005	2009
1996	17.5	2004	2008
1995	15.8	2000	2003
1994	18.0	2002	2006
1993	18.5	2001	2005

LEONAY WATERVALE RIESLING

Clare Valley $$$

1994	18.4	2002	2006
1992	18.5	2000	2004
1991	18.6		2003+
1990	18.0	1998	2002
1988	18.2	1996	2000
1981	14.5	1989	1993
1980	16.0	1988	1992
1973	18.4	1981	1985
1972	19.0	1992	1997

Leydens Vale

Vinoca Road
Avoca Vic 3467
Tel: (03) 5465 3202
Fax: (03) 5465 3529

Region: Pyrenees Winemaker: Kim Hart
Viticulturist: Kim Hart Chief Executive: Kim Hart

Leydens Vale is a multi-regional label of Blue Pyrenees Estate. It has featured a delicious and almost sour merlot from time to time, but at present offers a limey, musky Riesling and a spicy, earthy Shiraz.

1997 Riesling

RIESLING

Southern Australia $$

1998	17.5	2000	2003+
1997	18.0	2002	2005
1995	15.0	1997	2000
1994	16.8	1999	2002

1996 Shiraz

SHIRAZ

Pyrenees $$$

1998	16.5	2000	2003+
1997	14.5	1999	2002
1996	16.2	2001	2004
1995	15.0	2000	2003
1994	16.0	1999	2002

Region: Yarra Valley Winemakers: Max McWilliam, Jim Brayne
Viticulturist: Alex Van Driel Chief Executive: Kevin McLintock

The Yarra Valley outpost of the McWilliams family operation is a steadily expanding affair which serves more as an entry point to the qualities of Yarra wines than as their ultimate destination. Each of the Lillydale Vineyards wines are fresh, vibrant and fruit-driven and destined for relatively early drinking. One wonders what could occur should the team pay the same attention to ultimate quality here as they have at Brand's in Coonawarra.

Lillydale Vineyards

Lot 10 Davross Court
Seville Vic 3139
Tel: (03) 5964 2016
Fax: (03) 5964 3009
Website:
www.mcwilliams.com.au
E-mail:
liloffice@mcwilliams.
com.au

CABERNET MERLOT

Yarra Valley $$

1998	15.0	2000	2003
1997	16.8	2002	2005
1996	15.8	1998	2001
1995	15.3	1997	2000
1994	16.9	1999	2002
1992	17.5	1997	2000
1991	17.6	1999	2003
1990	16.5	1995	1998

CHARDONNAY

Yarra Valley $$

1998	16.6	1999	2000
1997	17.0	1999	2002
1996	16.2	1998	2001
1995	15.7	1997	2000
1994	15.0	1996	1999
1992	16.8	1994	1997

GEWURZTRAMINER

Yarra Valley $$

1998	16.8	2000	2003
1996	17.0	2001	2004
1995	18.4	2000	2003
1993	15.5	1995	1996

PINOT NOIR

Yarra Valley $$

1999	16.8	2001	2004
1998	16.2	1999	2000
1997	16.8	1999	2002
1996	17.2	1998	2001
1995	16.2	1997	2000
1994	16.5	1996	1999

Lindemans

Riddoch Highway
Coonawarra SA 5263
Tel: (08) 8736 3205
Fax: (08) 8736 3250

Regions: Coonawarra and Padthaway Winemaker: Greg Clayfield
Viticulturist: Max Arney Chief Executive: Tom Park

One of Australia's classic red wine labels, Lindemans is becoming a more consistent performer with its sought-after trio of St George Cabernet Sauvignon, Limestone Ridge Shiraz Cabernet and the Pyrus Cabernet blend. Their style is rich, ripe and oaky, and they usually benefit handsomely from a decade in the cellar.

LIMESTONE RIDGE SHIRAZ CABERNET SAUVIGNON

Coonawarra $$$$

1997	17.8	2005	2009+
1996	18.5	2004	2008+
1994	18.6		2006+
1993	17.4	2001	2005
1992	16.6	1997	2000
1991	18.4		2003+
1990	16.5	1995	1998
1989	16.8	1991	1994
1987	16.0	1989	1992
1986	16.5	1994	1998
1985	16.0	1990	1993
1984	16.0	1989	1992
1982	17.0	1987	1990
1981	17.0	1989	1993
1980	18.5	1998	1992

PADTHAWAY CABERNET SAUVIGNON/MERLOT

Padthaway $$$

1997	16.6	2002	2005+
1996	17.0	2001	2004
1995	17.3	2003	2007
1994	16.7	1999	2002
1993	16.7	1998	2001
1992	17.0	1997	2000

PADTHAWAY CHARDONNAY

Padthaway $$

1999	17.3	2004	2007
1998	18.0	2003	2006
1997	18.0	2002	2005
1996	16.0	2001	2004
1995	15.5	1997	2000
1994	16.8	1999	2002
1993	17.7	1998	2001
1992	18.2	1997	2000

PYRUS

Coonawarra $$$$

1997	18.0	2005	2009
1996	16.9	2004	2008
1995	18.1	2003	2007
1994	18.4	2002	2006
1993	16.8	1998	2001
1992	16.5	1997	2000
1991	17.5	1996	1999
1990	17.8	1995	1998
1988	16.5	1993	1996
1987	14.5	1989	1992
1986	16.0	1988	1991
1985	18.0	1987	1990

RESERVE PORPHYRY

Coonawarra and Padthaway $$$

1994	17.3	1999	2002
1993	16.0	1998	2001
1990	16.0	1992	1995
1989	16.0	1994	1997
1988	17.8	1993	1996
1987	17.0	1995	1999
1983	17.0	1991	1995

ST. GEORGE CABERNET SAUVIGNON

Coonawarra $$$$

1997	17.2	2005	2009
1996	18.0	2001	2004+
1995	18.5	2003	2007+
1994	18.5		2014+
1993	16.8	1998	2001
1992	16.7	2000	2004
1991	19.0		2011+
1990	17.6	1995	1998
1989	16.0	1994	1997
1988	18.0	1993	1996
1987	15.0	1989	1992
1986	16.5	1991	1994
1985	17.0	1990	1993
1984	16.0	1986	1989
1982	16.5	1990	1994
1981	16.0	1989	1993
1980	18.0	1992	1997

Region: Lower Hunter Valley Winemaker: Patrick Auld
Viticulturist: Jerome Scarborough Chief Executive: Tom Park

Until the early 1970s Lindemans was synonymous with the very best the Hunter Valley stood for, boasting a remarkable legacy of differently labelled classic semillons and a welter of incredibly flavoursome and enduring shiraz labelled as 'Burgundy'. After two decades of rudderless management it is beginning to reclaim its past, with some fine Steven Vineyard Shirazes and Semillons.

SEMILLON (FORMERLY RIESLING)

Lower Hunter Valley, Young $$

1998	17.5	2003	2006+
1996	17.4	2001	2004
1995	16.6	2000	2003
1994	17.8	2002	2006
1993	17.2	1998	2001
1992	17.0	2000	2004
1991	18.0	1999	2003
1990	16.5	1995	1998

SHIRAZ

Lower Hunter Valley $$$

1996	15.8	1998	2001
1994	18.0	1999	2002
1993	15.3	1995	1998
1991	18.3		2003+
1990	17.5		2002+
1989	14.5	1991	1994
1988	15.0	1993	1996
1987	17.0	1995	1999

STEVEN VINEYARD SHIRAZ

Lower Hunter Valley $$$

1997	16.6	2002	2005+
1996	16.5	2001	2004+
1995	18.5	2003	2007
1994	18.0	2002	2006
1991	18.6		2003+
1990	18.2		2002+
1989	16.0	1994	1997
1988	16.5	1996	2000
1987	17.0	1999	2004
1986	18.0	1998	2003

Region: McLaren Vale Winemaker: John Loxton
Viticulturist: Chris Dundon Chief Executive: Terry Davis

Another successful medium sized brand now swimming in the
Mildara Blass pond, Maglieri has a simply awesome recent track
record with its red wines, especially with the McLaren Vale
speciality, shiraz. The Steve Maglieri Shiraz represents
some very fine reserve parcels of this wine.

SHIRAZ

McLaren Vale $$$

1998	16.0	2000	2003
1997	16.8	2002	2005
1995	18.1	2000	2003

STEVE MAGLIERI SHIRAZ

McLaren Vale $$$$$

1998	17.2	2003	2006
1997	18.0	2002	2005+
1995	18.7	2003	2007
1994	18.3	2002	2006
1993	15.0	1995	1998

Region: Mornington Peninsula Winemaker: Nat White
Viticulturist: Nat White Chief Executives: Rosalie & Nat White

Nat and Rosalie White are making the best wines of their lives.
The Mornington Peninsula's recent run of warm seasons and some
painstaking viticulture has helped lift the Main Ridge Half Acre
Pinot Noir into the top bracket, while the 1998 Chardonnay takes
this wine to a new level of texture and integration. If only other
Peninsula growers and makers paid similar attention to detail!

CHARDONNAY

Mornington Peninsula $$$$

1998	18.6	2006	2010
1997	16.6	1999	2002+
1996	16.4	1998	2001
1995	15.0	1997	2000
1994	18.3	1999	2002
1993	16.8	1998	2001
1992	18.7	2000	2004
1991	16.4	1996	1999
1990	16.7	1995	1998
1989	16.0	1997	2001
1988	16.8	1993	1996

HALF ACRE PINOT NOIR

Mornington Peninsula $$$$

1998	18.1	2003	2006
1997	18.8	2002	2005+
1996	16.0	2001	2004
1995	16.4	1997	2000
1994	18.2	2002	2006
1993	17.2	2001	2005
1992	16.8	2000	2004
1991	17.0	1996	1999
1990	16.0	1992	1995

**Region: Coonawarra Winemaker: Bruce Gregory
Viticulturist: Brian Lynn Chief Executive: Brian Lynn**

Majella must surely be the envy of the countless new entrants to the wine industry, many of whom would be awestruck by its apparent overnight success. If they were to look closer they would discover that Majella's wines are sourced from very mature quality vineyards, they have been consistently excellent in quality and value, and their packaging has been strong, simple and consistent.

CABERNET

Coonawarra $$$

1998	18.6	2006	2010+
1997	18.0	2005	2009
1996	18.0	2001	2004
1995	15.7	1997	2000
1994	15.0	1996	1999

SHIRAZ

Coonawarra $$$

1998	18.7	2002	2006+
1997	18.3	2002	2005+
1996	18.5	2001	2004
1994	18.2	2002	2006
1993	15.9	1995	1998
1992	15.4	1994	1997
1991	15.8	1993	1996

THE MALLEEA

Coonawarra $$$$$

1998	18.8	2006	2010+
1997	17.8	2002	2005+
1996	18.3	2001	2004

Region: Adelaide Hills Winemaker: Reg Tolley
Viticulturist: Reg Tolley Chief Executive: Reg Tolley

Malcolm Creek's Chardonnay is a soft, reserved and creamy wine with attractive peach and citrus flavours and buttery oak. Warmer vintages of Cabernet Sauvignon tend to produce fine-grained and elegant wines with a pleasing intensity of small berry fruits.

CABERNET SAUVIGNON

Adelaide Hills $$$

1997	15.2	1999	2002+
1996	17.3	2004	2008+
1995	16.3	2000	2003
1994	14.5	1996	1999
1992	13.5	1997	2000
1991	15.0	1999	2003
1990	16.3	1998	2002
1989	16.8	1997	2001
1988	17.8	1993	1996
1987	16.0	1992	1995
1986	18.0	1994	1998

CHARDONNAY

Adelaide Hills $$$

1998	17.4	2003	2006
1997	16.8	2002	2005
1996	15.2	1998	2001
1995	16.8	2000	2003
1993	17.0	1995	1998
1991	14.7	1993	1996
1990	17.9	1998	2002
1989	17.1	1994	1997

Born and bred in the Barossa, Nigel Dolan is performing great
feats with one of the Valley's most treasured wine labels. But
where once there was but a single Mamre Brook red there are now
two, since the Cabernet Sauvignon and Shiraz are now made and
bottled separately. While I clearly have a soft spot for the Cabernet
Sauvignon, whose 1998 release is quite brilliant, I actually
prefer the Shiraz, which makes its debut in this edition.

CABERNET SAUVIGNON (FORMERLY CABERNET SHIRAZ)

Barossa Valley $$$

1998	18.9	2010	2018+
1997	18.2	2005	2009
1996	18.3	2004	2008
1995	16.5	1997	2000
1994	17.0	2002	2006
1993	17.5	1998	2001
1988	15.5	1993	1998
1986	18.2		2006+
1985	16.0	1990	1993
1984	18.3	1996	2001

CHARDONNAY

South Australia (Early vint. some Hunter V.) $$$

1998	16.0	2000	2003
1997	15.2	1998	1999
1996	16.7	1998	2001
1995	16.0	1997	2000
1994	18.0	1999	2002
1993	18.4	1998	2001
1990	17.5	1995	1998

SHIRAZ

Barossa Valley $$$

1998	18.6	2006	2010
1997	18.7	2005	2009+
1996	18.3	2004	2008

Region: Mornington Peninsula Winemakers: Ian Home & Daniel Greene
Viticulturist: David Jordan Chief Executive: Ian Home

Massoni

RMB 6580
Mornington-Flinders Road
Red Hill Vic 3937
Tel: (03) 5989 2352
Fax: (03) 5989 2014

Massoni continues to build on its reputation as one of the small number of top-class Mornington Peninsula brands by carefully selecting small parcels of fruit for its two principal wines. The company's style has typically been to present rich, thickly layered Chardonnay and more robust Pinot Noir than we are perhaps used to seeing from the Peninsula. Recent releases, especially from the excellent 1997 and 1999 vintages, have seen a lightening of style and new-found refinement.

PINOT NOIR

Mornington Peninsula $$$$

1999	18.6	2004	2007+
1998	16.6	2000	2003
1997	18.2	2002	2005+
1996	15.2	1997	2000
1995	16.1	1997	2000
1994	18.5	1999	2002
1993	18.2	1998	2001
1992	17.5	2000	2004
1991	16.5	1999	2003

RED HILL CHARDONNAY

Mornington Peninsula $$$$

1999	17.5	2001	2004
1998	18.2	2000	2003+
1997	18.6	2002	2005+
1996	16.6	1998	2001
1995	16.2	1997	2000
1994	18.8	2002	2006
1993	18.2	1998	2001+
1992	18.0	1997	2000
1991	18.6	1996	1999
1990	18.5	1995	1998
1989	18.2	1994	1997

1996
MASSONI

RED HILL PINOT NOIR
MORNINGTON PENINSULA

1996
MASSONI

RED HILL CHARDONNAY
MORNINGTON PENINSULA

McAlister Vineyards

RMB 6810 Golden Beach Road Longford South-East Gippsland Vic 3851
Tel: (03) 5149 7229
Fax: (03) 5149 7229

Region: Gippsland Winemaker: Peter Edwards
Viticulturist: Peter Edwards Chief Executive: Peter Edwards

The McAlister is a small Gippsland vineyard dedicated to making fine, restrained red wines from the Bordeaux varieties. The annual blend can be tight, elegant and long-living, while the occasional releases of straight Merlot (only bottled separately when the blend doesn't require the entire merlot crush) can be excellent.

THE McALISTER

Gippsland $$$$

1997	16.2	2005	2009
1996	15.3	1998	2001
1995	16.3	2000	2003
1994	18.7	2002	2006
1993	17.0	1998	2001
1992	18.1	2000	2004
1991	18.1	1999	2003
1990	18.5		2002+
1989	16.0	1997	2001
1988	18.0	2000	2005
1987	17.8	1999	2004
1986	17.0	1994	1998

Meadowbank

Glenora Tas 7140
Tel: (03) 6286 1234
Fax: (03) 6286 1133

Region: Derwent Valley Winemaker: Andrew Hood
Chief Executive: Gerald Ellis

Meadowbank is a small Tasmanian maker of tight-knit and elegant wines which shares with many of its neighbours the difficulties encountered in cooler years. This vineyard is capable of excellent wine in warmer seasons.

CHARDONNAY

Derwent Valley $$$$

1998	15.8	2000	2003
1997	15.0	1998	1999
1995	16.2	1997	2000
1994	16.6	1999	2002
1993	17.3	1998	2001

GRACE ELIZABETH CHARDONNAY

Derwent Valley $$$$$

1998	15.0	2000	2003
1997	15.2	1998	1999
1995	18.7	2003	2007

HENRY JAMES PINOT NOIR

Derwent Valley $$$$

1999	16.7	2001	2004+
1998	15.0	2000	2003+
1997	15.3	1999	2002

Region: Langhorne Creek Winemaker: Nigel Dolan
Viticulturists: Tom and Guy Adams Chief Executive: Terry Davis

Another brand of Mildara Blass Ltd, the Stonyfell Metala continues
to be released under its historic white label. A section of the
vineyard's original plantings is allocated to the Original Vines label,
which commenced so successfully with the very refined, silky and
concentrated 1994 wine. The rather deluxe 1996 effort
is a very worthy successor indeed.

SHIRAZ CABERNET

Langhorne Creek $$

1998	18.1	2006	2010
1997	16.8	2002	2005
1996	17.4	2001	2004
1995	17.0	2000	2003
1994	17.5	2002	2006
1993	17.9	2001	2005
1992	17.5	2000	2004
1991	16.3	1999	2003
1988	14.5	1993	1996
1987	16.0	1992	1995
1986	17.0	1994	1998
1985	16.5	1993	1997
1984	17.3	1996	2001
1983	17.7	1995	2000

Metala

Nuriootpa Road
Angaston SA 5353
Tel: (08) 8564 3355
Fax: (08) 8564 2209

Mildara Coonawarra

Riddoch Highway
Coonawarra SA 5263
Tel: (08) 8736 3380
Fax: (08) 8736 3307

Region: Coonawarra Winemakers: David O'Leary, Scott Rawlinson
Viticulturist: Vic Patrick Chief Executive: Terry Davis

The famous white label of Mildara Coonawarra is all that remains of an historic collection of wines once given similar packaging. The wine has traditionally epitomised the elegance of the Coonawarra palate structure and the brightness and intensity of its fruit, although recent vintages haven't lived up to their predecessors.

CABERNET SAUVIGNON

Coonawarra $$$

1997	15.2	1999	2002
1996	16.6	2004	2008
1995	16.3	2000	2003
1994	18.2	2002	2006
1993	18.7	2001	2005
1992	18.3	2000	2004
1991	17.0	1996	1999
1990	18.5	1995	1998
1989	16.0	1994	1997
1988	18.3	1996	2000

Miramar

Henry Lawson Drive
Mudgee NSW 2850
Tel: (02) 6373 3874
Fax: (02) 6373 3854

Region: Mudgee Winemaker: Ian MacRae
Viticulturist: Ian MacRae Chief Executive: Ian MacRae

Like several other smaller Mudgee makers, Miramar's robust and generously proportioned reds, citrusy chardonnay and tangy semillon offer genuine value for money at a time when most wine prices are simply spiralling upwards.

CABERNET SAUVIGNON

Mudgee $$

1997	16.6	2005	2009
1996	15.8	2001	2004
1995	15.0	2000	2003
1994	18.2		2006+
1991	16.8	1999	2003
1990	17.1	1995	1998

CHARDONNAY

Mudgee $$

1996	16.2	2001	2004
1995	16.7	2000	2003
1994	15.0	1996	1999
1993	17.7	1998	2001
1992	17.5	1997	2000

SEMILLON
Mudgee $$

1997	17.5	2005	2009
1996	18.1	2004	2008
1995	17.9	2003	2007
1993	17.1	1998	2001
1992	16.5	1997	2000
1990	14.8	1995	1998

SHIRAZ
Mudgee $$

1997	15.7	2002	2005+
1996	15.3	2001	2004
1995	18.4	2003	2007
1994	17.6	2002	2006
1993	18.0		2005+
1991	17.4		2003+
1988	17.0	2000	2008
1986	17.0	1998	2006
1985	17.0	1997	2005

Region: Various Winemaker: Luis Simian
Viticulturist: Ross Turkington Chief Executive: Lou Miranda

Miranda is one of the most dynamic of contemporary Australian
wine companies, today with significant investments in Victoria's
King Valley, the Barossa Valley and at its home base of Griffith. Its
Golden Botrytis is an intensely flavoured, luscious
dessert wine of consistent quality.

GOLDEN BOTRYTIS
Griffith $$$$$

1998	17.2	2003	2006
1997	18.5	2002	2005
1996	17.8	1998	2001
1995	16.2	1997	2000
1994	16.2	1996	1999
1993	18.3	1998	2001
1987	16.5	1992	1995

As you might expect, 1998 was a fine year for this small maker of finely crafted Clare Valley wines. Mitchell focuses on the two classic Clare Valley whites of semillon and riesling, plus the wild and exotic The Growers Grenache, a fine-grained Cabernet Sauvignon and a favourite of mine, the Peppertree Vineyard Shiraz.

CABERNET SAUVIGNON

Clare Valley $$$

1998	17.1	2006	2010
1997	15.6	2002	2005
1996	16.7	2004	2008
1995	15.0	2000	2003
1994	17.6	2002	2006
1992	17.4		2004+
1991	18.0		2003+
1990	18.5		2002+
1988	16.5	1996	2000

PEPPERTREE VINEYARD SHIRAZ

Clare Valley $$$

1998	17.9	2006	2010
1997	16.0	1999	2002
1996	18.0	2001	2004
1995	15.0	2000	2003
1994	17.3	1999	2003
1993	18.0	2001	2005
1992	17.9	2000	2004
1991	17.5	1996	1999
1990	18.5	1998	2002
1989	18.0	1994	1997
1988	16.0	1993	1996

THE GROWERS GRENACHE

Clare Valley $$$

1999	15.8	2001	2004
1998	16.5	2000	2003
1997	17.0	1999	2002
1996	15.7	1998	2001
1995	15.2	1997	2000

THE GROWERS SEMILLON/SAUVIGNON BLANC BLEND

Clare Valley $$

1999	16.8	2001	2004+
1998	16.6	2000	2003
1997	16.8	2002	2005
1996	17.2	2001	2004
1995	16.5	2000	2003
1994	18.2	2002	2006
1993	18.7	2001	2005
1992	16.5	1997	2000
1991	18.5	1996	1999
1990	18.0	1995	1998

WATERVALE RIESLING

Clare Valley $$

1999	14.5	2001	2004
1998	17.0	2003	2006+
1997	17.8	2005	2009
1996	16.0	2001	2004
1995	18.3	2003	2007
1994	16.5	1999	2003
1993	18.0	2001	2005
1992	17.4	1997	2000
1991	18.5	1996	1999
1990	18.5	1995	1998
1989	16.0	1997	2001
1988	16.0	1990	1993

Region: Nagambie Lakes - Goulburn Valley
Winemakers: Don Lewis, Alan George
Viticulturist: John Beresford Chief Executive: Brian Croser

Now part of Petaluma Ltd, Mitchelton is a large and significant maker of contemporary Goulburn Valley wines with a number of different brands including Preece and Thomas Mitchell.

BLACKWOOD PARK RIESLING

Nagambie Lakes - Goulburn Valley $$

1999	16.0	2001	2004
1998	18.2	2006	2010
1997	17.0	2002	2005+
1996	18.0	2004	2008
1995	18.2	2000	2003
1994	18.0	1999	2002
1993	18.3	1998	2001
1992	17.7	1994	1997
1991	18.5	1999	2003
1990	17.5	1995	1998

CABERNET SAUVIGNON

Nagambie Lakes - Goulburn Valley $$$

1996	18.0	2004	2008+
1995	18.0		2007+
1994	18.2		2006+
1993	18.3		2005+
1992	18.1	2000	2004
1991	18.3	1999	2003
1990	17.6	1998	2002

CHARDONNAY

Nagambie Lakes - Goulburn Valley $$$$

1998	16.7	2003	2006
1997	18.3	2002	2005
1996	16.8	1998	2001
1994	18.2	1999	2002
1993	18.0	1998	2001
1992	18.5	1997	2000
1991	18.0	1996	1999
1990	17.5	1995	1998

MARSANNE

Nagambie Lakes - Goulburn Valley $$$

1998	16.7	2000	2003
1997	16.2	1998	1999
1996	16.6	1997	1998

PRINT SHIRAZ

Nagambie Lakes - Goulburn Valley $$$$

1996	16.7	2001	2004
1995	17.9	2003	2007
1994	16.6	2002	2006
1993	18.4		2005+
1992	17.8	2000	2004
1991	18.5		2003+
1990	17.2	1998	2002

SHIRAZ

Nagambie Lakes - Goulburn Valley $$$

1997	15.6	1999	2002
1996	15.2	1998	2001
1995	16.0	2000	2003
1994	15.6	1996	2001

WOOD MATURED MARSANNE

Nagambie Lakes - Goulburn Valley $$$$

1994	15.0	1995	1996
1993	18.6	1998	2001
1992	18.5	2000	2004
1991	16.6	1996	1999
1990	17.5	1998	2002
1989	15.8	1994	1997
1988	17.0	1996	2000
1987	15.0	1995	1999
1986	16.0	1994	1998

Region: Barossa Valley Winemaker: Natasha Mooney
Chief Executive: Bruce Richardson

Moculta

Heaslip Road
Angle Vale SA 5117
Tel: (08) 8284 7000
Fax: (08) 8284 7219

Formerly sold under the 'Barossa Valley Estate' label and still made at Angle Vale, the Moculta wines are forward and fruity, destined for early enjoyment. With two excellent vintages in 1997 and 1998, its Shiraz is clearly its leading wine.

CABERNET MERLOT

Barossa Valley $$

1998	14.5	2000	2003
1997	16.6	1999	2002
1996	15.0	1998	2001
1995	16.0	1997	2000
1994	15.4	1996	1999
1993	15.0	1995	1998
1992	17.3	1994	1997
1990	16.3	1992	1995

CHARDONNAY

Barossa Valley $$

1998	16.2	1999	2000
1997	17.1	1998	1999
1996	15.6	1997	1998

SHIRAZ

Barossa Valley $$

1998	17.0	2003	2006
1997	17.8	1999	2002
1996	16.4	1998	2001
1995	16.0	2000	2003
1993	15.2	1998	2001
1992	17.5	1997	2000

Montara

Chalambar Rd
Ararat Vic 3377
Tel: (03) 5352 3868
Fax: (03) 5352 4968

Region: Grampians Winemaker: Mike McRae
Viticulturist: Mike McRae Chief Executive: Mike McRae

Montara is a long established vineyard just to the south of the Victorian western district town of Ararat which has specialised largely in red wines, with a focus on shiraz and pinot noir. Its Shiraz is consistently its best red, typically packed with small berries and spice and smooth enough to enjoy relatively young.

SHIRAZ

Grampians $$$

1997	15.9	1999	2002
1996	16.0	2001	2004
1995	16.7	2000	2003
1994	17.4	2002	2006
1993	18.4		2005+
1992	17.2	2000	2004
1990	17.0	1992	1995

Montrose

Henry Lawson Drive
Mudgee NSW 2850
Tel: (02) 6373 3853
Fax: (02) 6373 3795

Region: Mudgee Winemaker: Brett McKinnon
Viticulturist: Stephen Guilbaud-Oulton Chief Executive: Christian Porta

Montrose is another of Orlando Wyndham's substantial investments at Mudgee. It's a maker of sound, flavoursome and perfectly reliable table wines which occasionally rise well above the pack, but its red wines from the Italian varieties of Barbera and Sangiovese can be excellent. While they begin life bursting with fruit, with time they settle down into leaner, astringent wines of true varietal authenticity.

BLACK SHIRAZ

Mudgee $$

1997	16.8	2005	2009
1996	16.9	1998	2001
1995	16.5	1997	2000
1994	16.0	1996	1999

SANGIOVESE

Mudgee $$$$

1998	16.7	2000	2003+
1997	17.9	1999	2002
1996	16.8	2001	2004

Region: Gingin Winemaker: Larry Cherubino
Viticulturist: Tony Kennar Chief Executive: Stephen Millar

From the rather warm region of Gingin, a short trip north of Perth, Moondah Brook's wines are clean, fresh and vibrant. My pick remains the Verdelho which, typical of several Western Australian verdelhos, develops mouthfilling richness of flavour and texture after just a few short years in the bottle, a feat occasionally matched by the Chenin Blanc.

Moondah Brook Estate

Dale Road
Middle Swan WA 6056
Tel: (08) 9274 5372
Fax: (08) 9274 5372

CABERNET SAUVIGNON

Gingin $$

1998	16.5	2003	2006+
1997	15.0	1999	2002
1996	17.2	2004	2008
1995	16.0	2000	2003
1993	15.3	1995	1998
1992	17.7	1997	2000
1991	17.4	1999	2003
1990	15.6	1995	1998

CHARDONNAY

Gingin $$

1999	15.2	2000	2001
1998	17.0	2000	2003
1997	15.8	1998	1999
1996	15.0	1997	1998

CHENIN BLANC

Gingin $$

1998	15.8	2000	2003+
1997	15.8	2002	2005
1996	16.0	2001	2004
1995	15.3	1997	2000
1994	16.5	1999	2002
1993	15.4	1994	1995
1992	16.2	1997	2000

SHIRAZ

Gingin $$

1998	16.1	2003	2006
1997	15.8	1999	2002
1996	16.5	2001	2004

Moorilla
Estate

655 Main Road
Berriedale Tas 7011
Tel: (03) 6249 2949
Fax: (03) 6249 4093

VERDELHO

Gingin $$

1999	16.0	2001	2004+
1998	16.8	2000	2003+
1997	15.1	1999	2002
1996	15.6	1998	2001
1995	15.8	1997	2000
1994	17.5	1999	2002
1993	17.5	1998	2001
1992	17.4	1997	2000
1991	16.0	1993	1996

Region: Southern Tasmania Winemaker: Alain Rousso
Viticulturist: Alain Rousso Chief Executive: Tim Goddard

The brightness and intensity of Moorilla Estate's fragrant Rieslings and Gewürztraminers, each made in a style atypical of those found on the Australian mainland, present the sort of clarity and accent of fruit one might more associate with Marlborough in New Zealand. Its red wines are skilfully and stylishly presented, but typically generate more genuinely ripe fruit quality in warmer seasons. The team at Moorilla takes its pinot noir very seriously and has produced some excellent results.

CABERNET SAUVIGNON

Southern Tasmania $$$

1998	16.6	2003	2006
1997	15.8	2002	2005+
1995	14.8	2000	2003
1994	18.0	2002	2006
1993	15.0	2001	2005
1992	17.9	2000	2004
1991	16.5	1999	2003
1990	17.0	1998	2002

CHARDONNAY

Southern Tasmania $$$$

1999	15.2	2001	2004
1998	14.8	2000	2003+
1996	15.2	1998	2001
1995	18.4	2003	2007
1994	16.0	2002	2006
1993	17.0	1998	2001
1992	18.0	1997	2000
1991	17.0	1999	2003
1990	17.0	1998	2002
1989	18.0	1997	2001

GEWÜRZTRAMINER

Southern Tasmania $$$$

1999	17.0	2004	2007
1998	16.8	2003	2006
1997	17.0	2002	2005
1996	15.0	1997	1998
1995	18.5	2003	2007
1994	17.5	2002	2006
1993	18.0	1998	2001
1992	16.8	1997	2000
1991	18.0	1993	1996

PINOT NOIR

Southern Tasmania $$$$

1999	16.0	2001	2004
1998	16.2	2000	2003
1997	17.8	2002	2005
1996	17.0	2001	2004
1995	16.5	2000	2003
1994	17.4	1999	2002
1993	13.5	1995	1998
1992	15.0	1994	1997
1991	17.0	1999	2003
1990	17.5	1995	1998

RESERVE PINOT NOIR

Southern Tasmania $$$$

1998	16.7	2000	2003
1997	15.2	1999	2002
1996	18.0	2001	2004

RIESLING

Southern Tasmania $$$

1999	16.2	2004	2007
1998	17.2	2003	2006
1997	16.0	1999	2002
1996	17.6	2001	2004
1995	16.6	1997	2000
1994	18.6		2006+
1993	18.2	1998	2001
1992	16.0	1997	2000
1991	17.5	1996	1999
1990	16.5	1995	1998
1989	17.0	1997	2001

Moorooduc Estate

501 Derril Road
Moorooduc Vic 3933
Tel: (03) 5971 8506
Fax: (03) 5971 8550
E-mail:moorooduc
@ozemail.com.au

Region: Mornington Peninsula Winemaker: Dr Richard McIntyre
Viticulturist: Ian Macrae Chief Executive: Dr Richard McIntyre

Rick McIntyre takes full advantage of his comparatively warm location on the Mornington Peninsula to develop succulent and fleshy table wines from Chardonnay and Pinot Noir which are right at the forefront of the region's quality leader-board. Like those from other Peninsula makers, its Cabernet needs a warm season to really produce. Moorooduc Estate opened its attractively designed winery restaurant in 2000.

CABERNET

Mornington Peninsula $$$$

1995	14.5	2000	2003
1994	14.5	1999	2002
1993	16.2	2001	2005
1992	16.7	2000	2004
1991	18.3	1999	2003
1990	18.0	1995	1998
1989	16.0	1991	1994
1988	17.0	1993	1997

CHARDONNAY

Mornington Peninsula $$$$

1998	16.8	2000	2003
1997	16.5	2002	2005
1996	18.2	2001	2004
1995	18.2	2000	2003
1994	18.7	1999	2002
1993	17.8	1998	2001
1992	17.7	1994	1997
1991	18.0	1996	1999
1990	18.3	1999	2002
1989	18.0	1994	1997

PINOT NOIR

Mornington Peninsula $$$$

1998	16.5	2003	2006
1997	18.2	2002	2005
1996	16.0	2001	2004
1995	18.2	2000	2003
1994	17.8	1999	2002
1993	18.0	1998	2001
1992	18.7	2000	2004
1991	15.3	1996	1999

Region: NE Victoria Winemaker: David Morris
Viticulturist: Stephen Guilbaud-Oulton Chief Executive: Christian Porta

Morris

Mia Mia Road
Rutherglen Vic 3685
Tel: (02) 6026 7303
Fax: (02) 6026 7445

Morris is an Orlando Wyndham brand based in Rutherglen which is entirely left to its own devices concerning the making of its richly flavoured and thickly textured regional reds, of which the Shiraz and Durif are both regional classics, and of course its spectacular collection of fortifieds where many agree it has no peer.

CABERNET SAUVIGNON

NE Victoria $$

1997	15.0	1999	2002+
1996	16.6	2004	2008+
1995	16.2	2003	2007
1994	16.8		2006+
1993	16.2		2005+
1992	16.6	2000	2004
1990	17.5		2002+
1989	17.5	2001	2009
1988	17.5	2000	2005
1987	16.5	1995	1999
1986	17.0	1994	1998

CHARDONNAY

NE Victoria $$

1998	15.8	2000	2003
1997	15.1	1999	2002
1996	16.0	1998	2001
1995	15.7	1997	2000
1994	17.0	1999	2002
1991	15.0	1993	1996

DURIF

NE Victoria $$

1997	17.4		2009+
1996	16.6	2004	2008+
1995	18.2		2007+
1994	18.1	2002	2006
1993	16.3	2001	2005
1992	17.0		2004+
1991	18.0		2003+
1990	18.2	2002	2010
1989	16.6	2001	2009
1988	16.5	2000	2005
1987	17.0	1999	2004
1986	16.5	1998	2003
1985	18.0	1997	2002
1984	17.0	1996	2001

SEMILLON

NE Victoria $$

1998	16.0	2000	2003
1996	17.1	2001	2004
1995	17.0	2000	2003
1994	16.5	1999	2002

SHIRAZ

NE Victoria $$

1997	15.6	2005	2009
1996	16.8	2004	2008+
1995	16.0	2000	2003
1994	16.3	2002	2006
1993	15.0	1998	2001
1992	17.5		2004+
1991	17.0		2003+
1990	16.4	1998	2002
1989	15.8	1994	1997

Moss Wood

Metricup Road
Willyabrup via Cowaramup
WA 6284
Tel: (08) 9755 6266
Fax: (08) 9755 6303

Region: Margaret River Winemaker: Keith Mugford
Viticulturist: Ian Bell Chief Executive: Keith Mugford

Moss Wood is one of Australia's premier cabernet vineyards able to produce exceptional Chardonnay from time to time, while its Semillon and Pinot Noir can also be excellent wines. Moss Wood does occasionally fight against the leafy characters associated with cooler and later cabernet seasons, but its mature vineyard and fastidious approach ensure that most vintages maintain a high standard of quality and longevity. Typically the Moss Wood Cabernet Sauvignon needs a decade in the bottle, by which time it will usually have reached a style and standard only challenged by Mount Mary and Cullen within these shores.

CABERNET SAUVIGNON

Margaret River $$$$$

1997	18.2	2005	2009
1996	18.7	2008	2016
1995	19.0	2007	2015
1994	19.2		2014+
1993	18.0	2005	2013
1992	18.5	2004	2012
1991	18.8	2003	2011+
1990	19.0	2002	2010+
1989	18.3	2001	2009
1988	17.0	1996	2000
1987	18.3	1999	2007
1986	18.1	1998	2006
1985	17.3	1993	1997

CHARDONNAY
Margaret River $$$$

1999	18.9	2007	2011
1998	17.0	2003	2006+
1997	18.7	2005	2009
1996	18.0	1998	2001
1995	18.2	2003	2007
1994	18.8	2002	2006
1993	17.8	1998	2001
1992	18.5	2000	2004
1991	17.5		2003+
1990	18.5		2002+
1989	17.0	1997	2001

PINOT NOIR
Margaret River $$$$

1997	15.8	2002	2005
1996	16.8	2001	2004
1995	18.0	2003	2007
1994	16.0	1999	2002
1993	15.2	1998	2001
1992	15.0	1997	2000
1991	15.5	1993	1998
1990	18.5	1998	2002

Region: Pyrenees Winemaker: Matthew Barry
Viticulturists: Matthew Barry & Graeme Miles Chief Executive: John Barry

Mount Avoca is a large-ish small vineyard and winery owned by the Barry family, which now has a greater collective role in its wine production than ever before. The 1998 Shiraz is the vineyard's best red for several years. Its wild, brambly fruit and firm ripe tannins are carefully integrated with vanilla oak.

CHARDONNAY
Pyrenees $$$

1999	15.3	2000	2001
1998	16.0	2000	2003
1997	16.6	1999	2002+

Mount Avoca

Moates Lane
Avoca Vic 3467
Tel: (03) 5465 3282
Fax: (03) 5465 3544
Website: mountavoca.com
E-mail:
mountavoca@bigpond.com

Mount Gisborne

Waterson Road
Gisborne Vic 3437
Tel: 03 5428 2834
Fax: 03 5428 2834

SAUVIGNON BLANC

Pyrenees $$$

1999	15.8	2000	2001
1998	16.8	2000	2003
1997	17.8	1998	1999

SHIRAZ

Pyrenees $$

1998	17.2	2003	2006
1997	15.0	2002	2005
1996	16.5	1998	2001
1995	15.0	1997	2000
1994	15.9	1996	1999
1993	16.0	1998	2001
1992	17.2	2000	2004
1991	17.0	1996	1999
1990	15.8	1995	1998
1989	15.5	1994	1997
1988	17.5	1993	1996

Region: Macedon Winemaker: Stuart Anderson
Viticulturist: David Ell Chief Executives: David & Mary Ell

David and Mary Ell own and manage this immaculate Macedon property which in its relatively short existence has created some rich, heady Pinot Noir and reserved, complex and minerally Chardonnay which simply bursts with intense citrusy fruit.

CHARDONNAY

Macedon $$$$

1998	18.7	2003	2006+
1997	18.5	2002	2005
1995	18.0	2000	2003

PINOT NOIR

Macedon $$$$

1998	17.0	2003	2006
1997	18.4	2002	2005+
1996	17.6	2004	2008
1995	18.1	2000	2003+

Region: Strathbogie Ranges Winemaker: Nick Walker
Chief Executive: Terry Davis

Mount Helen is a Victorian brand owned by Mildara Blass, but the actual vineyard itself in the Strathbogie Ranges has since passed into the hands of Normans Wines Ltd. In 1998 it continued its new-found consistency with its Cabernet Merlot, creating a wine whose deep dark berry and plum flavours and firm structure are ideally suited to cellaring.

CABERNET MERLOT

Strathbogie Ranges $$$

1998	17.5	2006	2010
1997	18.3	2005	2009
1996	17.3	2004	2008
1994	18.2		2006+
1991	17.6	1996	1999
1990	17.9	1995	1998

Region: Clare Valley Winemakers: Jeffrey Grosset, Stephanie Toole
Chief Executive: Stephanie Toole

Some of the most honest, approachable and generously flavoured of all Clare Valley wines come from Mount Horrocks, although I wouldn't want to sell short the quality of first-rate wines like its 1996 Cabernet Merlot and 1999 Riesling.

CABERNET MERLOT

Clare Valley $$$

1996	18.4	2004	2008+
1995	17.0	2000	2003
1994	17.6	1999	2002
1993	16.0	1998	2001
1992	16.9	1997	2000

CORDON CUT

lare Valley $$$$

1999	17.6	2001	2004
1998	17.2	1999	2000
1997	16.0	1999	2002
1996	18.2	2001	2004
1995	17.3	2000	2003
1994	18.8	1999	2002
1993	18.6	1998	2001
1992	17.1	1994	1997

RIESLING

Clare Valley $$

1999	18.2	2004	2007
1998	18.1	2003	2006
1997	17.0	2002	2005
1996	17.3	1998	2001
1995	17.0	1997	2000
1994	18.0	1999	2002
1993	18.5	2001	2005
1992	17.5	2000	2004
1991	16.8	1996	1999

SEMILLON (SAUVIGNON BLANC)

Clare Valley $$$

1999	17.8	2004	2007+
1998	17.3	2000	2003
1997	16.6	1999	2002
1996	16.4	1998	2001
1995	16.7	1997	2000
1994	18.5	2000	2006
1993	17.7	1998	2001

Region: Bendigo Winemaker: Nick Walker
Chief Executive: Terry Davis

Mildara Blass, not a company largely focused towards small production individual vineyard wines, must be absolutely delighted with the consistently excellent Shiraz from the Mount Ida vineyard. Typically musky and spicy, brightly flavoured with red and dark berry/plum fruits, it's chock-full of pepper and spice, and married with well-handled oak.

SHIRAZ

Heathcote $$$$

1998	18.9	2003	2006+
1997	17.6	2002	2005
1996	18.0	2001	2004
1995	18.9	2003	2007
1994	18.5	1999	2002
1992	18.6	1997	2000
1991	18.3	1999	2003
1990	18.1	1995	1998
1989	15.0	1991	1994

Region: Grampians Winemakers: Trevor Mast, Andrew McLoughney
Viticulturist: Damias Sheehan Chief Executive: Trevor Mast

Mount Langi Ghiran is one of the premier vineyards in central western Victoria. Best known for its remarkably spicy and peppery Langi Shiraz, which hasn't presented its usual depth in the 1998 release, it also makes an under-rated Cabernet Sauvignon Merlot Blend and a fragrant, limey Riesling. The company is expanding rapidly to take advantage of substantial export opportunities helped by flattering but deserved coverage in overseas media, especially within the United States.

CABERNET SAUVIGNON MERLOT

Grampians $$$$

1997	17.4	2005	2009+
1996	17.2	2004	2008+
1994	18.7		2006+
1993	18.5	2001	2005
1992	18.7	2000	2004
1991	18.2	1999	2003
1990	17.7	1995	1998
1989	17.5	1997	2001
1988	17.0	1993	1996

CHARDONNAY

Grampians $$$

1997	15.6	1999	2002+
1996	16.5	1998	2001
1995	16.2	1996	1997
1994	18.3	1999	2002
1993	18.5	1995	1998
1992	16.5	1994	1997
1991	17.0	1992	1995

LANGI SHIRAZ

Grampians $$$$$

1998	17.0	2003	2006
1997	18.0	2005	2009+
1996	18.5	2004	2008
1995	18.3	2003	2007
1994	19.3		2006+
1993	16.5	2001	2005
1992	18.0		2004+
1991	17.1	1999	2003
1990	18.0		2002+
1989	18.6		2001+
1988	17.5	1996	2000

RIESLING

Grampians $$

1999	14.5	2000	2001
1998	15.2	2000	2003
1997	15.0	1999	2002
1996	18.4	2004	2008
1995	18.3	2003	2007
1994	17.5	1999	2002
1993	18.5	1998	2001
1992	15.2	1994	1997

Region: Yarra Valley Winemakers: John Middleton & Macgregor Forbes
Viticulturists: John Middleton & Macgregor Forbes
Chief Executive: John Middleton

John Middleton's incredible attention to detail continues to inspire the making of some of Australia's greatest wines, especially from the red Bordeaux varieties. Recent tastings of his mature wines from lesser seasons show how strongly a top vineyard can still perform under adverse conditions. While its Quintet and Pinot Noir are as well known and sought after as any made in Australia, Mount Mary's white wines are now approaching comparable stature. The Triolet blend of sauvignon blanc, semillon and muscadelle now rivals some of the most exceptional white Bordeaux wines and the 1998 is no exception. The Chardonnay, while stylistically about as far from the mainstream Australian example as it is possible to travel, has enjoyed a brilliant decade in the 1990s.

CABERNET 'QUINTET'

Yarra Valley $$$$$

1997	17.5	2005	2009
1996	18.7	2004	2008+
1995	18.2	2003	2007+
1994	19.0		2006+
1993	18.0	2005	2013
1992	18.7	2000	2004
1991	18.8	1999	2003
1990	19.4		2002+
1989	15.5	1994	1997
1988	19.2	2000	2008
1987	17.3	1995	1999
1986	18.8		1998+
1985	17.5	1997	2002
1984	18.7		2004+
1983	16.0	1991	1995
1982	18.6	1994	1999
1981	16.5	1993	1998
1980	17.0	1992	1997

CHARDONNAY

Yarra Valley $$$$$

1998	17.5	2003	2006
1997	18.0	2002	2005
1996	18.1	2004	2008
1995	18.7	2003	2007
1994	18.3	2002	2006
1993	17.2	1998	2001
1992	18.8	2000	2004
1991	17.9	1999	2003
1990	18.0	1998	2002
1989	16.0	1994	1997
1988	17.0	1993	1996

PINOT NOIR

Yarra Valley $$$$$

1997	15.9	2002	2005
1996	16.7	1998	2001
1995	16.6	2000	2003
1994	18.4	2002	2006
1993	16.5	1998	2001
1992	18.5	2000	2004
1992	18.6	1997	2000
1991	18.2	1999	2003
1990	17.8	1995	1998
1989	18.7	1997	2001
1988	18.8	1996	2000

TRIOLET (FORMERLY SAUVIGNON)

Yarra Valley $$$$$

1998	18.8	2003	2006+
1997	17.9	2002	2005
1996	18.7	2001	2004
1995	18.6	2000	2003
1994	18.0	1999	2002
1993	18.6	1995	1998
1992	18.7	1997	2000+
1992	18.5	2000	2004
1991	18.3	1996	1999
1990	18.5	1998	2002
1989	18.0	1994	1997

Region: Lower Hunter Valley Winemaker: Phillip Ryan
Viticulturist: Graham Doran Chief Executive: Kevin McLintock

While its Elizabeth (semillon) remains the benchmark entry-level wine for anyone wanting to discover the benefits of bottle-age, this McWilliams label has revitalised its stylish Rosehill Shiraz and has improved its standard Philip Shiraz. Rare releases of Lovedale Semillon and Maurice O'Shea Shiraz are well worth finding.

CHARDONNAY

Lower Hunter Valley $$

1997	16.6	1999	2002
1996	17.0	2001	2004
1995	16.2	2000	2003
1994	15.5	1996	1999
1993	17.6	1998	2001
1992	16.6	1997	2000

ELIZABETH

Lower Hunter Valley $$

1997	18.0	2005	2009
1996	18.0	2004	2008+
1995	18.2	2003	2007+
1994	18.6		2006+
1993	18.6	2001	2005+
1992	17.9	2000	2004
1991	16.5	1993	1996
1990	15.4	1992	1995
1989	17.7	1994	1997
1988	16.6	1990	1993
1987	17.1	1995	1999
1986	18.6	1994	1998+
1985	14.0	1990	1993
1984	18.0	1996	2001

HUNTER VALLEY MERLOT

Lower Hunter Valley $$

1998	15.7	2000	2003
1997	15.0	1999	2002
1996	16.9	1998	2001

LOVEDALE SEMILLON

Lower Hunter Valley $$$$

1996	18.7		2008+
1995	18.7	2003	2007+
1986	18.8	1998	2006+
1984	19.0	1997	2005+

MAURICE O'SHEA SHIRAZ

Lower Hunter Valley $$$

1997	17.6	2005	2009
1996	16.6	2001	2004+
1994	18.0	2002	2006
1993	17.6	1998	2001

OLD PADDOCK & OLD HILL SHIRAZ

Lower Hunter Valley $$$$

1997	16.6	2002	2005
1996	17.8	2004	2008+
1995	17.2	2003	2007

PHILIP

Lower Hunter Valley $$

1997	16.0	1999	2002
1996	15.4	1998	2001
1995	16.5	2000	2003
1994	15.2	1999	2002
1993	14.0	1995	1998

ROSEHILL SHIRAZ

Lower Hunter Valley $$$

1998	18.2	2006	2010+
1997	18.0	2002	2005
1996	18.2	2004	2008
1995	15.3	1997	2000
1991	17.6	1996	1999
1990	14.6	1992	1995
1988	15.8	1990	1993
1987	17.6	1992	1995

Region: Eden Valley Winemakers: Adam Wynn, Andrew Ewart
Viticulturist: Adam Wynn Chief Executive: Adam Wynn

Mountadam is a specialist maker of ripe and generously flavoured wines from a warm site in the High Eden Valley, which incidentally is less of a valley than a ridge of hills. The vineyard has been responsible for some of Australia's most powerfully flavoured and structured Chardonnay, some juicy ripe blend of merlot and cabernet sauvignon labelled as The Red, and some gamey, briary Pinot Noir. Its sparkling and typically pinkish Pinot Noir Chardonnay can be superb. A fine Pinot Noir from 1998 is the best of the current Mountadam releases.

CHARDONNAY

Eden Valley $$$$

1997	16.6	1999	2002
1996	17.2	1998	2001
1995	16.0	2000	2003
1994	18.3	2002	2006
1993	18.6	2001	2005
1992	18.2	2000	2004
1991	18.8		2003+
1990	18.2	1998	2002
1989	17.3	1994	1997

PINOT NOIR

Eden Valley $$$$

1998	17.8	2003	2006
1997	16.3	2002	2005
1996	16.0	2004	2008
1995	16.3	2000	2003
1994	16.7	1999	2002
1993	17.0	2001	2005
1992	16.9	1997	2000
1991	18.0	1999	2002

PINOT NOIR CHARDONNAY

Eden Valley $$$$

1994	14.5	1999	2002
1992	18.4	1997	2000
1991	18.2	1996	1999
1990	18.4	1995	1998

THE RED

Eden Valley $$$$

1997	14.5	1999	2002
1996	15.9	2001	2004
1995	17.0	2000	2003
1994	18.4		2006+
1992	16.7	2000	2004
1990	18.0	1995	1998
1989	16.0	1994	1997
1988	17.0	1996	2000

Region: Central Victoria Winemaker: Hugh Cuthbertson
Viticulturist: Alan Cuthbertson Chief Executive: Janet Cuthbertson

Murrindindee is a small specialist maker of Chardonnay and a red
Bordeaux blend sited in the foothills of the Great Dividing Range
in Victoria. Its Chardonnay is given the full leesy Burgundian
treatment, while the red is elegant, supple and finely-tuned.

CABERNETS

Central Victoria $$$$

1997	14.6	1999	2002
1995	18.1	2003	2007
1994	17.1	2002	2006
1992	15.1	1994	1997
1985	15.3	1993	1997

CHARDONNAY

Central Victoria $$$$

1998	16.9	2003	2006
1997	18.3	2002	2005+
1996	17.1	2001	2004
1994	17.3	1999	2002

Region: Adelaide Hills Winemaker: Peter Leske
Viticulturist: Wayne Stewart Chief Executive: James Tweddell

Nepenthe is the first substantial winery to have been built within the water catchment area of the Adelaide Hills for several years. It has established itself as a reliable maker of fresh, zesty white wines from a number of varieties, especially Sauvignon Blanc, while its Pinot Noir, made from young vines, has a little catching up to do.

CHARDONNAY

Adelaide Hills $$$

1999	16.6	2001	2004+
1998	17.0	2000	2003
1997	16.0	1998	1999

PINOT NOIR

Adelaide Hills $$$

1999	16.2	2001	2004+
1998	16.5	2000	2003+
1997	14.7	1998	1999

SAUVIGNON BLANC

Adelaide Hills $$$

1999	18.4	2000	2001
1998	17.7	1999	2000+
1997	17.9	1997	1998

SEMILLON

Adelaide Hills $$$

1999	17.6	2001	2004
1998	16.5	2000	2003
1997	16.1	1998	1999

Region: McLaren Vale Winemakers: Peter Fraser, Stuart Auld
Viticulturist: Roger Polkinghorn Chief Executive: Robert Hay

Normans is a medium-sized winery whose latest red wine releases show a pleasing improvement across the board, especially with the premium Chais Clarendon wines and the Langhorne Creek Cabernet Sauvignon, which makes its debut in this edition. The White Label reds are a drinkable lot with fine flavour and value.

Normans

Grants Gully Road
Clarendon SA 5157
Tel: (08) 8383 6138
Fax: (08) 8383 6089

CABERNET SAUVIGNON

South Australia $$

1999	16.6	2001	2004
1998	15.8	2003	2006
1997	14.7	1999	2002+
1996	16.0	2001	2004
1995	15.4	1997	2000
1994	15.0	1996	1999

MERLOT

South Australia $$

1999	16.9	2001	2004
1998	16.7	2000	2003
1997	16.5	1999	2002
1996	16.0	1998	2001

SHIRAZ

South Australia $$

1999	16.3	2001	2004
1998	15.0	2000	2003
1997	14.9	1998	1999

CHAIS CLARENDON
CABERNET SAUVIGNON

McLaren Vale $$$$

1998	17.6	2006	2010
1996	16.6	2004	2008
1995	15.7	1997	2000
1994	18.0	2000	2006
1992	17.3	2000	2004
1991	18.4		2003+
1990	18.2		2002+
1989	18.0	1997	2001
1988	18.0	1996	2000
1987	15.0	1992	1995
1986	16.0	1994	1998
1984	18.0	1992	1996

CHAIS CLARENDON CHARDONNAY

Padthaway $$$

1999	16.6	2001	2004
1997	17.2	1999	2002
1996	17.2	2001	2004
1995	17.7	2000	2003
1994	17.5	1999	2002
1991	17.5	1996	1999
1990	18.5	1998	2002
1989	16.0	1994	1997

CHAIS CLARENDON SHIRAZ

McLaren Vale $$$$

1998	18.3	2006	2010
1997	16.7	1999	2002
1996	17.1	2001	2004
1995	18.2	2003	2007
1994	16.7	1999	2002
1992	17.3	1997	2000
1991	18.0	1999	2003
1990	18.2		2002+
1989	18.0	1997	2001
1988	18.5		2000+

LANGHORNE CREEK CABERNET SAUVIGNON

Langhorne Creek $$$

1998	18.3	2006	2010
1997	16.2	1999	2002
1996	15.4	2001	2004

OLD VINE SHIRAZ

South Australia $$$$

1998	16.6	2000	2003
1997	15.9	1999	2002+
1996	16.0	1998	2001

Oakridge is a small but ambitious Yarra Valley winery which moved
its base from its initial cool and elevated site to a warmer location
on the Yarra Valley floor, adjacent to the Maroondah Highway.
Once it gains access to more mature vineyards I would anticipate
more strength and structure in its Reserve wines.
I expect big things from Oakridge Estate.

CABERNET SAUVIGNON MERLOT

Yarra Valley $$$

1998	16.1	2000	2003
1997	15.4	2002	2005
1995	16.0	1997	2000
1994	15.0	1996	1999
1993	16.3	1998	2001
1992	18.2	2000	2004
1991	17.8	1999	2003
1990	16.5	1992	1995

CHARDONNAY

Yarra Valley $$$$

1998	16.0	2000	2003
1997	18.2	2002	2005
1996	18.3	2001	2004
1995	15.6	1997	2000
1994	16.0	1996	1999

RESERVE CABERNET SAUVIGNON

Yarra Valley $$$$

1997	16.6	2005	2009+
1995	16.8	2000	2003+
1994	18.0	2002	2006
1991	18.9	2003	2011
1990	18.5	2002	2010
1987	15.0	1992	1995
1986	18.5	1994	1998

Region: Barossa Valley Winemaker: Philip Laffer
Viticulturist: Joy Dick Chief Executive: Christian Porta

Orlando is one of the three largest wine companies in Australia, a position it maintains with a relatively small number of large-selling mid-priced brands and a small number of flagship wines, each of which I presently rate very highly indeed. The 'Saint series' offers exceptional value, especially with white wine, while the RF and Jacobs Creek range maintain their standards despite enormous increases in scale of production. Jacobs Creek is presently the largest-selling brand of bottled wine in the entire UK wine market.

CENTENARY HILL SHIRAZ

Barossa Valley $$$$$

1996	18.2	2004	2008
1995	17.6	2000	2003+
1994	18.9	2002	2006+

JACARANDA RIDGE CABERNET SAUVIGNON

Coonawarra $$$$$

1996	19.2		2008+
1994	18.8		2006+
1992	16.8	2000	2004
1991	18.3		2003+
1990	18.5		2002+
1989	18.1	1997	2001
1988	17.4	1993	1996
1987	17.5	1995	1999
1986	16.0	1991	1994
1982	17.8	1987	1990

JACOB'S CREEK RIESLING

Southern Australia $

1999	16.6	2001	2004
1998	15.7	1999	2000
1997	16.7	1999	2002
1996	16.8	1998	2001
1995	15.0	1997	2000
1994	15.8	1996	1999

JACOB'S CREEK SHIRAZ CABERNET

Southern Australia $

1998	15.5	2000	2003+
1997	15.6	2002	2005
1996	15.0	1998	2001
1995	16.0	2000	2003
1994	15.5	1999	2002

LAWSON'S SHIRAZ

Padthaway $$$$$

1997	18.2	2005	2009+
1996	19.2		2008+
1995	17.2	2003	2007
1994	18.9	2006	2014+
1993	18.0	2001	2005
1992	16.8	2004	2012
1991	18.9	1999	2003
1990	18.1	2002	2010
1989	16.9	1997	2001
1988	18.4	2000	2008
1987	17.2	1995	1999
1986	18.3	1998	2006

ST HELGA RIESLING

Eden Valley $$

1999	18.6	2007	2011
1998	18.5	2006	2010
1997	16.9	2002	2005
1996	18.7	2004	2010
1995	16.7	2003	2007
1994	18.6	2002	2006+
1993	16.2	1995	1998
1992	18.7	2000	2004+
1991	17.7	1999	2003+
1990	18.0	1995	1998
1989	17.0	1991	1994

ST HILARY CHARDONNAY

Padthaway $$

1999	16.5	2001	2004
1998	17.3	2003	2006
1997	17.0	1999	2002
1996	17.2	2001	2004
1995	15.6	1996	1997
1994	16.7	1996	1999

ST HUGO CABERNET SAUVIGNON

Coonawarra $$$

1997	16.9	2005	2009
1996	18.0	2004	2008+
1994	18.6	2006	2014
1993	17.6	2001	2005
1992	16.5	1997	2000
1991	18.8	2003	2011+
1990	18.5		2002+
1989	18.3	1997	2001
1988	17.5	1996	2000
1987	16.8	1995	1999
1986	17.0	1994	1998
1985	17.8	1990	1993
1984	18.0	1989	1992
1983	15.5	1985	1988
1982	18.4	1990	1994

STEINGARTEN RIESLING

Eden Valley $$$

1999	18.4	2007	2011
1998	19.3	2010	2018+
1997	18.7	2005	2009
1996	19.2	2004	2008+
1995	17.6	2000	2003
1994	19.0	1999	2002+
1992	18.2	2004	2012
1991	18.9	2003	2011
1990	18.6	1998	2002+
1989	16.5	1991	1994
1988	17.0	1993	1996
1987	17.0	1999	2004

Region: Riverlands Winemaker: Hugh Reimers
Viticulturist: Bill Wilksch Chief Executive: Robert Hill Smith

Oxford Landing is owned by S. Smith & Son. It offers some of the best value around in the 'fighting varietal' section with a well-handled chardonnay and a red blend of cabernet sauvignon and shiraz that does justice to some time in the cellar.

CABERNET SHIRAZ

Riverlands $

1999	15.3	2000	2001
1998	14.8	1999	2000
1997	16.7	1998	1999
1996	16.1	1998	2001
1995	14.5	1996	1997
1994	15.0	1996	1999
1993	16.0	1998	2001

CHARDONNAY

Riverlands $

1999	15.8	2000	2001
1998	16.0	1999	2000+
1997	16.0	1998	1999

Region: Mornington Peninsula Winemaker: Lindsay McCall
Viticulturist: Lindsay McCall Chief Executives: Lindsay & Margaret McCall

Paringa Estate is a leading small Mornington Peninsula vineyard whose red wines are frequently amongst the region's finest. Its relatively warm site helps fashion a typically intense, concentrated and very spicy Pinot Noir, while its Shiraz can reveal heady berry fruit, dark pepper characters and a fine-grained bony leanness.

CHARDONNAY

Mornington Peninsula $$$$

1999	16.8	2002	2004
1998	17.5	2003	2006
1997	18.2	2002	2005
1996	15.4	1997	1998
1995	17.8	2000	2003
1994	18.2	1996	1999
1993	17.9	1998	2001
1992	16.9	1997	2000

PINOT NOIR

Mornington Peninsula $$$$$

1999	16.8	2004	2007
1998	18.6	2003	2006+
1997	19.0	2005	2009
1996	16.0	1998	2001
1995	18.0	2000	2003
1994	16.0	1996	1999
1993	18.2	1998	2001
1992	17.7	1997	2000
1991	14.7	1996	1999

SHIRAZ

Mornington Peninsula $$$$$

1999	16.5	2001	2004+
1998	16.6	2003	2006
1997	18.7	2005	2009
1996	16.5	2001	2004
1995	16.4	2000	2003
1994	18.4	1999	2002
1993	18.3	2001	2005
1992	15.8	2000	2004
1991	17.4	1999	2003

Region: Coonawarra Winemaker: Chris Cameron
Viticulturist: Doug Balnaves Chief Executive: John Parker

With the 1998 vintage Parker's First Growth moves up a notch in concentration and strength, while my personal favourite remains the very complete and long-living classic made in 1996. Parker regularly downgrades wine to the second Cabernet Sauvignon brand when it doesn't cut the mustard for the First Growth label.

CABERNET SAUVIGNON

Coonawarra $$$

1998	16.0	2003	2006
1997	15.8	1999	2002+
1996	15.3	1998	2001
1995	16.1	2000	2003
1994	15.4	1999	2002
1992	15.0	1997	2000
1991	16.5	1999	2003

TERRA ROSSA FIRST GROWTH

Coonawarra $$$$$

1998	18.6	2010	2018
1996	19.0	2008	2016
1994	15.3	1999	2002
1993	17.0	2001	2005
1991	18.6	2003	2011+
1990	19.2	2002	2010
1989	17.9	1994	1997
1988	18.8	2000	2008

Region: Bendigo Winemakers: Graeme Leith, Greg Bennett
Viticulturists: Graeme Leith, Greg Bennett
Chief Executives: Graeme Leith, Sue Mackinnon

Passing Clouds is a mature central Victorian vineyard that crops low yields of intensely flavoured fruit which it consistently turns into dark, powerful, brooding and inky reds for long-term cellaring.

ANGEL BLEND

Bendigo $$$$

1998	17.2		2010+
1997	18.1	2005	2009+
1996	17.0		2008+
1995	18.4		2007+
1994	17.4		2006+
1992	18.2	2000	2004
1991	17.3	1999	2003
1990	16.8		2002+
1987	16.0	1995	1999
1985	18.0	1993	1997

er
awarra
te

Highway
arra SA 5263
) 9357 3376
) 9358 1517

PARKER
COONAWARRA
ESTATE

TERRA ROSSA
CABERNET SAUVIGNON
1994

750ml

PARKER
COONAWARRA
ESTATE

TERRA ROSSA
FIRST GROWTH
1993

750ml

sing
ds

0 Kurting Road
r Vic 3517
) 5438 8257
) 5438 8246

Passing Clouds

Angel Blend
1994
Product of Australia

GRAEME'S BLEND

Bendigo $$$

1998	17.4	2006	2010+
1997	17.2	2005	2009
1996	16.9	2004	2008+
1995	18.3	2003	2007
1994	16.4		2006+
1992	18.3		2004+
1991	17.5	1996	1999
1990	18.0	1995	1998
1989	15.5	1994	1997

SHIRAZ

Bendigo $$$$

1998	16.0		2010+
1997	16.0	2005	2009
1996	16.8	2004	2008
1994	18.0	2002	2006+

Region: Clare Valley Winemaker: Neil Paulett
Viticulturist: Matthew Paulett Chief Executive: Neil Paulett

Neil Paulett is one of a group of skilled Clare Valley winemakers who fashion sophisticated reds with delightful clarity of fruit, minty regional influences and fine-grained tannins plus, of course, the regional speciality of riesling. His is a typically zesty, citrusy wine which usually appreciates at least five years in the bottle.

CABERNET MERLOT

Clare Valley $$

1997	16.5	2002	2005
1996	18.2	2004	2008
1995	16.7	2000	2003
1994	17.0	1996	1999
1993	15.3	1995	1998
1992	18.2	2000	2004
1991	18.1	1999	2003
1990	18.5	1995	1998
1989	18.0	1994	1997
1988	17.0	1993	1996
1987	16.0	1992	1995

Pauletts

Polish Hill Road
Polish Hill River SA 5453
Tel: (08) 8843 4328
Fax: (08) 8843 4202
E-mail:
paulwine@rbe.net.au

RIESLING

Clare Valley $

1999	16.8	2004	2007
1998	16.8	2000	2003+
1997	15.0	2002	2005
1996	16.6	2001	2004
1995	18.0	2003	2007
1994	18.2	2002	2006
1993	17.0	1995	1998
1992	18.2	2000	2004
1991	17.3	1999	2003
1990	18.0	1998	2002
1989	15.0	1994	1997
1988	16.5	1996	2000
1987	17.0	1999	2004

SHIRAZ

Clare Valley $$

1998	15.8	2000	2003+
1997	15.9	2002	2005
1996	16.4	2001	2004
1995	16.8	2000	2003
1994	17.4	1999	2002
1993	18.5	2001	2005
1992	17.6	2000	2004
1991	17.5	1996	1999
1990	17.5	1995	1998
1989	17.0	1994	1997

Pendarves

110 Old North Road
Belford NSW 2335
Tel: (02) 9913 1088
Fax: (02) 9970 6152

Region: Lower Hunter Valley Winemaker: Greg Silkman
Viticulturist: Ray Dibley Chief Executive: Dr Philip Norrie

Pendarves Estate is the vineyard owned and managed by Dr Philip Norrie, GP, wine historian and author, and one of the medical front men in the ongoing tussle with Australia's neo-prohibitionist movement. The overall standard of Pendarves' wines has not been helped by several recent changes in contract winemaking.

CHARDONNAY

Lower Hunter Valley $$

1999	14.0		2000
1998	16.8	2000	2003
1997	15.3	1999	2002
1996	16.3	1998	2001
1995	17.8	2000	2003
1994	17.8	1999	2002
1993	16.9	1998	2001

Region: Barossa Valley Winemaker: John Duval
Viticulturist: Andrew Pike Chief Executive: Tom Park

Penfolds

Tanunda Road
Nuriootpa SA 5355
Tel: (08) 8560 9389
Fax: (08) 8560 9494

The first release of the so-called 'Baby Grange', rather aimlessly christened RWT (from Red Winemaking Trial), has stolen much of the thunder from the 1995 Grange itself. The RWT is a Barossa shiraz from 1997 selected to make a more supple, elegant wine than expected of Grange. Furthermore, it's been matured in French oak casks rather than the small American cooperage we usually associate with Penfolds and Grange. As for the 1995 Grange? Good enough, but by no means a classic. The most important Penfolds release of the last year is unquestionably the 1997 Yattarna Chardonnay, the first really convincing wine of excellence under this label.

ADELAIDE HILLS CHARDONNAY (FORMERLY TRIAL BIN)

Adelaide Hills $$$

1998	15.7	2000	2003
1997	16.4	2002	2005
1996	18.2	2001	2004
1995	16.7	1997	2000

ADELAIDE HILLS SEMILLON (FORMERLY TRIAL BIN)

Adelaide Hills $$$

1997	16.4	1999	2002
1996	17.5	1998	2001
1995	16.8	1997	2000
1994	16.5	1996	1999
1993	18.5	2001	2005

BIN 128 COONAWARRA SHIRAZ

Coonawarra $$$

1997	16.0	2002	2005
1996	18.4		2008+
1995	15.9	2000	2003
1994	18.2	2002	2006
1993	16.4	2001	2005
1992	18.0	2000	2004
1991	16.8	1999	2003
1990	17.9	1998	2002
1989	15.8	1994	1997
1988	17.0	2000	2005
1987	15.0	1992	1995
1986	18.0	1994	1998
1985	16.5	1993	1997

BIN 389 CABERNET SHIRAZ

South Australia $$$

1997	18.0	2005	2009+
1996	19.2	2008	2016
1995	17.7	2004	2008
1994	18.2		2006+
1993	18.1		2005+
1992	17.8		2004+
1991	18.4		2003+
1990	18.6	2002	2010
1989	16.0	1994	1997
1988	18.0	1996	2000
1987	17.5	1995	1999
1986	18.6	1998	2006
1985	15.7	1993	1997
1984	15.0	1989	1992
1983	18.2	1995	2003

BIN 407 CABERNET SAUVIGNON

Barossa Valley $$$

1997	16.7	2005	2009
1996	18.6	2004	2008
1995	17.0	2000	2003
1994	18.3	2002	2006
1993	18.1	2001	2005
1992	16.5	1997	2000
1991	18.3		2003+
1990	18.0		2002+

BIN 707 CABERNET SAUVIGNON

Barossa Valley & Coonawarra $$$$$

1997	17.0	2005	2009+
1996	19.5		2016+
1994	18.8		2004+
1993	18.8		2005+
1992	18.4		2004+
1991	19.2	2003	2011+
1990	18.9		2010+
1989	17.5	1997	2001
1988	18.7	2000	2008
1987	18.0	1999	2007
1986	18.8		2006+
1985	17.5	1997	2005
1984	18.0	1996	2004
1983	17.5	1995	2003
1982	16.8	1994	2002
1980	18.2	1992	2000
1978	17.5	1990	1998
1977	17.5	1989	1997
1964	19.0	1994	1999

CLARE ESTATE

Clare Valley $$$

1996	18.2	2004	2008+
1995	18.2	2003	2007
1994	18.1	2002	2006
1993	18.2		2005+
1992	17.5	2000	2004
1991	18.2	1999	2003
1990	16.8	1998	2002
1989	16.0	1994	1997
1988	17.5	1993	1996
1987	16.5	1992	1995
1986	18.1	1994	1998

CLARE ESTATE CHARDONNAY

Clare Valley $$

1996	16.4	1998	2001
1995	16.3	1997	2000
1994	17.6	1999	2002
1993	17.5	1998	2001
1992	16.4	1994	1997

Barossa Valley (predominantly) $$$$$

1995	18.3	2007	2015
1994	19.3	2006	2014+
1993	18.6		2013+
1992	18.8	2004	2012
1991	18.6		2011+
1990	19.1		2010+
1989	18.3	2001	2006
1988	18.2	2000	2005
1987	17.8	1999	2007
1986	19.0		2006+
1985	18.0	1997	2005
1984	18.2	1996	2004
1983	19.0		2003+
1982	17.8	1994	2002
1981	16.4	1993	2001
1980	18.1	2000	2005
1979	17.7	1987	1991
1978	18.5	1998	2003
1977	16.0	1989	1994
1976	18.4	1996	2006
1975	17.7	1995	2000
1974	15.0	1982	1986
1973	15.3	1985	1990
1972	17.2	1984	1989
1971	19.0	2001	2006
1970	17.0	1982	1990
1969	17.5	1989	1994
1968	18.3	1988	1998
1967	18.7	1987	1997
1966	19.0	1996	2001
1965	17.8	1985	1995
1964	17.5	1984	1989
1963	18.6	1993	2003
1962	19.0	1992	1997
1961	17.2	1981	1986
1960	18.0	1990	1995
1959	16.2	1979	1984
1958	15.6	1978	1983
1957	18.2	1977	1982
1956	16.4	1976	1981
1955	19.0	1985	1990
1954	18.6	1974	1979
1953	19.6	1983	1988
1952	18.8	1972	1982
1951	16.0	1963	1971

KALIMNA BIN 28 SHIRAZ

Barossa Valley $$$

1997	17.4	2005	2009
1996	18.5		2008+
1995	17.0	2003	2007
1994	17.8	2002	2006
1993	15.3	1998	2001
1992	17.9	2000	2004
1991	18.0	1999	2003
1990	18.1	1998	2002
1989	16.0	1994	1997
1988	16.7	1996	2000
1987	16.5	1995	1999
1986	18.2	1998	2003
1985	16.0	1993	1997
1984	15.5	1989	1992
1983	15.0	1995	2000
1982	16.5	1990	1994

KOONUNGA HILL SHIRAZ CABERNET SAUVIGNON

South Australia $$

1998	16.1	2003	2006+
1997	15.9	2002	2005
1996	17.2	2004	2008
1995	16.0	2000	2003
1994	16.2	1999	2002
1993	16.5	2001	2005
1992	16.6	2000	2004
1991	17.7	1999	2003
1990	17.1	1998	2002
1989	16.4	1997	2001
1988	17.0	1996	2000
1987	15.0	1995	1999
1986	18.2	1998	2006
1985	15.3	1993	1997
1984	17.0	1996	2004
1983	16.7	1991	1995
1982	17.3	1994	2002
1981	16.5	1993	2001
1980	16.7	1992	2000+
1979	16.0	1987	1991
1978	18.2	1990	1998
1977	17.5	1989	1997
1976	16.5	1988	1996

MAGILL ESTATE SHIRAZ

Adelaide Metropolitan $$$$$

1997	17.9	2005	2009
1996	18.6		2008+
1995	18.2	2003	2007
1994	17.4	2002	2006+
1993	18.2		2005+
1992	17.2	2000	2004
1991	18.6		2011+
1990	18.5	2002	2010
1989	18.0	1997	2001
1988	17.6	2000	2005
1987	18.2	1995	1999
1986	18.5	1998	2003
1985	18.2	1993	1997
1984	17.2	1989	1992
1983	17.9	1995	2000

OLD VINE RED RHÔNE BLEND

Barossa Valley $$$

1997	17.2	2005	2009
1996	17.9	2004	2008
1995	15.8	1997	2000
1994	17.7	2002	2006
1993	16.8	2001	2005

RAWSON'S RETREAT RED

South Australia $

1998	15.8	2000	2003
1997	15.0	1998	1999
1996	15.6	1998	2001
1995	16.2	1997	2000

ST HENRI SHIRAZ (SHIRAZ CABERNET IN 1995)

Barossa Valley, Clare Valley, Coonawarra $$$$

1996	18.7		2008+
1995	17.6	2003	2007+
1994	18.3		2006+
1993	17.9	2003	2007
1992	17.0	2000	2004
1991	18.3		2003+
1990	18.9		2002+
1989	18.3	2001	2009
1988	18.0	2000	2005
1987	18.0	1999	2004
1986	18.0	1998	2006
1985	17.6	1997	2002
1984	14.5	1992	1996
1983	17.0	1995	2003
1982	17.0	1990	1994
1981	15.0	1993	1998
1980	17.0	1992	1997
1979	14.0	1987	1991
1978	14.5	1990	1995
1977	15.0	1989	1994
1976	18.0	1996	2001

THE VALLEYS CHARDONNAY

Clare and Eden Valleys $$

1998	16.8	2000	2003
1997	17.9	1999	2002
1996	16.5	1998	2001
1995	16.4	1997	2000
1994	17.8	1999	2002
1993	17.5	1998	2001
1992	17.0	1997	2000
1991	16.9	1993	1996

Led by its Cabernet Sauvignon, Penley Estate has emerged in recent years as one of the leading red wine makers in Coonawarra. Given his background and breeding, it's hardly surprising that Kym Tolley, related to the Penfold family, fashions his best wines in a Penfolds-like style, based around fruit richness and density almost bordering on the over-ripe, with an excellent integration of assertive chocolate oak. The Chardonnay is a full-blown, citrusy and creamy style which doesn't require cellar patience at all.

CABERNET SAUVIGNON
Coonawarra $$$$$

1997	17.0	2002	2005+
1996	17.5	2004	2008
1995	16.2	2000	2003
1994	17.0	1998	2002
1993	18.0		2005+
1992	18.1	2000	2004
1991	18.8		2003+
1990	18.3	1998	2002
1989	17.5	1994	1997

CHARDONNAY
Coonawarra $$$

1998	16.1	1999	2000
1997	17.0	1999	2002+
1996	16.3	1998	2001
1995	17.0	1997	2002
1994	16.5	1996	1999
1993	15.8	1995	1998
1991	15.0	1996	1999
1990	15.5	1995	1998
1989	15.3	1994	1997

HYLAND SHIRAZ
Coonawarra $$$

1998	16.3	2003	2006
1997	16.7	1999	2002+
1996	16.9	2001	2004
1994	14.9	1996	1999
1993	15.0	1995	1998

PHOENIX CABERNET SAUVIGNON

Coonawarra $$$

1998	16.8	2003	2006
1997	16.7	1999	2002+
1996	17.1	1998	2001+
1995	15.6	1997	2000

SHIRAZ CABERNET

Coonawarra $$

1997	15.3	1999	2002
1996	16.3	1998	2001
1995	16.9	1997	2000
1994	17.8	2002	2006
1993	16.8	1995	1998
1992	17.0	1997	2000
1991	18.2	1999	2003
1990	17.5	1995	1998

Region: Lower Hunter Valley Winemaker: Chris Cameron
Viticulturist: Carl Davies

Pepper Tree is an ambitious Hunter Valley-based winery which not only sources fruit from a number of regions in several states, but actually manages its Coonawarra vineyard by computer from Pokolbin! Its flagship wine is the Coonawarra Reserve Merlot, one of Australia's leading examples of this variety.

CHARDONNAY

Various $$$

1999	17.9	2004	2007
1998	17.4	2000	2003
1997	15.7	1998	1999
1996	15.3	1997	1998

COONAWARRA RESERVE MERLOT

Coonawarra $$$$$

1998	18.9	2006	2010
1996	18.7	2001	2004+
1995	16.5	1997	2000

RESERVE SEMILLON

Lower Hunter Valley $$$

1998	16.6	2006	2010
1997	18.2	2005	2009
1996	17.3	2004	2008
1995	18.6	2003	2007
1994	17.2	1999	2002
1993	16.5	1998	2001

Region: Adelaide Hills Winemakers: Brian Croser, Con Moshos
Viticulturist: Mike Harms Chief Executive: Brian Croser

Petaluma is hardly a 'small' winery, but has managed to keep its
premier wines well and truly in the small winery mindset. A recent
tasting of every Riesling, Coonawarra and Merlot ever made by
Petaluma revealed a number of things. Firstly, it was time that the
Coonawarra joined the Chardonnay amongst the top-rating wines
in this book. The 1997 and 1998 vintages of this wine, so different
in structure but so similar in breeding, are easily the two best
releases since the extraordinary first wine of the lineage from
1979. It was a surprise to discover how much more powerful and
densely structured the Coonawarra Merlot is than corresponding
vintages of the cabernet blend, while it was no surprise
whatsoever to enjoy so many classic vintages of the Riesling.
Petaluma has now joined the Rhône varietal stakes with its first
Viognier and an interesting preview of its first
Shiraz from the Adelaide Hills.

CHARDONNAY

Adelaide Hills $$$$$

1998	18.6	2006	2010
1997	18.9	2005	2009
1996	18.7	2004	2008
1995	18.8	2003	2007
1994	18.5	2002	2006
1993	18.2	1995	1998
1992	18.8	2000	2004
1991	16.0	1996	1999
1990	18.2	1998	2002
1989	17.0	1991	1994
1988	18.0	1993	1996
1987	17.9	1995	1999
1986	16.5	1991	1994
1985	16.0	1990	1993

COONAWARRA

Coonawarra $$$$$

1998	19.5		2018+
1997	19.2	2009	2017+
1996	18.6		2016+
1995	18.1	2007	2015
1994	18.8	2006	2014+
1993	17.8	2005	2013+
1992	18.8		2012+
1991	18.7	2003	2011+
1990	18.6		2010+
1988	17.8	2000	2008+
1987	16.3	1995	1999
1986	17.6	1998	2006
1985	15.0	1990	1993
1984	14.7	1986	1989
1982	16.0	1987	1990
1981	16.2	1986	1989
1980	15.3	1985	1988
1979	18.8	1991	1996+

CROSER

Adelaide Hills $$$$

1998	18.3	2003	2006
1997	17.7	1999	2002+
1996	18.2	1998	2001
1995	18.0	1997	2000
1994	18.3	1996	1999
1993	18.2	1995	1998
1992	18.4	1997	2000
1991	17.0	1993	1996
1990	18.3	1995	1998
1988	18.5	1990	1993
1987	17.5	1995	1999

MERLOT

Coonawarra $$$$$

1998	19.2	2010	2018+
1997	19.0		2009+
1996	18.3	2004	2008
1995	17.2	2003	2007
1994	18.2	2006	2014+
1993	16.7	2001	2005+
1992	18.7	2004	2012+
1991	17.2		2003+
1990	17.8	2002	2010

1999	18.7	2011	2019
1998	17.6	2006	2010
1997	18.8	2005	2009+
1996	18.6	2008	2016
1995	18.9	2007	2015
1994	18.3	2006	2014
1993	16.0	2001	2005
1992	17.0	2000	2004
1991	18.2	1996	1999
1990	18.8	2002	2010+
1989	17.1	1997	2001+
1988	17.8	2000	2008
1987	15.7	1992	1995
1986	19.2	1998	2006+
1985	18.8	1997	2005
1984	15.9	1989	1992
1983	16.2	1988	1991
1982	18.7	1994	2002+
1981	16.0	1989	1993
1980	18.9	1992	2000
1979	15.8	1987	1991

Region: Barossa Valley
Winemakers: Andrew Wigan, Peter Scholz, Ian Hongell & Leonie Lange
Viticulturist: Peter Nash Chief Executive: Douglas Lehmann

In similar fashion to Penfolds, which with its RWT Shiraz made its first foray into a French oak-matured Barossa red, Peter Lehmann recently released its own French oak-matured shiraz, labelled Eight Songs. It's from the 1996 vintage and is simply a wonderful, deep, and seamless red of rare quality, but priced well beneath the company's premier Stonewell Shiraz. At the other end of the scale, the 1998 Lehmann reds offer typical value for money.

CABERNET SAUVIGNON

Barossa Valley $$

1998	18.0	2006	2010
1997	18.1	2002	2005+
1996	17.2	2001	2004
1995	16.6	2000	2003
1994	18.1	1999	2002
1993	18.0	2001	2005
1992	18.3	2000	2004
1991	16.9	1999	2003
1990	18.2		2002+
1989	17.5	1997	2001
1988	18.0		2000+
1987	17.0	1995	1999
1986	18.0	1998	2003

CHARDONNAY

Barossa Valley $$

1998	16.5	2000	2003
1997	16.5	1998	1999
1996	15.2	1997	1998
1995	15.0	1996	1997
1994	16.3	1996	1999
1993	16.0	1995	1998
1992	16.5	1994	1997
1991	16.3	1993	1996
1990	17.5	1998	2002

CLANCY'S

Barossa Valley $$

1998	15.5	2000	2003
1997	17.9	2002	2005
1996	16.8	1998	2001
1995	16.8	1997	2000
1994	17.0	1996	1999
1993	15.3	1995	1998

EDEN VALLEY RIESLING

Eden Valley $

1999	15.6	2000	2001
1998	17.0	2003	2006
1997	16.0	1999	2002
1996	17.2	2001	2004
1995	15.0	1997	2000
1994	16.5	1999	2002
1993	18.0	1998	2001
1992	17.9	1997	2000
1991	17.5	1996	1999
1990	17.0	1995	1998

MENTOR (FORMERLY CELLAR COLLECTION CABERNET BLEND)

Barossa Valley $$$$

1996	18.6	2008	2016
1995	16.8		2007+
1994	18.0		2006+
1993	16.0	2001	2005+
1992	16.5	2000	2004
1991	18.2	1999	2003
1990	18.4		2002+
1989	18.4	2001	2006
1986	18.6	1998	2003

NOBLE SEMILLON

Barossa Valley $$$$

1998	15.4	2003	2006
1997	15.8	1999	2002
1996	14.8	1997	1998
1995	16.0	2000	2003
1994	17.4	1999	2002
1992	15.4	1997	2000
1990	16.0	1995	1998
1989	16.0	1994	1997

RESERVE RIESLING

Eden Valley $$

1994	18.0	2002	2006
1993	18.5	2001	2005+
1992	18.4	2000	2004
1991	18.0	1996	1999
1990	17.8	1992	1997
1989	17.5	1991	1996
1987	17.5	1992	1995

SEMILLON

Barossa Valley $

1999	16.8	2001	2004
1998	16.8	2000	2003
1997	17.1	1999	2002
1996	16.8	1998	2001
1995	16.5	2000	2003
1994	18.0	1999	2002
1993	16.5	2001	2005
1992	17.0	2000	2004
1990	16.0	1995	1998

SHIRAZ

Barossa Valley $$

1998	17.9	2003	2006
1997	18.0	2002	2005+
1996	17.5	1998	2001
1995	16.2	1997	2000
1994	17.5	1999	2002
1993	17.3	2001	2005
1992	18.2	2000	2004
1991	17.4	1996	1999
1990	17.0	1995	1998
1989	16.0	1994	1999
1988	18.5	1996	2000

STONEWELL SHIRAZ

Barossa Valley $$$$$

1995	18.5	2007	2015+
1994	19.0	2002	2006+
1993	18.6	2005	2013
1992	18.2	2000	2004
1991	18.8		2011+
1990	17.6	2002	2010
1989	18.8	2001	2006+
1988	18.6	2000	2008
1987	18.5	1999	2004

Region: Eden Valley Winemaker: Louisa Rose
Viticulturist: Robin Nettelbeck Chief Executive: Robert Hill Smith

Pewsey Vale is best known for its Riesling and the 1999 edition doesn't let the side down. It's a knockout expression of the tight-knit, fragrant and steely Eden Valley style, with apple, pear and lime juice fruit just waiting to explode. One of the S. Smith & Son brands made at the Yalumba winery at Angaston, Pewsey Vale also makes a tight, fine-grained Cabernet Sauvignon usually given smoky coffee oak influences to complement its sweet berry flavours.

Pewsey Vale

Brownes Rd
Pewsey Vale SA 5353
Tel: (08) 8561 3200
Fax: (08) 8561 3393

CABERNET SAUVIGNON

Eden Valley $$

1998	16.9	2006	2010
1997	18.2	2005	2009+
1996	17.3	2004	2008
1995	16.0	2003	2007
1994	18.2	2002	2006
1993	17.8		2005+
1992	16.6	2000	2004
1991	17.8	1999	2003
1990	17.5	1998	2002
1989	15.3	1990	1991
1988	16.0	1996	2000
1986	17.0	1991	1994

Phillip Island
Vineyard

**414 Berry's Beach Road
Phillip Island Vic 3922
Tel: (03) 5956 8465
Fax: (03) 5956 8465
Website:
www.phillipisland
wines.com.au
E-mail: enq@phillipisland
wines.com.au**

RIESLING

Eden Valley $

1999	18.6	2007	2011+
1998	16.6	2003	2006
1997	18.3	2005	2009
1996	18.3		2008+
1995	17.8	2003	2007
1994	18.1		2006+
1993	18.3	1998	2001
1992	18.0	1997	2000
1991	18.1	1999	2003
1990	18.5	1998	2002
1989	16.7	1997	2001
1988	17.0	1993	1996
1987	17.0	1992	1995
1986	18.0	1991	1994
1985	16.8	1993	1997
1984	18.7	1996	2004
1983	16.8	1991	1995
1981	16.6	1989	1993
1979	18.3	1991	1999
1978	18.5	1990	1998
1973	17.8	1985	1993
1969	18.6	1981	1989

**Region: Gippsland Winemakers: David Lance, James Lance
Viticulturist: Michael Bentley Chief Executives: Joanne & Michael Bentley**

The first vineyard and winery development on Phillip Island, home to hundreds of families' holiday homes and the Australian Motor Cycle Grand Prix, Phillip Island Wines produces its fragrant and punchy Sauvignon Blanc from grapes grown on site and its occasionally excellent The Nobbies Pinot Noir from Gippsland fruit.

SAUVIGNON BLANC

Gippsland $$$

1999	15.6		2000
1998	17.4	2000	2003
1997	18.0	1999	2002

THE NOBBIES PINOT NOIR

Gippsland $$$$

1999	15.9	2001	2004
1998	17.0	2000	2003
1997	15.3	1998	1999
1996	17.2	1998	2001+

Pierro is a small but highly significant Margaret River vineyard widely and rightly feted for the consistent excellence of its statuesque Chardonnay, a wine now emulated the length and breadth of this country. Rare bottlings are released as 'Unfiltered' batches, which typically offer even more complexity and character in the wine's youth. Pierro's next best wine is its characteristically barrel fermented and matured LTC Semillon Sauvignon Blanc, which receives just a splash of Chardonnay before bottling.

CABERNETS

Margaret River $$$$$

1998	17.2	2006	2010+
1997	15.8	2002	2005
1996	18.2	2004	2008+
1995	16.0	2000	2003

CHARDONNAY

Margaret River $$$$$

1998	18.1	2000	2003+
1997	18.6	2002	2005+
1996	19.2	2004	2008
1995	18.2	2000	2003
1994	18.6	2002	2006
1993	18.8	2001	2005
1992	19.0	2000	2004
1991	18.5	1996	1999
1990	18.5	1998	2002
1989	17.6	1994	1997
1988	16.5	1990	1995
1987	18.3	1995	1999
1986	18.7	1994	1998

PINOT NOIR

Margaret River $$$$

1998	16.0	2000	2003+
1997	16.8	2002	2005
1996	16.5	2001	2004
1995	15.3	2000	2003
1994	16.0	1999	2002
1993	17.2	2001	2005
1992	17.0	2000	2004
1990	18.5	1995	1998
1988	15.0	1989	1990
1987	18.0	1992	1995

SEMILLON SAUVIGNON BLANC

Margaret River $$$

1999	16.8	2001	2004
1998	17.5	2000	2003
1997	18.0	2002	2005
1996	18.2	2001	2004
1995	18.2	1997	2000
1994	18.0	1999	2002
1993	18.2	1998	2001
1992	17.5	1997	2000
1991	17.5	1996	1999
1990	17.0	1998	2002

Region: Clare Valley Winemaker: Neil Pike
Viticulturist: Andrew Pike Chief Executive: Neil Pike

Now a worthy entrant in the Australian sangiovese stakes, Pikes is a successful small Clare Valley winery (and even specialist brewery!) which focuses on all the right things for this region: riesling, shiraz and cabernet (plus pale ale). The latest releases include an exceptional Riesling from 1999 and a brace of excellent reds from the fine 1998 season.

CABERNET

Clare Valley $$$

1998	17.5	2006	2010+
1997	16.8	2005	2009
1996	17.6	2004	2008+
1995	16.0	1997	2000
1994	18.3	2002	2006
1993	18.0	1998	2001
1992	18.4	2000	2004
1991	18.2	1999	2003
1990	18.0	1998	2002

RIESLING

Clare Valley $$

1999	18.6	2007	2011
1998	18.1	2003	2006+
1997	16.7	2002	2005
1996	17.2	2001	2004
1995	14.7	1997	2000
1992	16.1	1997	2000
1990	18.0	1998	2002
1988	18.0	1993	1996

SHIRAZ
Clare Valley $$$

1998	17.6	2006	2010+
1997	17.0	2005	2009
1996	16.0	2001	2004
1995	18.2	2000	2003
1994	17.6	1999	2002
1993	17.2	2001	2005
1992	18.3	2000	2004
1991	18.5		2003+
1990	18.3		2002+

Region: Pipers River Winemaker: Andrew Pirie
Viticulturist: Andrew Pirie Chief Executive: Andrew Pirie

Pipers Brook

1216 Pipers Brook Road
Pipers Brook Tas 7254
Tel: (03) 6382 7527
Fax: (03) 6382 7226
Website: www.pbv.com.au
E-mail: info@pbv.com.au

Pipers Brook is Tasmania's most significant winery whose best recent wines have come from the Alsatian grapes of Riesling, Gewürztraminer and Pinot Gris, as well as the Champagne varieties which it has crafted into two very complete and elegant Pirie sparkling wines from 1995 and 1996. In 1998 Pipers Brook also made its best Summit Chardonnay for some time, a taut and sophisticated wine that will develop over the next five years.

CHARDONNAY
Pipers River $$$$

1999	16.5	2001	2004
1998	17.0	2003	2006
1997	17.8	1999	2002
1996	15.8	1998	2001
1995	18.4	2003	2007
1994	15.0	1996	1999
1993	18.2	1998	2001
1992	18.0	1997	2000
1991	18.5	1999	2003

PIPERS BROOK VINEYARD
1995 CHARDONNAY
Tasmania

GEWURZTRAMINER
Pipers River $$$

1999	18.2	2004	2007
1998	18.5	2003	2006+
1997	17.2	1999	2002
1996	18.3	2001	2004
1995	18.3	2000	2003
1993	17.0	1995	1998
1992	18.2	2000	2004
1991	17.0	1999	2003
1990	16.8	1995	1998
1989	16.0	1994	1997

PIPERS BROOK VINEYARD
1996 GEWÜRZTRAMINER
Tasmania

PIPERS BROOK VINEYARD
1995 OPIMIAN
Tasmania

OPIMIAN (FORMERLY CABERNET SAUVIGNON)

Northern Tasmania $$$$

1998	14.7	2003	2006
1997	15.3	2002	2005
1995	18.4	2003	2007
1992	16.3	1994	1997
1991	17.0	1999	2003
1989	16.0	1994	1997
1988	17.0	1996	2000
1987	15.0	1992	1995
1986	15.5	1994	1998

PIPERS BROOK VINEYARD
1995 PELLION
Pinot Noir
Tasmania

PELLION (FORMERLY PINOT NOIR)

Northern Tasmania $$$$

1998	16.3	2000	2003+
1997	16.8	2002	2005
1996	15.0	2001	2004
1995	16.8	1997	2000
1994	17.3	1999	2002
1993	16.8	1995	1998
1992	17.5	1997	2000
1991	18.0	1999	2003
1990	16.5	1992	1995
1988	17.0	1993	1996

PIPERS BROOK VINEYARD
1996 RIESLING
Tasmania

RIESLING

Pipers River $$$

1999	18.2	2007	2011
1998	18.6	2006	2010
1997	17.2	2002	2005
1996	18.1	2004	2008
1995	18.2	2003	2007
1994	17.5	2002	2006
1993	18.3	1998	2001
1992	18.8		2004+
1991	16.5	1996	1999
1990	17.0	1995	1998
1989	18.0	1994	1997
1988	16.5	1993	1996

Region: Great Southern Winemakers: Gavin Berry, Gordon Parker
Viticulturists: Roger Pattenden, Peter Glen Chief Executive: Gavin Berry

A classically elegant and complete 1998 Shiraz is clearly the best
from this excellent Mount Barker vineyard since 1994, while its
1999 Riesling and Chardonnay are both genuine achievements from
this rather dampish vintage. Broadly speaking, Plantagenet is a
marvellously consistent and reliable small winery given the
marginality of its area whose wines can usually
be cellared with total confidence.

Plantagenet

Albany Highway
Mount Barker WA 6324
Tel: (08) 9851 2150
Fax: (08) 9851 1839

CABERNET SAUVIGNON

Great Southern $$$$

1997	16.5	2005	2009
1996	16.0	2001	2004
1995	16.5	2003	2007
1994	18.7	2006	2014+
1993	17.3	2001	2005
1992	18.5		2004+
1991	17.9		2003+
1990	18.3		2002+
1989	18.0	2001	2009
1988	17.5	2000	2008
1987	16.5		2007+
1986	18.0	1998	2003
1985	18.0	1997	2002

CHARDONNAY

Great Southern $$$

1999	18.3	2004	2007+
1998	16.8	2003	2006
1997	17.5	2002	2005
1996	16.0	2001	2004
1995	18.1	2000	2003
1994	17.0	1996	1999
1993	18.2	1998	2001
1992	16.7	1994	1997

PINOT NOIR

Great Southern $$$$

1998	16.0	2000	2003+
1997	17.0	1999	2002+
1996	17.5	2001	2004
1995	17.4	2000	2003
1994	16.7	1996	1999
1993	17.0	1998	2001
1991	16.6	1999	2003

RIESLING

Great Southern $$

1999	18.1	2007	2011
1998	18.7	2006	2010
1997	18.5	2005	2009
1996	18.5	2004	2008
1995	18.3	2003	2007
1994	18.5		2006+
1993	18.4	1998	2001
1992	18.1	1997	2000
1991	17.8	1996	1999
1990	16.5	1992	1995
1989	18.5	1991	1994

SHIRAZ

Great Southern $$$$

1998	18.8	2006	2010
1997	15.8	1999	2002
1996	16.0	2002	2008
1995	18.2	2003	2007
1994	19.0	2002	2006
1993	18.5		2005+
1991	17.4	1999	2003
1990	18.0	1998	2002
1989	17.0	2001	2009
1988	17.0		2000+
1987	17.0	1999	2007
1986	16.5	1998	2007

Region: Mudgee Winemaker: James Manners
Viticulturist: Stephen Guilbaud-Oulton Chief Executive: Christian Porta

Such has been the success in the marketplace of Montrose's Poet's Corner white and red wines that they now form the backbone of a new Orlando Wyndham range made from Mudgee fruit. Their consistency and value for money remains.

SEMILLON SAUVIGNON BLANC CHARDONNAY

Mudgee $$

1999	15.0	2001	2004
1998	15.0	1999	2000
1997	16.0	1998	1999
1996	16.0	1997	1998

Poet's Corner

Craigmoor Road
Mudgee NSW 2850
Tel: (02) 6372 2208
Fax: (02) 6372 4464

SHIRAZ CABERNET SAUVIGNON CAB. FRANC

Great Southern $$$$

1998	15.1	2000	2003
1997	15.7	1999	2002
1996	16.4	2001	2004
1995	16.0	1997	2000

Region: Lower Hunter Valley Winemaker: Phil Ryan
Viticulturist: Evan Powell Chief Executive: David Clarke

A specialist in clear, bright and uncluttered chardonnay wines with generous, mouthfilling flavours, elegance and focus, Poole's Rock is a highly rated Hunter Valley vineyard owned by Macquarie Bank chairman, David Clarke.

CHARDONNAY

Lower Hunter Valley $$$$

1999	16.8	2001	2004
1998	17.2	2003	2006
1997	17.0	2002	2005
1996	17.8	1998	2001
1995	16.0	1997	2000

Region: Goulburn Valley Winemakers: Don Lewis, Alan George
Viticulturist: John Beresford Chief Executive: Brian Croser

Preece is a mid-priced Mitchelton label which stands for several attractive early-drinking bistro styles of wine. Look out for the occasional surprise under the Cabernet Sauvignon label and some supple and intense varietal Merlot releases of great appeal.

CABERNET SAUVIGNON

Goulburn Valley $$

1998	16.3	2000	2003+
1997	15.2	2002	2005
1996	15.7	1998	2001
1995	16.2	2000	2003
1994	16.7	1999	2002
1993	16.2	1998	2001
1992	17.5	1997	2000
1991	17.2	1996	1999

Goulburn Valley $$

1999	15.3	2000	2001
1998	15.8	1999	2000
1997	16.4	1998	1998
1996	15.0	1997	1998
1995	15.7	1997	2000
1994	16.5	1996	1999
1993	15.9	1995	1998

MERLOT

Goulburn Valley $$

1998	16.9	2000	2003
1997	16.8	2002	2005
1995	17.2	2000	2003
1994	16.5	1999	2002
1993	16.0	1998	2001
1992	17.7	1997	2000

SAUVIGNON BLANC

Goulburn Valley $$

1999	16.8	2000	2001
1997	15.0	1998	1999
1996	15.0	1997	1998
1995	15.4	1995	1996

**Region: Adelaide Winemakers: Joe Grilli, Grant Harrison
Viticulturist: Peter Cox Chief Executive: Joe Grilli**

Joe Grilli is one of Australia's most innovative winemakers whose
Joseph range includes a sumptuously proportioned and long-living
Cabernet Sauvignon Merlot, and an idiosyncratic Sparkling Red
blend of young red wines and older wines bought at auction.

JOSEPH CABERNET SAUVIGNON MERLOT

Adelaide Plains $$$$$

1998	16.7	2006	2010
1997	18.5		2009+
1996	18.2		2008+
1995	16.5	2000	2003
1994	19.2		2006+
1993	18.7		2005+
1992	17.8	2004	2012
1991	19.2		2003+
1990	18.5		2002+
1989	18.5	2001	2009
1988	17.0	1996	2000
1987	16.6	1995	1999

JOSEPH 'LA MAGIA' BOTRYTIS RIESLING

Adelaide Plains $$$

1998	15.7	2003	2006
1996	17.2	2001	2004
1995	18.6	2000	2003
1994	18.3	1999	2002
1993	18.8	2001	2005
1991	18.4	1999	2003
1989	16.5	1994	1998

Region: Geelong Winemaker: Bruce Hyett
Viticulturist: Bruce Hyett Chief Executive: Bruce Hyett

Prince Albert is a small vineyard of mature vines in Victoria's Geelong region planted exclusively to pinot noir, from which Bruce Hyett makes a delicate, willowy and occasionally exotic wine with genuine varietal qualities.

PINOT NOIR

Geelong $$$$

1999	16.9	2007	2011
1998	17.5	2003	2006
1997	18.0	2002	2005
1996	15.0	1998	2001
1995	18.0	2000	2003
1994	17.0	1999	2002
1993	15.8	1995	1998
1992	18.3	1997	2000
1991	15.5	1996	1999
1990	15.5	1992	1995

Region: East Coastal Tasmania Winemaker: Claudio Radenti
Viticulturist: Geoff Bull

Claudio Radenti oversees the making of this creamy, complex and savoury sparkling wine from the Freycinet winery on Tasmania's east coast. It is only introduced to the market with considerable age and the two most recent releases have been excellent.

CHARDONNAY PINOT NOIR

Pyrenees $$$$

1995	18.2	2000	2003
1994	18.6	1999	2002
1993	16.0	1998	2001

Region: Pyrenees Winemaker: Neill Robb
Viticulturist: Neill Robb Chief Executive: Neill Robb

Sally's Paddock is the small dry land in front of Neill and Sally
Robb's winery at Redbank, planted to a largely Bordeaux-based mix
of red varieties which just happens to include shiraz. The firm, wild
and brambly 1998 vintage has received more new oak treatment
than most of its predecessors without sacrificing a minute of the
wine's legendary longevity, and maintains the excellent and
consistent run from this mature vineyard.

SALLY'S PADDOCK

Pyrenees $$$$

1998	18.5		2010+
1997	16.5	2005	2009
1996	18.0	2008	2016
1995	18.8		2007+
1994	18.5		2006+
1993	18.5		2005+
1992	17.9	2000	2004
1991	17.6		2011+
1990	18.0		2020+
1989	16.0	2001	2009
1988	16.6	2000	2008
1987	15.0	1999	2004
1986	18.2		2006+
1985	16.6	1997	2005
1984	15.5	1989	1992
1983	16.0		2003+

Region: Margaret River Winemaker: Andrew Forsell
Viticulturist: Jeffrey Cottle Chief Executive: Bill Ullinger

Redgate is another of Margaret River's group of emerging top-class
wineries which tends to specialise in the Bordeaux varieties, red
and white. Recent vintage have not really reflected
the vineyard's true potential.

CABERNET FRANC

Margaret River $$$$

1998	15.0	2000	2003
1996	16.2	1998	2001
1995	18.2	2000	2003+
1994	14.8	1996	1999

CABERNET SAUVIGNON

Margaret River $$$$

1998	14.5	2000	2003
1996	15.8	2001	2004
1995	18.5	2003	2007
1994	17.8	2002	2006
1993	15.3	1995	1998

SAUVIGNON BLANC RESERVE

Margaret River $$$

1999	15.0		2000
1998	17.2	1999	2000
1997	16.1	1998	1999

Region: Coonawarra Winemakers: Bruce & Malcolm Redman
Viticulturists: Bruce & Malcolm Redman Chief Executives: Bruce & Malcolm Redman

Redman's wines have faded in and out rather more than they might have over recent vintages, with the Redman brothers focusing on restrained, more reserved expressions of Coonawarra red wine.

CABERNET SAUVIGNON

Coonawarra $$$

1998	16.8	2006	2010
1997	16.5	2002	2005
1996	16.7	2004	2008
1994	18.0	2002	2006
1993	18.2	2001	2005
1992	17.8		2004+
1991	15.3		2003+
1990	18.0		2002+
1989	15.0	1997	2001
1988	16.5		2000+
1987	16.5	1999	2004

CABERNET SAUVIGNON MERLOT

Coonawarra $$$

1997	15.7	2002	2005
1996	17.3	2004	2008+
1995	15.9	2000	2003
1994	18.1		2006+
1993	18.2	2001	2005
1992	18.4	2000	2004
1991	17.6	1999	2003
1990	16.0	1995	1998

SHIRAZ ■

Coonawarra $$

1998	15.8	2003	2006
1997	14.8	1998	1999
1996	15.3	1998	2001
1995	15.8	1997	2000
1994	15.4	1996	1999
1993	17.0	2001	2005
1992	17.5	2000	2004
1991	16.5	1993	1996
1990	17.5	1995	1998
1989	15.0	1991	1994
1988	17.0	1993	1996

Region: Margaret River Winemaker: Keith Mugford
Viticulturist: Ian Bell Chief Executives: Keith & Clare Mugford

Recently bought by Moss Wood, Ribbon Vale will be operated by Keith Mugford and his team, but kept entirely separate as a stand-alone brand. Mugford is especially keen to explore the potential latent in the vineyard's dry whites and merlot. He could hardly have had a better start with the 2000 vintage.

CABERNET SAUVIGNON ■

Margaret River $$$

1998	16.0	2000	2003
1997	16.0	2002	2005
1996	14.7	2001	2004
1995	17.0	2003	2007
1994	17.2	2002	2006
1993	17.2	2001	2005
1992	15.8	2000	2004
1991	16.8	1999	2003
1990	18.0	1998	2002

CABERNET MERLOT ■

Margaret River $$$

1997	18.0	2005	2009
1996	17.0	2004	2008+
1995	16.0	2003	2007+
1994	16.3	2002	2006
1993	15.3	1995	1998
1992	16.8	1997	2000
1991	16.5		2003+
1990	18.0	1995	1998
1989	17.0	1994	1997

MERLOT

Margaret River $$$

1998	16.0	2003	2006
1997	14.7	1999	2002
1996	17.0	2004	2008
1995	17.3	2000	2003
1994	14.5	1999	2002
1993	16.8	2001	2005
1992	17.7	2000	2004
1991	18.1	1999	2003
1990	16.5	1995	1998

SAUVIGNON BLANC

Margaret River $$$

1999	17.2	2000	2001
1998	15.3	1999	2000
1997	17.5	1998	1999
1996	17.8	1997	1998
1995	18.4	1996	1997

SEMILLON

Margaret River $$$

1999	17.3	2001	2004
1998	18.0	1999	2000
1997	16.7	1999	2002
1996	18.3	1998	2001
1995	17.3	1997	2000
1994	17.4	1999	2002
1993	18.0	1995	1998
1992	18.3	1997	2000
1991	18.0	1996	1999

SEMILLON SAUVIGNON BLANC

Margaret River $$$

1999	15.3	2000	2001
1998	18.4	2000	2003
1997	15.2		1998
1996	17.9	1998	2001

Richmond Grove

Para Road
Tanunda SA 5352
Tel: (08) 8563 7300
Fax: (08) 8563 2804

Region: Various Winemaker: John Vickery
Viticulturist: Joy Dick Chief Executive: Christian Porta

Richmond Grove is a major national brand owned by Orlando Wyndham. It retains few labels from its Hunter origins, its better wines being sourced and made elsewhere. Take for example the pair of rieslings supervised by John Vickery, one of Australia's foremost riesling specialists, the Coonawarra Cabernet Sauvignon, the Barossa Shiraz and the refreshingly flavoured white wines sourced from the company's massive developments at Cowra. The Watervale Riesling, sometimes found bottled under a Stelvin screw-top seal, is clearly the brand's leading wine.

BAROSSA RIESLING
Barossa Valley $$

1997	16.7	2003	2006
1998	17.6	2006	2010
1997	17.6	2002	2005+
1996	16.9	2001	2004+
1995	16.3	1997	2000+
1994	17.8	2002	2006
1993	16.9	1995	1998

BAROSSA SHIRAZ
Barossa Valley $$

1997	16.3	1999	2002
1996	17.0	1998	2001
1995	16.0	1997	2000
1994	17.6	1999	2002

COONAWARRA CABERNET SAUVIGNON
Coonawarra $$

1997	14.9	1999	2002
1996	16.4	1998	2001
1995	16.0	2000	2003
1994	18.3	2002	2006
1993	16.5	1998	2001
1992	16.8	1997	2000

COWRA CHARDONNAY
Cowra $$

1998	15.8	1999	2000
1997	16.6	1999	2002
1996	16.0	1998	2001
1995	15.0	1996	1997

COWRA VERDELHO

Cowra $$

1998	16.0	1999	2000
1997	15.0	1998	1999
1996	16.8	1998	2001
1995	16.0	2000	2003
1994	17.5	1996	1999
1993	17.1	1995	1998

WATERVALE RIESLING

Clare Valley $$

1999	18.5	2004	2007+
1998	18.4	2006	2010
1997	18.5	2005	2009
1996	16.8	2001	2004
1995	18.1	2003	2007
1994	16.4	1999	2002

**Region: Coonawarra Winemaker: Wayne Stehbens
Viticulturist: Leon Oborne Chief Executive: David Yunghanns**

Owned and made by the Wingara Wine Group at their Katnook Estate winery, Riddoch offers two fine early-drinking red wines including a delicious, ready-to-go 1998 Shiraz. Recent white releases have lacked their customary freshness.

CABERNET SHIRAZ

Coonawarra $$

1998	16.5	2000	2003+
1997	14.8	1998	1999
1996	16.6	1998	2001
1995	15.3	1997	2000
1994	17.0	1996	1999
1993	16.4	1998	2001
1992	17.4	1997	2000
1991	18.3	1996	1999
1990	17.7	1995	1998

SHIRAZ

Coonawarra $$

1998	17.0	2003	2006
1997	15.2	1999	2002
1996	17.0	1998	2001
1995	15.5	1996	1997
1994	17.0	1999	2002
1993	15.0	1995	1998
1992	16.6	1997	2000
1991	18.0	1999	2003
1990	17.5	1995	1998

Region: Coonawarra Winemaker: David O'Leary
Viticulturist: Vic Patrick Chief Executive: Terry Davis

Robertson's Well is a premium Mildara Blass label given to a finely crafted and long-living Coonawarra Cabernet Sauvignon plus a deeply flavoured, spicy Shiraz. Recent vintages haven't quite lived up to the promise of the 1994 wine.

CABERNET SAUVIGNON

Coonawarra $$$

1998	17.5	2006	2010
1996	16.2	2001	2004
1995	16.0	1997	2000
1994	18.3	2002	2006
1993	17.5	2001	2005
1992	17.8	2000	2004

SHIRAZ

Coonawarra $$$

1998	17.5	2003	2006
1997	16.0	1999	2002
1996	16.8	1998	2001

Region: Upper Hunter Valley Winemaker: Philip Shaw
Viticulturist: Richard Hilder Chief Executives: Sandy Oatley, Keith Lambert

Rosemount is an exemplarily operated and managed wine business whose recent growth has been little short of incredible. It is now a strong claimant for the title of Australia's largest family-owned wine business. Not only does it boast some of the most prominent and visible Australian exported wine brands, but its range of wines from its premier collection of labels to the less expensive Diamond range and red and white blends consistently present excellent value and quality when measured against their competitors. Simply put, you just don't often see an ordinary bottle of Rosemount wine.

BALMORAL SYRAH

McLaren Vale $$$$$

1997	17.0	2002	2005
1996	18.4	2004	2008
1995	19.2		2007+
1994	18.7	2002	2006+
1993	16.5	1998	2001
1992	19.0	2000	2004+
1991	18.8		2003+
1990	18.5	2002	2010
1989	18.4	1997	2003+

CABERNET SAUVIGNON

South Australia $$

1999	16.1	2000	2001
1998	16.2	2000	2003
1996	15.3	1998	2001
1995	15.0	1997	2000
1994	16.5	1999	2002
1993	16.6	1998	2001
1992	17.0	1997	2000
1991	16.5	1999	2003

CHARDONNAY

Upper Hunter Valley $$

1999	16.3	2000	2001
1998	17.3	2000	2003
1997	16.2	1999	2002
1996	16.5	1998	2001
1995	15.5	1996	1997
1994	17.0	1996	1999

GIANT'S CREEK CHARDONNAY

Upper Hunter Valley $$$$

1997	17.3	2005	2009+
1996	17.2	2001	2004
1995	16.7	1997	2000
1994	17.3	1999	2002
1993	18.5	1998	2001
1992	15.3	1994	1997
1989	17.0	1997	2001
1988	16.8	1996	2000
1987	17.8	1995	1999

GSM

McLaren Vale $$$

1997	16.6	1999	2002+
1996	17.0	2001	2004
1995	15.9	2003	2007
1994	16.4	1999	2002

MOUNTAIN BLUE

Mudgee $$$$$

1997	18.6	2005	2009
1996	18.8		2008+
1995	18.6		2007+
1994	18.2		2006+

ORANGE VINEYARD CABERNET SAUVIGNON

Orange $$$

1998	18.0	2006	2010
1997	16.7	2005	2009
1996	17.5	2004	2008
1995	16.0	2003	2007

ORANGE VINEYARD CHARDONNAY

Upper Hunter Valley $$$

1998	18.0	2003	2006
1997	18.5	2005	2009
1996	18.0	2001	2004
1995	18.0	2003	2007
1994	18.4	1999	2002

ROXBURGH CHARDONNAY

Upper Hunter Valley $$$$$

1997	18.2	2002	2005
1996	18.5	2001	2004
1995	18.5	2000	2003
1994	17.6	1999	2001
1993	16.6	1998	2001
1992	16.5	1997	2000
1991	18.3		2003+
1990	17.9	1998	2002
1989	18.3	1997	2001

SHIRAZ

McLaren Vale $$

1999	16.2	2000	2001
1998	16.8	2000	2003+
1997	16.3	1999	2002
1995	16.8	1997	2000
1994	15.7	1996	1999
1993	17.0	1998	2001
1992	16.5	1997	2000
1991	16.3	1996	1999

SHOW RESERVE CABERNET SAUVIGNON

Coonawarra $$$$

1997	17.3	2002	2005+
1996	18.7	2004	2008+
1995	16.5	2000	2003
1994	18.8	2006	2014
1993	18.0	2001	2005
1992	18.3		2004+
1991	16.0	2003	2011
1990	18.1	2002	2010
1989	16.3	1994	1997
1988	17.5	1996	2000+
1987	18.0	1999	2004
1986	18.2	1998	2006
1985	18.1	1993	1997+
1982	17.7	1994	2002

SHOW RESERVE CHARDONNAY

Upper Hunter Valley $$$$

1999	18.3	2004	2007
1998	18.2	2006	2010
1997	18.0	2002	2005+
1996	18.8	2004	2008+
1995	18.1	2003	2007
1994	17.1	2002	2006
1993	17.6	1998	2001
1992	17.2	1997	2000
1991	16.1	1999	2003+
1990	18.4	1998	2002

SHOW RESERVE SEMILLON

Upper Hunter Valley $$$$

1996	18.0	2004	2008
1995	18.2	2003	2007
1991	16.8	1996	1999
1990	18.1	1998	2002
1989	18.3	1997	2001+

The former focus of Len Evans' winemaking aspirations is now rather languishing as part of Mildara Blass. Its Hunter Valley Semillon and Brokenback Shiraz (especially from the first-rate 1998 vintage) remain as excellent examples of what the Hunter is all about, but there's now an awful lot of rubbish from various NSW regions now bottled under the Rothbury brand. One hopes that somebody can come up with the right formula to steer what was once known as the Pokolbin Opera House back on track.

BROKENBACK SHIRAZ (FORMERLY RESERVE SHIRAZ)

Lower Hunter Valley $$$

1998	18.1	2006	2010
1996	15.6	1998	2001
1995	14.5	1997	2000
1994	18.0		2006+
1993	18.7		2008+
1991	18.3		2003+
1989	18.4	2001	2009

COWRA CHARDONNAY

Cowra $$

1999	15.6		2000
1998	15.0		1999
1997	17.0	1999	2002
1996	16.6	1998	2001
1995	17.0	2000	2003
1994	15.0	1995	1996
1993	17.0	1998	2001

HUNTER VALLEY CHARDONNAY (FORMERLY BARREL FERMENT CHARDONNAY)

Lower Hunter Valley $$

1999	15.6	2000	2001
1997	16.6	1998	1999
1996	17.5	2001	2004
1994	18.4	1996	1999
1993	16.3	1995	1998
1992	17.2	1997	2000
1991	17.0	1996	1999
1990	17.0	1992	1995

HUNTER VALLEY SEMILLON

Lower Hunter Valley $$

1998	15.1	2000	2003
1997	17.5	2004	2009
1996	18.2	2004	2008
1995	17.7	2000	2003
1994	16.9	1999	2002
1993	18.0		2005+
1992	15.0	1994	1997
1991	18.1	1999	2003
1990	16.0		2002+
1989	18.1	2001	2009
1988	15.0	1990	1995
1987	16.0	1995	1999
1986	18.6	1994	1998

MUDGEE CABERNET MERLOT

Mudgee $$

1998	14.5	1998	1999
1997	14.5	1998	1999
1996	15.0	1998	2001
1995	15.3	2000	2003

Region: Coonawarra Winemaker: Paul Gordon
Viticulturist: Max Arney Chief Executive: Tom Park

Made alongside the Lindemans individual vineyard wines, Rouge Homme's reds and whites have been deliberately made in earlier-drinking styles, offering uncomplicated, easy-drinking marriages of fruit and oak, if deployed. The excellent 1996 Cabernet Sauvignon showed what these vineyards could really be capable of, so it's sometimes hard not to wonder if more couldn't be done with the fruit the brand has access to.

CABERNET SAUVIGNON

Coonawarra $$$

1998	16.8	2006	2010+
1997	16.8	1999	2002+
1996	18.2		2008+
1995	17.0	2000	2003
1994	16.1	1999	2002
1993	14.5	2001	2005
1992	17.7	2000	2004
1991	16.8	1999	2003
1990	16.8	1995	1998
1989	16.0	1994	1997
1988	17.0	1996	2000

PINOT NOIR

Coonawarra $$

1998	14.8	1999	2000
1997	16.0	1999	2002
1996	14.0	1997	1998
1995	15.7	1997	2000
1994	16.0	1996	1999

SHIRAZ CABERNET

Coonawarra $$

1998	16.0	2000	2003
1997	16.9	2002	2005
1996	17.0	1998	2001
1995	14.8	1997	2000

Region: Coonawarra Winemaker: Philip Laffer
Viticulturist: Joy Dick Chief Executive: Christian Porta

Russet Ridge is another Coonawarra-based brand, this time owned and operated by Orlando Wyndham. The cabernet blend is generally lighter and earlier to mature than the St Hugo Cabernet Sauvignon, while the Chardonnay is an attractive peachy early-drinking style.

CABERNET SHIRAZ MERLOT

Coonawarra $$

1996	17.8	2001	2004+
1995	15.6	2000	2003
1994	17.8	1999	2002
1993	17.2	2001	2005
1992	16.8	2000	2004
1991	17.6	1996	1999

CHARDONNAY

Coonawarra $$$

1998	16.5	2000	2003
1997	16.1	1998	1999
1996	15.6	1997	1998

Region: Coonawarra Winemaker: John Innes
Viticulturist: Grant Oschar Chief Executive: John Innes

Rymill

The Riddoch Run
Coonawarra SA 5
Tel: (08) 8736 5
Fax: (08) 8736 5

Rymill is a rapidly expanding Coonawarra wine company initially based around the extensive vineyard holdings of its founder, Peter Rymill. While Rymill does release some charming and easy-drinking red wines and some punchy, vibrant Sauvignon Blancs, it hasn't yet fulfilled its unquestioned potential.

CABERNET SAUVIGNON

Coonawarra $$$$

1997	16.8	2005	2009
1996	16.0	2001	2004
1995	16.2	2000	2003
1994	16.4	2002	2006

JUNE TRAMINER

Coonawarra $$$$

1998	16.2	2000	2003
1997	16.7	1999	2002+
1996	15.0	1998	2001

MERLOT CABERNETS

Coonawarra $$$

1997	17.4	1999	2002
1996	16.8	1998	2001
1995	16.6	1997	2000
1994	16.0	1996	1999

SAUVIGNON BLANC

Coonawarra $$

1999	15.6		2000
1998	15.7		1999
1997	16.8	1998	1999
1996	15.4	1997	1998
1992	17.5	1994	1997+

SHIRAZ

Coonawarra $$$

1997	17.4	2002	2005
1996	15.8	2001	2004
1995	16.5	2000	2003
1994	15.0	1999	2002+

tram

ston Road
ston SA 5353
(08) 8564 3355
(08) 8564 2209

Region: Barossa Valley Winemaker: Nigel Dolan
Viticulturist: Murray Heidenreich Chief Executive: Terry Davis

It's really only for the No. 1 reds of Cabernet Sauvignon and Shiraz that Saltram remains of interest to the drinker of serious wine. The Classic label of cheaper varietal wines has lost its early gloss and now hosts a set of uninteresting, if sound and drinkable beverage wines, but Nigel Dolan deserves every encouragement to keep up his excellent work with these very ripe, concentrated and assertively oaked modern Barossa classics.

NO. 1 SHIRAZ

Barossa Valley $$$$

1997	17.8	2005	2009
1996	18.4	2002	2006
1995	17.2	2000	2003
1994	18.2	2002	2006

ndalford

West Swan Road
sham WA 6055
(08) 9274 5922
(08) 9274 2154

Region: Various, WA Winemaker: Bill Crappsley
Viticulturist: Ian Davies Chief Executive: Peter Prendiville

Sandalford is a medium-sized independent Western Australian wine company of some standing with access to a wide range of vineyard resources from most WA regions. It has chosen to pursue the varietal option in creating its premium wines, blending together various parcels of fruit from these regions as seasonal changes dictate.

CABERNET MERLOT

Mount Barker, Margaret River $$$$

1998	16.6	2000	2003+
1997	16.6	2005	2009
1996	18.2	2004	2008
1995	17.8	2000	2003
1994	17.7	2002	2006
1993	14.8	1998	2001
1992	16.0	1994	1997
1991	16.2	1999	2003
1990	17.0		2002+
1989	15.5	2001	2009

CHARDONNAY

Margaret River, Mount Barker, Pemberton blend $$$

1997	16.6	1999	2002+
1996	16.9	1998	2001
1995	18.3	2000	2003
1994	17.2	1999	2002
1993	18.5	1998	2001
1992	15.4	1993	1994

SHIRAZ

Margaret River, Mount Barker $$$$

1997	15.0	1999	2002+
1996	16.3	2001	2004
1995	16.7	2003	2007
1994	17.3	2002	2006
1993	16.8	1998	2001
1992	14.5	1994	1997
1991	14.7	1996	1999

VERDELHO

Margaret River $$$

1998	16.4	2003	2006
1997	15.2	1998	1999
1996	17.4	1998	2001
1995	15.7	1997	2000
1994	16.2	1999	2002
1993	18.0	2001	2005
1992	16.0	1997	2000
1991	16.5	1996	1999
1990	17.7	1998	2002

Region: Margaret River Winemakers: Mike & Jan Davies
Chief Executive: Mike Davies

Sandstone's Semillon is one of the finest of the wood-matured Margaret River styles, with distinctive richness derived from fruit quality, oak and yeast lees contact after fermentation. The 1998 Cabernet Sauvignon might herald a move towards a tighter and finer-grained style based around sweeter, fresher fruit qualities. It's considerably more supple and elegant than previous releases.

CABERNET SAUVIGNON

Margaret River $$$$

1998	17.7	2006	2010
1996	16.9	2004	2008
1995	16.0	2003	2007
1993	16.4	2001	2005
1992	17.9		2004+
1991	17.0		2003+
1990	16.8	1998	2002
1989	17.5	1997	2001
1988	16.3	1993	1996

SEMILLON

Margaret River $$$$

1999	17.3	2004	2007
1998	18.3	2003	2006
1997	18.5	2002	2005
1995	18.5	2003	2007
1994	18.0	1999	2002
1993	18.2	2001	2005
1992	18.2	1994	1997

Region: McLaren Vale   Winemakers: Michael & Filippo Scarpantoni
Viticulturist: Filippo Scarpantoni Chief Executive: Domenico Scarpantoni

There's been a change in the approach at Scarpantoni towards the
making of very assertively oaked red wines which tend to stifle
their rich and concentrated fruit, even from the
excellent 1998 season.

BLOCK 3 SHIRAZ

McLaren Vale $$$

1998	14.5	2000	2003
1997	16.2	2002	2005
1996	17.0	2001	2004
1995	16.3	1997	2000
1994	16.5	1999	2002
1993	16.3	1998	2001
1992	16.5	1997	2000

CABERNET SAUVIGNON

McLaren Vale $$$

1998	15.3	2003	2006
1997	16.6	2002	2005
1996	15.4	1998	2001
1995	15.3	1997	2000
1994	18.3	2002	2006
1993	16.5	1998	2001
1992	16.9	2000	2004
1991	17.2		2003+

Region: Geelong Winemakers: Robin Brockett, Matthew Browne
Viticulturist: Robin Brockett Chief Executive: Matthew Browne

Scotchmans Hill is a booming small winery on Victoria's Bellarine Peninsula whose wines have a devoted market and are found on dozens of cafe wine lists, where their early-maturing and very approachable qualities are best appreciated. Scotchmans Hill is also associated with the spectacularly restored Spray Farm property and vineyard on the Bellarine Peninsula.

Scotchmans Hill

Scotchmans Road
Drysdale Vic 3222
Tel: (03) 5251 3176
Fax: (03) 5253 1743

CABERNET SAUVIGNON MERLOT

Geelong $$$$

1998	16.6	2003	2006
1996	14.7	1998	2001
1995	15.8	2000	2003
1994	14.4	1996	1999
1993	18.1	2001	2005
1992	15.2	1994	1997

CHARDONNAY

Geelong $$$$

1999	16.0	1999	2000
1998	16.4	1999	2000
1997	17.6	1998	2002
1996	15.6	1997	1998
1995	16.5	1996	1997
1994	16.0	1996	1999
1993	18.3	1998	2001
1992	15.9	1994	1997
1991	17.0	1993	1996
1990	16.0	1995	1998

PINOT NOIR

Geelong $$$$

1999	16.0	2000	2001+
1998	15.8	1999	2000
1997	17.6	1999	2002
1996	15.0	1998	2001
1995	17.5	1996	1997
1994	16.0	1995	1996

Seaview

**Chaffeys Road
McLaren Vale SA 5171
Tel: (08) 8323 8250
Fax: (08) 8323 9308**

SAUVIGNON BLANC

Geelong $$$

1999	15.6		2000
1998	15.2		1998
1997	16.6	1998	1999
1996	16.8	1997	1998
1995	15.5	1996	1997

Region: McLaren Vale Winemaker: Fiona Donald
Viticulturist: Brian Hill Chief Executive: Tom Park

Seaview certainly isn't what it used to be. This historic label has been split apart, with most of its wines now corralled into the new Edwards & Chaffey brand. The 'reserve' wines which used to carry the 'Edwards & Chaffey' tag now sport another – 'section 353', whatever that's supposed to mean. Meantime, the Seaview sparkling wines more or less continue their fine form of the last decade, with the possible exception of a slightly disappointing 1997 Pinot Noir Chardonnay.

CHARDONNAY VINTAGE RESERVE

South Australia $$$

1995	17.8	2000	2003
1994	18.1	1999	2002
1993	18.1	1995	1998
1992	18.3	1997	2000
1991	16.0	1995	1998
1990	18.6	1995	1998
1988	16.8	1990	1993

PINOT NOIR CHARDONNAY

South Australia $$$

1997	16.0	1999	2002
1995	17.5	2000	2003
1994	18.1	1999	2002
1993	17.6	1995	1998
1992	18.2	1997	2000
1991	17.0	1993	1996
1990	18.6	1995	1998
1989	18.0	1991	1994

Regions: Great Western, Barooga, Barossa
Winemakers: Ian McKenzie, James Godfrey, Andrew Fleming
Viticulturist: Trudy Traveena Chief Executive: Tom Park

A glance at the scores allocated to the current and forthcoming
Seppelt releases is testimony to the fine work of Ian McKenzie and
Andrew Fleming. There's no doubt in my mind that the present
Seppelt collection is the best I have seen in fifteen years of wine
writing, the jewels in the crown being the Great Western Shiraz,
the Dorrien Cabernet Sauvignon, the Salinger and the very
reasonably priced Chalambar Shiraz.

CHALAMBAR SHIRAZ

Great Western $$

1998	18.1	2006	2010+
1997	16.8	2002	2005+
1996	15.2	1998	2001
1995	17.5	2003	2007
1994	16.5	1999	2002
1993	15.4	1995	1998
1992	17.2	1997	2000
1991	17.0	1999	2003
1990	17.8	1998	2002
1989	17.0	1998	2001

CORELLA RIDGE CHARDONNAY

Victoria $$

1998	16.3	2000	2003
1997	16.6	1999	2002
1996	16.4	1998	2001
1995	16.0	1996	1997

DORRIEN CABERNET SAUVIGNON

Barossa Valley $$$$

1996	18.8	2008	2016
1994	18.7	2006	2014
1993	17.0	2001	2005
1992	17.8	2000	2004
1991	18.6		2003+
1990	18.0	2002	2010
1989	17.9	1997	2001
1988	15.3	1993	1996
1987	17.4	1995	1999
1986	17.5	1998	2003
1984	18.3	1996	2001
1982	18.0	1990	1994

DRUMBORG CABERNET SAUVIGNON

Western Districts $$$$

1996	16.7	2001	2004+
1994	14.6	1999	2002
1993	17.1	2001	2005
1991	17.2	1999	2003
1989	18.2	2001	2009
1985	18.5	1997	2002
1982	18.0	1990	1994

GREAT WESTERN SHIRAZ

Great Western $$$$

1996	18.6		2008+
1995	18.0		2007+
1993	17.6	1998	2001
1992	18.0	2000	2004
1991	18.4		2003+
1988	16.5	1993	1996
1987	14.5	1992	1995
1986	17.0	1998	2003
1985	16.5	1997	2002

HARPERS RANGE CABERNET BLEND

Victoria $$$

1998	17.1	2006	2010
1997	17.4	2002	2005+
1996	16.3	2001	2004
1995	16.9	2003	2007
1994	16.4	1999	2002
1993	15.0	1995	1998
1992	17.0	1997	2000
1991	18.2	1996	1999
1990	16.5	1995	1998

ORIGINAL SPARKLING SHIRAZ (FORMERLY HARPERS RANGE SPARKLING BURGUNDY

Victoria $$$

1995	18.3	2003	2007
1994	18.0	2002	2006+
1993	17.8	2001	2005
1992	16.0	1997	2000
1991	18.0		2003+
1990	17.6	1998	2002
1989	15.5	1997	2001
1988	16.5	1996	2000
1987	16.5	1995	1999

SALINGER

Southern Australia $$$$

1993	18.7	1998	2001
1992	18.7	1997	2000
1991	18.3	1996	1999
1990	18.6	1995	1998
1989	17.0	1991	1994

SHOW SPARKLING SHIRAZ

Great Western $$$$$

1987	17.0	1995	1999+
1986	18.7	1998	2006
1985	17.0	1993	1997
1984	18.3	1999	2001
1983	17.6	1995	2000
1982	18.3	1990	1994
1972	18.2	1992	1997

SUNDAY CREEK PINOT NOIR

Victoria $$$

1998	16.8	2000	2003
1997	17.5	1999	2002
1996	17.7	1998	2001

TERRAIN CABERNET SAUVIGNON

Southern Australia $

1998	15.9	2000	2003
1997	15.8	2002	2005
1996	15.2	1998	2001
1995	15.4	1997	2000
1994	15.0	1996	1999
1993	17.7	1998	2001

Sevenhill

**College Road
Sevenhill via
Clare SA 5453**
Tel: (08) 8843 4222
Fax: (08) 8843 4382

Region: Clare Valley Winemakers: Brother John May & John Monten
Viticulturist: Brother John May Chief Executive: Brother John May

Sevenhill has made Riesling from its Clare Valley vineyards for several decades, but the wines from recent years have shown new refinement and poise. Sevenhill's red wines have also developed nicely in recent years and while they didn't suffer too much of a dip with the 1997 vintage, the 1998s are as ripe, generous and open as ever before.

CABERNET SAUVIGNON

Clare Valley $$$

1998	15.8	2003	2006
1997	15.8	2002	2005+
1996	16.6	2004	2008
1995	15.3	1997	2000
1994	17.0		2006+
1993	17.3		2005+
1992	17.2	2000	2004
1991	16.3	1999	2003
1990	16.0	1998	2002

RIESLING

Clare Valley $$

1999	16.6	2004	2007
1998	17.5	2003	2006
1997	18.1	2002	2005
1996	18.2	2004	2008
1995	18.3	2000	2003
1994	18.2	2002	2006
1993	16.8	1998	2001
1992	18.5	1997	2000
1991	17.0	1993	1996
1990	15.0	1995	1998

SEMILLON

Clare Valley $$

1999	17.0	2005	2007+
1998	16.8	2003	2006
1996	16.0	1998	2001
1995	15.0	1997	2000
1994	16.0	1999	2002
1993	17.2	1998	2001

SHIRAZ

Clare Valley $$$

1998	17.0	2003	2006
1997	16.7	2002	2005+
1996	17.6	2001	2004
1995	17.4	2003	2007
1994	17.5	2002	2006
1993	18.2		2005+
1992	17.3	2000	2004
1991	18.0		2003+
1990	15.8	1995	1998

SHIRAZ TOURIGA GRENACHE

Clare Valley $$

1998	16.0	2003	2006
1997	15.7	2002	2005
1996	16.6	2001	2004
1995	16.5	2002	2006
1994	16.8	2002	2006
1993	17.2		2005+
1992	17.2	2000	2004
1991	19.0	1996	1999
1990	16.0	1995	1998

ST. ALOYSIUS

Clare Valley $$

1999	15.3	2000	2001
1998	15.2	1999	2000
1997	16.0	1998	1999
1996	15.2	1997	1998
1995	16.6	1997	2000
1994	16.7	1996	1999
1993	16.8	1995	1998
1992	16.2	1997	2000
1991	18.0	1996	1999

ST. IGNATIUS

Clare Valley $$

1998	16.8	2006	2010
1997	15.6	2002	2005
1996	15.8	1998	2001
1995	16.2	1997	2000
1994	17.3	1999	2002
1993	17.8		2005+

Seville Estate was one of the first wineries of the modern Yarra Valley revival which began in the early 1970s. Established by Dr Peter McMahon, after whose profession the company's 'GP' series of multi-regional Victorian wines is named, it was purchased by the Hunter Valley's Brokenwood winery. Since that time Seville Estate's Shiraz has moved towards a deliciously dark, savoury and spicy red of medium weight and structure but intense flavours. An especially cool site, it will always deliver more vintage variation than most Yarra vineyards.

CABERNET SAUVIGNON

Yarra Valley $$$$

1997	16.8	2005	2009
1995	15.8	2000	2003+
1994	16.7	2002	2006
1992	18.3	2004	2012
1991	18.0	1999	2003
1990	17.5	1994	1998
1989	16.0	1993	1997
1988	18.0	1992	1996
1987	15.0	1991	1995
1986	17.0	1990	1994

CHARDONNAY

Yarra Valley $$$

1998	16.8	2003	2006
1997	18.3	2002	2005+
1996	17.5	2001	2004
1995	17.8	2000	2003
1994	18.3	2002	2006
1993	17.7	1998	2001
1992	17.6	2000	2004
1991	18.2	1996	1999
1990	17.5	1995	1998
1989	16.0	1991	1994

PINOT NOIR

Yarra Valley $$$$

1998	16.0	2000	2003+
1995	16.3	2000	2003
1993	18.1	1998	2001
1992	16.5	2000	2004
1991	18.2	1996	1999

SHIRAZ

Yarra Valley $$$$

Year	Score	Drink from	Drink to
1997	16.5	2002	2005+
1996	18.0	2004	2008
1995	18.2	2003	2007
1994	16.7	1996	1999
1993	18.6	2001	2005
1992	18.4	1997	2000
1991	18.3	1996	1999
1990	18.0	1995	1998
1989	15.0	1991	1994
1988	17.5	1996	2000
1986	17.6	1994	1998

Region: Yarra Valley Winemakers: Shan & Turid Shanmugam
Viticulturists: Shan & Turid Shanmugam Chief Executive: Turid Shanmugam

It's typically one of the Yarra Valley's finer Chardonnays, but Shantell's is made without a malolactic fermentation, giving it a distinctive minerally texture, while the Cabernet Sauvignon harks back to an older style, with eucalypt/mint flavours and a long, linear tannic backbone. Shantell's Pinot Noir frequently tastes highly spiced, with fruit flavours of cherries and cooked plums.

CABERNET SAUVIGNON

Yarra Valley $$$$

Year	Score	Drink from	Drink to
1997	16.3	2002	2005
1996	15.4	2001	2004
1995	15.3	2000	2003
1994	17.4	2002	2006
1993	16.4	1998	2001
1992	18.6		2004+
1991	18.0	1999	2003
1990	18.0	1998	2002
1989	16.5	1991	1994
1988	18.1	1993	1996

CHARDONNAY

Yarra Valley $$$

Year	Score	Drink from	Drink to
1999	15.9	2000	2001
1997	16.3	2002	2005
1996	16.7	1998	2001
1995	18.2	2000	2003
1994	18.4	1999	2002
1993	18.4	1998	2001
1992	18.2	1997	2000
1991	17.8	1996	1999
1990	18.7	1995	1998

PINOT NOIR

Yarra Valley $$$$

1998	16.8	2000	2003+
1997	16.2	2002	2005
1996	16.4	2001	2004
1995	16.0	2000	2003
1994	15.0	1996	1999
1993	17.6	1998	2001
1992	16.0	1994	1997
1991	17.3	1996	1999
1990	17.4	1995	1998

**Region: Adelaide Hills Winemakers: Martin Shaw, Willy Lunn
Viticulturist: Martin Shaw Chief Executives: Martin Shaw, Michael Hill Smith**

The 2000 vintage marked the first in its new winery at Balhannah
in the Adelaide Hills for white wine specialist, Shaw and Smith, a
company that combines the winemaking and marketing talents of
two cousins, Martin Shaw and Michael Hill Smith. Its leading wine
is the Reserve Chardonnay, a superbly complex and elegant wine
of genuine finesse, while the Sauvignon Blanc is a benchmark in
the less overtly grassy style. The cousins have also dipped into the
red wine game with a fine-grained 'Incognito' Merlot.

RESERVE CHARDONNAY

Adelaide Hills $$$$

1998	18.3	2003	2006
1997	18.4	2002	2005+
1996	17.5	2001	2004
1995	18.6	2000	2003
1994	17.0	1999	2002
1993	19.0	2001	2005
1992	18.9	2000	2004
1991	17.0	1993	1996

SAUVIGNON BLANC

Adelaide Hills $$$

1999	16.6	2000	2001
1998	17.5	1998	1999
1997	17.2	1998	1999
1996	18.1	1998	2001
1995	18.2	1997	2000
1994	18.5	1995	1996

UNOAKED CHARDONNAY

Adelaide Hills $$$

1999	15.0		2000
1998	17.0	1999	2000
1997	17.5	1998	1999
1996	17.3	1997	1998
1995	16.5	1996	1997

Region: McLaren Vale Winemaker: Nick Holmes
Viticulturist: Nick Holmes Chief Executive: Nick Holmes

Shottesbrooke

Bagshaws Road
McLaren Flat SA 5171
Tel: (08) 8383 0002
Fax: (08) 8383 0222

Maker of some of the McLaren Vale's most elegant and refined red wines, Nick Holmes has shown a deft touch with his very stylish 1998 Cabernet Sauvignon Merlot Malbec and recent vintages of Merlot and Sauvignon Blanc, although the 1999 Sauvignon Blanc appears to be sweeter than usual.

CABERNET SAUVIGNON MERLOT MALBEC

McLaren Vale $$$

1998	18.3	2006	2010
1997	16.7	2005	2009
1996	15.8	2001	2004
1995	18.1	2003	2007
1994	17.8	2002	2006
1993	16.0	1998	2001
1992	18.1	2000	2004
1991	18.5	1999	2003
1990	17.4	1998	2002
1989	17.2	1997	2001
1988	18.0	1993	1996
1987	14.5	1989	1992
1986	18.0	1994	1998

CHARDONNAY

McLaren Vale $$

1999	16.6	2001	2004
1998	16.8	2000	2003+
1997	16.0	1999	2002
1996	17.0	2001	2004
1995	15.0	1997	2000
1994	18.2	1999	2002
1993	18.5	2001	2005
1992	16.0	1997	2000

Skillogalee

**Trevarrick Road
Sevenhill via
Clare SA 5453
Tel: (08) 8843 4311
Fax: (08) 8843 4343**

MERLOT

McLaren Vale $$$

1999	16.8	2004	2007
1998	17.0	2003	2006
1997	17.9	2002	2005
1996	17.0	2001	2004
1995	17.2	2000	2003
1994	17.2	1999	2002
1993	18.0	2001	2005
1992	18.0	1997	2000
1991	17.0	1993	1996

SAUVIGNON BLANC

Fleurieu $$

1999	15.7	2000	2001
1998	17.8	1999	2000
1997	17.3	1998	1999
1996	16.7	1998	2001
1995	16.7	1997	2000
1994	18.5	1996	1999
1993	18.3	1994	1995

**Region: Clare Valley Winemaker: David Palmer
Viticulturist: David Chandler Chief Executive: David Palmer**

A most reliable small specialist maker of Clare Valley riesling and
dry red, Skillogalee's wines are usually elegant, crystal-clear in
their fruit expression and ideally suited to medium-term cellaring.
Its reds often reveal regional minty and eucalyptus flavours.

RIESLING

Clare Valley $$

1999	17.2	2004	2007
1998	17.0	2003	2006
1997	17.8	2005	2009
1996	17.5	2001	2004
1995	18.0	2003	2007
1994	18.5		2006+
1993	17.3	2001	2005
1992	18.0	1997	2000
1991	17.0	1996	1999
1990	18.5	1998	2002
1989	16.5	1991	1994

SHIRAZ

Clare Valley $$$

1998	15.4	2000	2003+
1997	17.9	2002	2005+
1996	16.4	1998	2001
1995	17.0	2000	2003
1994	17.6	1999	2002
1993	17.4	2001	2005
1992	17.5	2000	2004
1991	17.3	1996	1999
1990	18.0	1995	1998

THE CABERNETS

Clare Valley $$$

1998	16.4	2003	2006
1997	17.5	2002	2005+
1996	17.8	2004	2008
1995	16.0	2000	2003
1994	17.5	2002	2006
1993	16.4	2001	2005
1992	16.8	2000	2004
1991	17.0	1996	1999
1990	17.0	1998	2002

Region: East Coast Winemaker: Andrew Hood
Viticulturist: Rodney Lyne Chief Executive: Rodney Lyne

Spring Vale has its settings all worked out. Its tiny vineyard is situated near Freycinet on Tasmania's warm east coast, where fruit usually ripens more regularly than in much of Tasmania. Its wine is being made by consultant Andrew Hood, whose pinot noirs for Winstead and Wellington are already raising the levels of expectation in Tasmania. Furthermore, it has a great label. There's a little botrytis in the early-drinking and citrusy 1999 Chardonnay, while I thoroughly enjoy the juicy Pinot Gris from the same vintage.

CHARDONNAY

East Coast $$$

1999	16.8	2001	2004
1998	16.6	2000	2003
1997	18.0	2002	2005
1994	16.4	1996	1999
1993	16.4	1995	1996

PINOT NOIR

East Coast $$$$

1998	17.5	2003	2006
1997	17.8	2002	2005
1996	14.5	1998	2001
1995	15.0	1997	2000
1994	16.5	1996	1999
1993	16.8	1998	2001
1992	16.8	1997	2000
1991	16.5	1996	1999
1990	16.0	1992	1995

**Region: Barossa Valley Winemakers: Stuart Blackwell, Cathy Spratt
Viticulturist: Carl Lindner Chief Executive: Bob McLean**

In a move that will certainly strengthen both companies, St Hallett has announced its intentions to join forces with the energetic McLaren Vale-based winery of Tatachilla. Its present releases are pleasingly predictable, as the winemaking team has captured the ripeness and intensity of the fine 1998 Barossa vintage. I have an especially soft spot for the early-drinking and inexpensive Faith Shiraz from the same vintage and swear never to drink another bottle of Beaujolais while it is available.

BLACKWELL SHIRAZ

Barossa Valley $$$$

1998	17.7	2003	2006
1996	17.5	2004	2008
1995	16.0	2000	2003
1994	17.9	1999	2002+

CABERNET SAUVIGNON

Barossa Valley $$$

1998	16.8	2006	2010
1996	16.1	2001	2004
1995	16.0	1997	2000
1994	16.8	1996	1999
1993	17.0	1998	2001
1992	17.5	2000	2004
1991	16.4	1999	2003
1990	17.3	1995	1998

CHARDONNAY

Barossa Valley $$$

1999	16.8	2000	2001
1998	15.8	1999	2000
1997	15.6	1999	2002
1996	15.3	1997	1998
1995	16.1	1997	2000
1994	17.1	1996	1999
1993	16.5	1995	1998

EDEN VALLEY RIESLING

Eden Valley $$$

1999	17.0	2004	2007
1998	17.2	2003	2006+
1997	18.2	2002	2005+
1996	16.6	2001	2004

FAITH SHIRAZ

Barossa Valley $$$

1998	17.1	2003	2006
1997	16.5	1998	1999
1996	15.8	1998	2001
1995	16.6	2000	2003
1994	16.9	1996	1999+

OLD BLOCK SHIRAZ

Barossa Valley $$$$

1997	17.0	2002	2005
1996	16.8	2001	2004
1995	16.8	2000	2003+
1994	18.5	2002	2006
1993	17.6	1998	2001
1992	17.8	1997	2000
1991	18.6	2003	2011
1990	18.7	2002	2010
1989	17.6	1997	2001
1988	18.6	2000	2008
1987	17.0	1995	1999
1986	18.5	1998	2003
1985	17.5	1993	1997

SEMILLON SELECT

Barossa Valley $$$

1999	16.6	2001	2004
1998	15.4	1999	2000
1997	17.1	1999	2002
1996	16.5	1998	2001
1995	15.1	1996	1997

St Huberts

St Huberts Road
Coldstream Vic 3770
Tel: (03) 9739 1118
Fax: (03) 9739 1096

Region: Yarra Valley Winemaker: Fi Purnell
Viticulturist: Damien de Castella Chief Executive: Terry Davis

Since the early 1970s, when the Cester family adopted the name of one of Victoria's largest vineyards of last century for their Yarra Valley venture (the present vineyard is not planted on the previous St Huberts vineyard site), the property has had one of the most chequered careers imaginable, despite making the occasional head-turning wine in the process. Mildara Blass is delivering on its promises to restore St Huberts to the Yarra's elite, making its wines in a firmer and longer-living style than its near neighbour and stablemate of Yarra Ridge.

CABERNET SAUVIGNON

Yarra Valley $$$

1998	18.2	2006	2010
1997	17.9	2005	2009+
1996	16.0	1998	2001
1995	17.9	2000	2003
1994	18.3	2002	2006
1993	17.0	1998	2003
1992	18.2	2000	2004
1991	18.2	1999	2003
1990	16.8	1998	2002

CHARDONNAY

Yarra Valley $$$

1999	17.8	2004	2007
1997	15.3	1999	2002
1996	16.0	1998	2001
1995	17.5	2000	2003
1994	17.8	1999	2002
1993	17.4	1998	2001
1992	18.6	1997	2000+
1991	17.5	1996	1999

PINOT NOIR

Yarra Valley $$$

1999	16.9	2001	2004
1998	16.0	2000	2003
1997	16.0	2002	2005
1996	16.3	1998	2001
1995	16.8	2000	2003
1994	14.5	1995	1996
1993	18.1	1998	2001

Region: NE Victoria Winemaker: Peter Brown
Viticulturist: Peter Brown Chief Executive: Peter Brown

Peter Brown, one of Milawa's Brown Brothers, who purchased St Leonards from the family business, together with the historic and adjacent All Saints property, has stated his intentions to restore the once-popular St Leonards range of early-drinking fleshy white wines and sumptuous reds. The 1998 Shiraz appears to be an exaggerated version of its extremely oaky All Saints stablemates.

SHIRAZ

NE Victoria $$$$

1998	15.1	2000	2003
1997	17.5	2005	2009
1996	16.7	1998	2001
1995	15.7	2000	2003
1994	17.4	2004	2008

Region: NE Victoria Winemaker: Chris Killeen
Viticulturist: Lynton Enever Chief Executive: Norm Killeen

It's a pleasure to introduce the premium and very affordable Jack's Block Shiraz, which Chris Killeen only makes in exceptional vintages. My view is that they're virtually everything that a traditional Rutherglen red ought to be.

CABERNET SAUVIGNON

NE Victoria $$$

1996	16.0	2000	2003
1995	16.5	2000	2003
1992	17.8		2004+
1991	17.5	1999	2003
1990	16.4		2002+
1988	15.0	1996	2000
1987	17.0	1995	1999
1986	17.1	1994	1998
1985	16.1	1993	1997

CABERNET SHIRAZ BLEND

NE Victoria $$$

1998	16.6	2006	2010
1997	17.0	2005	2009+
1996	17.0	2004	2008+
1995	16.6		2007+
1994	16.5		2006+
1992	17.6		2004+

St Leonards

Wahgunyah Vic 3687
Tel: (02) 6033 1004
Fax: (02) 6033 3636

Stanton & Killeen

Murray Valley Highway
Rutherglen Vic 3685
Tel: (02) 6032 9457
Fax: (02) 6032 8018

DURIF

NE Victoria $$$

1998	16.0		2010+
1997	16.7		2009+
1996	17.0		2007+
1995	17.1		2007+
1994	16.4		2006+
1992	17.8		2004+
1991	15.8	1999	2003
1990	18.0		2002+
1988	18.0		2000+
1987	16.5	1999	2004
1986	17.0	1998	2003

JACK'S BLOCK SHIRAZ

NE Victoria $$$$

1998	18.3	2006	2010+
1997	18.1		2009+
1993	16.6	2001	2005+

SHIRAZ

NE Victoria $$$

1996	17.2	2004	2008
1995	16.8		2005+
1993	17.5		2005+
1992	18.3		2004+
1991	16.6	1999	2003
1990	17.8		2002+
1988	15.5	1996	2000
1987	17.5	1995	1999
1985	16.5	1993	1997

VINTAGE PORT

NE Victoria $$$

1995	18.8		2015+
1994	18.0	2006	2014
1993	18.4		2005+
1992	18.6		2004+
1991	18.5		2003+
1990	18.2	1998	2002
1989	17.2	1997	2001
1988	18.5	2000	2005
1987	16.5	1999	2004
1986	18.6		2006+
1985	17.0	1997	2002
1984	16.0	1996	2001

Today a part of Petaluma Ltd, Stonier's wines are amongst the finest and most consistent from Victoria's Mornington Peninsula region. It's my view that any Peninsula vineyard site able to adequately ripen cabernet sauvignon would be little short of princely for pinot noir, so it's no big deal to figure what I would do to Stonier's cabernet wines. Graft them over to make more of the excellent Reserve Pinot Noir and Chardonnay, that's what!

Stonier

362 Frankston-Flinders Rd
Merricks Vic 3916
Tel: (03) 5989 8300
Fax: (03) 5989 8709
Website:
www.stoniers.com.au
E-mail:
stoniers@stoniers.com.au

CABERNET

Mornington Peninsula $$$

1998	15.1	2000	2003
1997	15.0	1999	2002+
1995	14.5	1997	2000
1994	15.0	1998	2001
1993	16.7	1998	2001
1992	16.5	2000	2004
1991	17.0	1999	2003
1990	16.5	1992	1995

CHARDONNAY

Mornington Peninsula $$$

1998	16.5	1999	2000
1997	16.5	1998	2001
1996	17.0	1998	2001
1995	17.0	1997	2000
1994	16.5	1996	1999
1993	17.0	1995	1998
1992	16.6	1997	2000
1991	16.5	1996	1999

PINOT NOIR

Mornington Peninsula $$$

1999	16.8	2001	2004
1998	16.6	1999	2000
1997	16.5	1999	2002
1996	17.6	2001	2004
1995	16.0	1997	2000
1994	16.8	1996	1999
1993	17.4	1995	1998
1992	16.5	1994	1997
1991	17.0	1993	1996
1990	16.0	1992	1995

RESERVE CABERNET
Mornington Peninsula $$$$

1995	14.8	2000	2003
1993	17.6	2001	2005
1992	17.5	2000	2004
1991	16.6	1999	2003
1990	17.0	1998	2002
1989	16.0	1994	1997
1988	18.2	1996	2000
1987	15.7	1992	1995

RESERVE CHARDONNAY
Mornington Peninsula $$$$

1998	18.7	2003	2006
1997	18.6	2002	2005
1996	17.8	1998	2001
1995	17.8	2003	2007
1994	18.2	1996	1999
1993	17.5	1998	2001
1992	18.2	1994	1997
1991	17.0	1996	1999
1990	18.0	1995	1998
1989	16.0	1991	1994

RESERVE PINOT NOIR
Mornington Peninsula $$$$

1998	18.3	2003	2006
1997	18.7	2002	2005
1995	14.0	1997	2000
1994	17.2	1996	1999
1993	18.6	1998	2001
1992	18.2	1997	2000
1991	16.6	1993	1996
1990	17.5	1992	1995

Region: Pyrenees Winemakers: Shane Clohesy, David Crawford
Viticulturist: Philippe Bru Chief Executive: Chris Markell

Taltarni

Taltarni Road
Moonambel Vic 3478
Tel: (03) 5467 2218
Fax: (03) 5467 2306

Taltarni is one of the larger vineyards and wineries of the Pyrenees region and has long been associated with firm, occasionally unyielding and long-living red wines of great power. More recent vintages have seen a softening of the style, as exemplified by some excellent releases of Shiraz. Taltarni can usually be relied upon for a lively and varietal Sauvignon Blanc.

CABERNET SAUVIGNON

Pyrenees $$$$

1997	15.8	2002	2005+
1996	16.4	2004	2008
1995	18.0	2007	2015
1994	18.2	2006	2014+
1993	17.6	2005	2013
1992	18.0	2004	2012+
1991	18.3		2011+
1990	18.0	2002	2010+
1989	16.1	1997	2001
1988	18.5	2000	2008
1987	16.7	1999	2007
1986	16.8	1998	2006
1985	17.3	1987	2005
1984	18.2	1996	2004
1983	16.8		2003+
1982	17.5		2002+
1981	15.8	1989	1993
1980	16.0	1988	1992
1979	19.2		1999+

MERLOT CABERNET BLEND

Pyrenees $$$$

1998	15.3	2000	2003
1996	17.3	2001	2004
1995	17.9	2003	2007
1994	18.0	2002	2006
1993	17.9	2001	2005
1992	16.8	2000	2004
1991	16.8	1999	2003+
1990	18.2	1988	2002
1989	17.0	1994	1997
1988	18.3	2000	2008

RESERVE CABERNET SAUVIGNON

Pyrenees $$$$

1994	18.1		2004+
1992	18.6		2012+
1988	18.3		2008+
1984	18.4		2004+
1979	19.2	1999	2009

SAUVIGNON BLANC (FORMERLY FUME BLANC)

Pyrenees $$$

1999	18.2	2000	2001+
1998	16.3	1999	2000
1997	15.8	1997	1998
1996	16.5	1998	2001
1995	15.0	1997	2000
1994	17.9	1996	1999
1993	16.5	1998	2001
1992	17.0	1994	1997

SHIRAZ (FORMERLY FRENCH SYRAH)

Pyrenees $$$$

1998	18.7	2006	2010
1997	18.7	2005	2009+
1996	18.6	2004	2008
1995	16.0	2000	2003
1994	17.8	1999	2002
1993	18.4	2001	2005
1992	18.5		2004+
1991	18.2		2003+
1990	16.7	1998	2002+
1989	16.5	1997	2001
1988	18.5	2000	2008
1987	16.5	1995	1999
1986	18.5	1994	1998
1985	18.7	1997	2005+
1984	17.0	1992	1996
1983	16.5		2003+
1982	17.5	1990	1994
1981	18.0	1989	1993

TarraWarra's 1998 Chardonnay and Pinot Noir are two excellent examples of what this company does best, which is to create seamlessly textured and deeply flavoured wines from the two Burgundian varieties. Both should exhibit TarraWarra's characteristic longevity. While the Chardonnay's style has barely altered from the richly structured, creamy and secondary wines on which TarraWarra first made its name, the Pinot Noir has steadily acquired more suppleness and fleshiness. The 1998 is the perfect example.

CHARDONNAY
Yarra Valley $$$$

1998	18.7	2006	2010
1997	18.6	2005	2009
1996	17.5	2001	2004
1995	17.5	2000	2003+
1994	16.5	1996	1999
1993	18.3	1998	2001+
1992	18.8	2000	2004
1991	18.5	1996	1999
1990	17.6	1995	1998
1989	17.7	1997	2001
1988	18.5	1993	1996
1987	17.0	1995	1999
1986	17.3	1991	1994

PINOT NOIR
Yarra Valley $$$$

1998	18.7	2006	2010
1997	17.3	2002	2005
1996	18.6	2001	2004+
1995	18.2	2000	2003
1994	18.2	1999	2002
1993	16.7	1998	2001
1992	18.8	2000	2004
1991	16.5	1999	2003
1990	15.0	1998	2002
1989	15.3	1994	1997
1988	15.0	1993	1996

Region: McLaren Vale Winemakers: Michael Fragos, Justin McNamee
Viticulturist: Vic Zerella Chief Executive: Keith Smith

Tatachilla has won many friends with its uncompromisingly
generous and forward young red wines. While I agree that they
are fine drinking while relatively young, given their strength
and concentration, I doubt they have the complexity and
balance to become genuine cellaring wines.

CLARENDON VINEYARD MERLOT

McLaren Vale $$$$

1998	17.6	2003	2006
1997	16.0	2002	2005
1996	17.7	2001	2004+

FOUNDATION SHIRAZ

McLaren Vale $$$$

1998	17.6	2006	2010
1997	16.8	1999	2002+
1996	16.7	2001	2004
1995	16.0	1997	2000

KEYSTONE GRENACHE SHIRAZ

McLaren Vale $$

1999	15.0	2000	2001
1998	15.9	2000	2003
1997	14.5		1998

McLAREN VALE CABERNET SAUVIGNON

McLaren Vale $$$

1998	17.5	2003	2006+
1997	16.8	2002	2005
1996	17.8	2001	2004+

McLAREN VALE SHIRAZ

McLaren Vale $$$

1998	16.6	2003	2006
1997	16.8	2002	2005
1996	17.0	2004	2008

Region: Clare Valley Winemakers: Susan Mickan, Kelvin Budarick
Viticulturists: Ken Noack, Kate Strachan Chief Executive: Neil Jericho

I could hardly have been more delighted or surprised to taste the
new Taylors Cabernet Sauvignons from 1998 and 1999, each of
which are at the very least, very drinkable indeed. It would
be splendid if this large Clare Valley producer could
maintain this standard across its entire range.

CABERNET SAUVIGNON

Clare Valley $$

1999	18.0	2004	2007+
1998	17.0	2003	2006
1997	14.8	1999	2002
1996	15.0	1998	2001
1995	15.7	1997	2000
1994	16.3	1999	2002
1993	14.8	2001	2005
1992	15.2	2000	2004

CHARDONNAY

Clare Valley $$

1998	14.8	1999	2000
1997	14.0	1998	1999
1996	16.4	2001	2004
1995	16.2	2000	2003
1994	15.0	1996	1999
1993	16.5	1995	1998

CLARE RIESLING
(FORMERLY RHINE RIESLING)

Clare Valley $

1999	15.8	2001	2004
1998	15.6	2000	2003
1997	15.6	1999	2002
1996	17.8	2004	2008
1994	18.2	2002	2006
1993	16.8	1995	1998

SHIRAZ
(FORMERLY HERMITAGE)

Clare Valley $$

1999	16.6	2001	2004
1998	17.0	2003	2006
1997	16.5	2002	2005
1996	16.0	2001	2004
1995	16.5	2000	2003
1994	16.0	1996	1999
1993	16.3	1998	2001

Taylors

**Taylors Road
Auburn SA 5451
Tel: (08) 8849 2008
Fax: (08) 8849 2240**

I really enjoy the way David Robertson puts together his muscular, earthy and robust Cabernet Sauvignon and figgy, chalky Chardonnay, with its typically regional zesty citrus marmalade fruit.

CABERNET SAUVIGNON

Mudgee $$$

1995	17.5	2003	2007
1994	16.8	2002	2006+
1993	15.8	2001	2005
1992	16.8		2004+
1991	17.8		2003+
1990	18.2	1998	2002

CHARDONNAY

Mudgee $$$

1997	15.2	2002	2005
1996	17.3	2004	2008
1994	14.5	1999	2002
1993	16.9	2001	2005
1992	17.3	2000	2004
1991	16.4	1993	1996
1990	18.3	1995	1998

It would seem that with each passing vintage the Tim Adams wine business becomes more impressive. It's not just that its flagship The Aberfeldy Shiraz is fast becoming one of the classiest shirazes made in a country of good shiraz, but that virtually all the Tim Adams wines are constantly gaining in stature. My scores would suggest that if there's a weakness in the current range, I haven't found it.

BOTRYTIS AFFECTED SEMILLON

Clare Valley $$$

1998	18.3	2003	2006
1997	17.0	2002	2005
1994	17.0	2002	2006
1992	17.6	1997	2000
1991	17.5	1999	2003
1990	16.7	1995	1998

CABERNET

Clare Valley $$

1998	18.2	2006	2010+
1997	16.8	2002	2005
1996	16.9	2004	2008
1995	16.8	2003	2007
1994	16.5	2002	2006
1993	17.1	2001	2005
1992	17.7	2000	2004
1991	17.2		2003+
1990	17.2	1998	2002

RIESLING

Clare Valley $$

1999	18.2	2007	2011
1998	17.7	2006	2010
1997	18.5	2005	2009
1996	17.5	2004	2008
1995	15.3	1997	2000
1994	18.2	2002	2006
1993	18.2	2001	2005
1992	18.5	2000	2004
1991	17.0	1999	2003
1990	18.0		2002+

SEMILLON

Clare Valley $$

1999	17.3	2004	2007
1998	16.6	2003	2006
1997	18.5	2002	2005+
1996	17.9	2004	2008
1995	15.4	1997	2000
1994	18.3		2006+
1993	17.6	2001	2005
1992	17.7	2000	2004
1991	18.0	1999	2003
1990	17.5		2002+

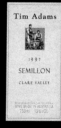

SHIRAZ
Clare Valley $$

1998	18.2	2003	2006
1997	17.8	2002	2005
1996	15.9	2001	2004
1995	17.4	2003	2007
1994	17.8	1999	2002
1993	17.2	1995	1998
1992	17.9	2000	2004
1991	17.5	1999	2003
1990	18.1	1998	2002
1989	17.2	1997	2001
1988	18.0	1996	2000
1987	17.7	1995	1999
1986	17.0	1994	1998

THE ABERFELDY
Clare Valley $$$$

1998	19.4	2010	2018+
1997	18.7	2005	2009+
1996	18.2	2008	2016
1995	18.0	2003	2007
1994	19.3	2006	2014+
1993	18.8	2005	2013
1992	18.5		2012+
1991	18.2	2003	2011
1990	16.7	1998	2002
1988	17.2	1996	2000+

THE FERGUS GRENACHE
Clare Valley $$

1999	18.0	2004	2007
1998	18.2	2003	2006+
1997	17.8	2002	2005
1996	17.4	2001	2004
1995	18.0	2000	2003
1994	17.9	2002	2006
1993	18.1	1998	2001

Region: Barossa Valley Winemaker: Neville Falkenberg
Viticulturist: Allen Jenkins   Chief Executive: Tom Park

Tollana

Tanunda Road
Nuriootpa SA 5355
Tel: (08) 8560 9389
Fax: (08) 8560 9494

Again I am left wondering about the way large wine companies go about their business. Southcorp clearly needs some reliable cheaper brands, so irrespective of its inherent quality, Tollana is sold well below its true worth. That can only mean good news for wine buyers, who want a very good reason indeed not to check out Tollana's excellent 1998 reds. The TR222 Cabernet Sauvignon is typically smooth and restrained, while the TR16 Shiraz simply bursts with exotic spice, dark cherry and cassis fruit.

BOTRYTIS RIESLING

Coonawarra and Eden Valley $$$

1998	17.4	2003	2006
1997	15.3	1999	2002
1996	16.0	1998	2001
1995	18.5	2000	2003
1994	17.0	1997	2000
1993	15.6	1995	1998
1992	18.3	1997	2000
1991	16.7	1996	1999
1990	17.5	1995	1998

CABERNET SAUVIGNON BIN TR222

Adelaide Hills $$$

1998	17.0	2006	2010
1997	18.5	2005	2009+
1996	17.4	2004	2008
1994	18.3		2006+
1993	18.1		2005+
1992	17.8	2000	2004
1991	17.0	2003	2011
1990	14.5	1992	1995
1988	17.8	1996	2000
1987	17.7	1992	1995
1986	18.0	1994	1998

CHARDONNAY

Eden Valley $$

1999	16.7	2001	2004
1998	15.6	2000	2003
1997	18.2	2002	2005
1996	16.3	1998	2001
1995	15.3	1996	1997
1994	16.8	1996	1999
1993	17.0	1995	1998

EDEN VALLEY RIESLING

Eden Valley $

1999	17.8	2001	2004+
1998	16.7	2000	2003
1995	16.5	1997	2000
1994	17.0	2002	2006
1993	16.6	1995	1998
1992	15.6	1993	1994

SHIRAZ BIN TR16

Eden Valley $$$

1998	17.9	2006	2010
1997	16.5	2002	2005
1996	16.2	2001	2004
1995	15.8	1997	2000
1994	15.8	1999	2002
1993	16.5	1998	2001
1992	18.4	2000	2004
1991	16.5	1999	2003
1990	16.0	1995	1998
1988	18.5	1993	1996

Trentham Estate

Sturt Highway
Trentham Cliffs NSW 2738
Tel: (03) 5024 8888
Fax: (03) 5024 8800
Website: www.trentham
estate.com.au

Region: Murray River Valley Winemaker: Anthony Murphy
Viticulturist: Pat Murphy Chief Executive: Anthony Murphy

The 1998 Merlot is the pick of Trentham Estate's current crop. This winery well deserves its reputation for its soft, approachable red wines from shiraz, cabernet sauvignon and merlot, most of which develop quite readily with bottle-aged complexity after just a couple of years.

CABERNET SAUVIGNON MERLOT

Murray River $$

1998	16.0	2000	2003
1997	15.0	1999	2002
1996	16.5	2001	2004
1995	15.0	1997	2000
1994	14.0	1995	1996
1993	16.6	1998	2001
1992	15.5	1994	1997
1991	16.1	1993	1996
1990	18.0	1992	1995

CHARDONNAY

Murray River $$

1998	15.0	1999	2000
1997	15.3	1998	1999
1996	17.0	1998	2001
1995	15.8	1997	2000
1994	16.5	1996	1999
1993	17.8	1995	1998
1992	16.2	1994	1997

MERLOT

Murray River $$

1998	17.0	2000	2003+
1997	15.6	1999	2002
1996	15.7	1998	2001
1995	16.0	1997	2000
1994	16.9	1996	1999
1993	16.2	1995	1998
1992	16.5	1993	1994
1991	17.0	1996	1999

SHIRAZ

Murray River $$

1998	15.0	2000	2003
1997	16.3	1999	2002
1996	18.1	2001	2004
1995	16.7	2000	2003
1994	16.0	1996	1999
1993	16.5	1995	1998
1992	16.8	1997	2000

Region: Mornington Peninsula Winemaker: Daniel Greene
Viticulturist: Shane Strange Chief Executive: Peter Hollick

Tuck's Ridge began as the largest vineyard and winery on the Mornington Peninsula and it is finally beginning to live up to its promises with some sumptuous, flavoursome wines from Chardonnay and Pinot Noir.

CHARDONNAY

Mornington Peninsula $$$$

1999	17.8	2001	2004
1998	15.9	2000	2003
1997	17.0	1999	2002
1996	14.5	1997	1998

PINOT NOIR

Mornington Peninsula $$$$

1999	16.6	2001	2004
1998	16.9	2000	2003
1997	17.5	1999	2002
1996	16.2	1998	2001

Region: Lower Hunter Valley Winemaker: Pat Auld
Viticulturist: Jerome Scarborough Chief Executive: Tom Park

Another of the Hunter Valley's traditional labels now struggling for recognition under a corporate umbrella, Tulloch is another of Southcorp's acquisitions. While it doesn't offer much in the cheaper market, with an outdated sparkling wine from semillon, a lean and ungenerous Verdelho and a simple and unsatisfying Unwooded Chardonnay, its Hector of Glen Elgin red still captures the essence of genuine Hunter shiraz.

HECTOR OF GLEN ELGIN

Lower Hunter Valley $$$$

1995	16.6	2003	2007
1994	18.2	2002	2006
1991	17.9		2003+
1989	16.5	1997	2001
1987	18.6	1999	2004
1986	16.7	1994	1998

VERDELHO

Lower Hunter Valley $$

1999	16.7	2000	2001+
1998	16.5	2000	2003
1997	14.5	1998	1999
1996	15.3	1996	1997
1995	16.6	1996	1997
1994	16.8	1996	1999
1993	16.3	1995	1998

Region: Yarra Valley Winemaker: Clare Halloran
Viticulturist: Lindsay Corby Chief Executive: Michael Matthews

Tunnel Hill is TarraWarra's second label, and has not lived up to its early wines in recent years, but its attractive 1999 Pinot Noir is handsomely its best release for some time. I don't believe it will be long before this brand is back on track.

PINOT NOIR			
	Yarra Valley $$$		
1999	17.3	2001	2004
1998	16.1	1999	2000
1997	16.7	1999	2002
1996	17.0	1998	2001
1995	15.4	1996	1997
1994	18.4	1996	1999
1993	17.0	1995	1998

Region: Mornington Peninsula Winemaker: David Leslie
Viticulturist: Paula Leslie Chief Executives: David & Paula Leslie

Turrumurra is another small Mornington Peninsula maker whose wines are usually very evolved and expressive by time of release. Winemaker David Leslie is clearly set upon the more briary and rustic expressions of Pinot Noir and Shiraz and these wines can deliver remarkably intense flavours.

PINOT NOIR			
	Mornington Peninsula $$$$		
1998	18.0	2003	2006
1997	17.3	2002	2005
1996	16.5	2001	2004

SHIRAZ			
	Mornington Peninsula $$$$		
1998	16.9	2003	2006
1997	17.1	2002	2005+
1996	14.6	1998	2001

Tunnel Hill

**Healesville Road
Yarra Glen Vic 3775
Tel: (03) 5962 3311
Fax: (03) 5962 3887
E-mail: enq@tarrawarra.
com.au**

Turramurra Estate

**RMB Wallaces Road
Dromana Vic 3936
Tel: (03) 5987 1146
Fax: (03) 5987 1286**

Tyrrell's

Broke Road
Pokolbin NSW 2320
Tel: **(02) 4993 7000**
Fax: **(02) 4998 7723**
E-mail:
admin@tyrrells.com.au

Region: Lower Hunter Valley Winemakers: Andrew Spinaze, Mark Richardson
Viticulturists: Cliff Currie, Rob Donoghue Chief Executive: Bruce Tyrrell

The quintessential Hunter winery, Tyrrell's is loaded with successful brands and quality vineyards, the best of which contribute to the company's enduring Vat series of wines. Tyrrell releases a brace of top semillons and shirazes, plus the region's best chardonnay, the provocatively named Vat 47 Pinot Chardonnay. Tyrrell's excellent performance over the last decade utterly belies the Hunter's inherent inconsistency, while its Rufus Stone reds certainly justify the company's expansion into other regions.

BROKENBACK SHIRAZ

Lower Hunter Valley $$$

1997	16.0	1999	2002
1996	15.1	1998	2001
1995	16.8	2000	2003
1994	17.2	2002	2006

LOST BLOCK SEMILLON

Lower Hunter Valley $$$

1999	16.7	2001	2004
1998	18.3	2003	2006+
1997	17.1	2002	2005+
1996	17.8	2004	2008
1995	16.7	2000	2003+

MOON MOUNTAIN CHARDONNAY

Lower Hunter Valley $$$

1998	17.0	2000	2003+
1997	17.4	1999	2002
1996	17.0	1998	2001

OLD WINERY CABERNET MERLOT

Various $$

1998	15.7	2000	2003
1997	16.6	2002	2005
1996	15.0	1998	2001
1995	15.8	1997	2000
1994	16.2	1996	1999
1993	15.8	1998	2001
1991	17.1	1996	1999

OLD WINERY CHARDONNAY

Lower Hunter Valley $$

1999	16.0	2000	2001
1998	14.0	1998	1999
1997	15.7	1998	1999
1996	15.6	1997	1998
1995	16.5	1997	1998

OLD WINERY SHIRAZ

Lower Hunter Valley $$

1997	15.2	1999	2002
1996	17.3	2001	2004
1995	16.8	1997	2000
1993	14.5	1995	1998
1992	17.0	2000	2004
1991	15.3	1996	1999

RUFUS STONE CABERNET SAUVIGNON

Coonawarra $$$$

1996	15.2	2001	2004
1995	15.1	2000	2003
1994	16.6	2002	2006
1993	16.0	1998	2001
1992	14.8	1994	1997

RUFUS STONE McLAREN VALE SHIRAZ

McLaren Vale $$$$

1998	18.2	2003	2006+
1997	18.0	2002	2005
1996	15.3	2001	2004

SHEE-OAK CHARDONNAY

Lower Hunter Valley $$$

1999	16.5	2000	2001
1998	15.4	1999	2000
1997	17.0	1998	1999
1996	16.8	1997	1998

STEVENS SEMILLON

Lower Hunter Valley $$$

1996	15.7	2001	2004
1995	17.0	2003	2007+
1994	16.2	1996	1999

VAT 1 SEMILLON

Lower Hunter Valley $$$

1999	18.6	2011	2019
1998	17.9	2006	2010+
1997	18.7		2009+
1996	18.8	2008	2016
1995	18.6		2007+
1994	18.0	2002	2006+
1993	16.8	1998	2001
1992	18.6	2004	2012
1991	17.4	1999	2003
1990	16.6	1998	2002
1989	15.8	1991	1994
1988	16.5	1993	1996
1987	17.8	1999	2007
1986	18.8	1998	2008
1985	16.5	1993	1997
1984	18.2	1996	2004
1983	16.7	1995	2003
1982	18.0	1994	2002
1981	17.0	1989	1993
1980	18.0	1992	2000

VAT 5 NVC SHIRAZ

Lower Hunter Valley $$$

1999	18.1	2007	2011
1998	16.5	2003	2006
1996	16.7	1998	2001
1995	17.7	2000	2003
1994	16.6	1996	1999
1993	16.2	1998	2001
1992	16.5	1997	2000
1990	16.5	1998	2002
1989	17.0	1997	2001
1988	14.5	1993	1996
1987	17.5	1995	1999
1986	14.0	1991	1994

VAT 6 PINOT NOIR

Lower Hunter Valley $$$$

1996	16.0	2003	2006
1997	17.9	2002	2005
1996	15.3	2001	2004
1994	17.2	1999	2002
1993	14.5	1995	1998
1992	15.6	1997	2000
1991	14.5	1993	1996
1990	16.9	1995	1998
1989	17.6	1994	1997

VAT 8 SHIRAZ CABERNET

Lower Hunter Valley, Coonawarra $$$

1998	18.6	2006	2010
1997	17.8	2005	2009+
1996	17.5	2001	2004
1995	18.1	2003	2007
1994	17.8	2002	2006
1993	18.0	2001	2005
1992	18.0	1997	2000

VAT 9 SHIRAZ

Lower Hunter Valley $$$$

1998	18.5	2006	2010
1997	18.4	2005	2009
1996	15.3	2001	2004
1995	18.1	2003	2007
1994	17.4	2002	2006+
1993	16.3	1998	2001
1992	18.0	1997	2000
1991	18.8		2003+

VAT 11 BAULKHAM SHIRAZ

Lower Hunter Valley $$$$

1999	17.8	2004	2007+
1998	18.5	2006	2010+
1996	17.6	2004	2008
1995	18.6	2003	2007
1994	18.1	2002	2006
1993	17.3	1998	2001
1992	18.2	2000	2004

VAT 47 PINOT CHARDONNAY

Lower Hunter Valley $$$$

1999	18.7	2007	2011
1998	18.8	2006	2010
1997	18.6	2002	2005
1996	18.4	2004	2008
1995	18.3	2000	2003
1994	18.0	1999	2002
1993	18.5	2001	2005
1992	18.4	2001	2005
1991	17.5	1999	2003
1990	18.0		2002+
1989	18.1	1997	2001
1988	14.0	1990	1993

Region: Margaret River Winemakers: Clive Otto, Will Shields
Viticulturist: Julia Ryan Chief Executive: Bob Baker

Owned by Janet Holmes a Court, Vasse Felix is a rapidly expanding Margaret River company with extensive new vineyards in an as-yet untested area of the region near Jindong. While some Vasse Felix wines are exceptional, the brand's performance remains enigmatic.

CABERNET MERLOT (FORMERLY CLASSIC DRY RED)

Margaret River $$$

1997	16.4	2002	2005
1996	16.5	2001	2004
1995	16.2	2000	2003
1994	16.6	1996	1999
1993	16.0	1995	1998
1992	17.5	2000	2004
1991	16.8	1999	2003
1990	16.0	1995	1998

CABERNET SAUVIGNON

Margaret River $$$$

1998	18.2	2006	2010
1997	16.7	2002	2005+
1996	15.7	2001	2004+
1995	16.0	2003	2007
1994	18.2		2006+
1993	16.5	1995	1998
1991	18.0		2003+
1990	17.9	1998	2002
1989	17.5	1997	2001
1988	18.5	1996	2000

sse Felix

Caves Road and
nans Road South
aramup WA 6284
(08) 9755 5242
(08) 9755 5425
site:
v.vassefelix.com.au
il:
@vassefelix.com.au

CHARDONNAY

Margaret River $$$

1998	14.5	1999	2000
1997	16.0	1999	2002
1996	16.6	1998	2001
1995	17.4	2000	2003
1994	18.1	1999	2002
1993	18.5	1998	2001
1992	16.0	1997	2000
1991	16.5	1993	1996
1990	16.5	1995	1998

CLASSIC DRY WHITE

Margaret River $$$

1999	15.2		2000
1998	16.0	1999	2000
1997	15.0	1998	1999
1996	15.7	1998	2001
1995	14.8	1996	1997
1994	16.2	1996	1999
1993	17.5	1995	1998

HEYTESBURY

Margaret River $$$$$

1998	16.8	2003	2006
1997	18.2	2005	2009
1996	16.7	2002	2008
1995	18.4	2003	2007+

HEYTESBURY CHARDONNAY

Margaret River $$$$$

1999	17.0	2001	2004
1998	16.6	2000	2003+
1996	15.8	1997	1998

SHIRAZ

Margaret River $$$$

1997	18.0	2005	2009
1996	17.1	2001	2004
1995	18.3	2000	2003
1994	18.2	2002	2006
1993	16.1	1998	2001
1992	16.7	2000	2004
1991	16.5	1999	2003

Region: Macedon Winemakers: David Watson, Mark Sheppard
Viticulturist: Mark Sheppard Chief Executive: John Quirk

Owned by the tiny publicly listed Vincorp organisation, Virgin Hills
is something of an under-performing asset whose recent wines are
a far cry from the occasionally brilliant, but often erratic
performance of vintages past. The current vintage is a typically
under-ripe example of why exceptional care needs to be
given to cabernet vineyards in marginal climates.

VIRGIN HILLS

Macedon $$$$

1998	15.8		2010+
1997	16.2	2002	2005
1995	14.8	1997	2000
1994	16.5	2002	2006
1993	16.3	2001	2005
1992	18.6	2000	2004
1991	18.4		2003+
1990	16.5	1998	2002
1988	18.2	1996	2000
1987	16.8	1999	2004
1985	18.3	1993	1997

Region: Margaret River Winemaker: Stuart Pym
Viticulturist: Steve James Chief Executive: Michael Wright

It would appear that Voyager Estate is being drawn irresistably
towards greatness. Greatness, mind, that will have come at some
price! The vast gaping hole on the otherwise pristine estate will
one day house huge underground oak cellars, themselves beneath
a brand new state of the art winery. As for the wines themselves,
their development over the last five years has
been little less than spectacular.

CABERNET MERLOT

Margaret River $$$$

1996	18.7	2004	2008+
1995	18.6	2003	2007+
1994	18.3		2006+

CHARDONNAY

Margaret River $$$$

1997	17.0	1999	2002
1996	17.6	1998	2001
1995	16.0	1997	2000
1994	17.0	1996	1999

Region: Yarra Valley Winemakers: Reg Egan, Maryann Egan
Viticulturist: Reg Egan Chief Executive: Reg Egan

Wantirna Estate is an oasis of a small but fully mature vineyard virtually surrounded by Melbourne suburbs. Its red wines from the excellent 1998 vintage are both exceptional in quality, but regrettably scarce in volume. Reg and Maryann Egan obviously share a common admiration for stylish and elegant wines able to conceal their strength behind a veil of subtlety and fineness.

AMELIA CABERNET SAUVIGNON MERLOT

Yarra Valley $$$$

1998	18.8		2010+
1997	19.0	2005	2009
1996	15.2	1998	2001
1995	18.0	1998	2001

ISABELLA CHARDONNAY

Yarra Valley $$$$

1999	16.8	2004	2007
1998	18.9	2003	2006+
1997	18.2	2002	2005+
1996	18.7	2001	2004+

LILY PINOT NOIR

Yarra Valley $$$$

1999	18.8	2004	2007+
1998	17.8	2003	2006+
1997	18.7	2002	2005+
1996	17.9	2001	2004

Region: Yarra Valley Winemakers: Jack Church, David Church
Viticulturist: Jack Church Chief Executive: Jack Church

Warramate is a small family-owned vineyard sited above the same slope as the Yarra Yering and Underhill vineyards and below that of the Coldstream Hills 'amphitheatre' block. Its red wines are generally light and herby.

CABERNET SAUVIGNON

Yarra Valley $$$

1997	15.0	2002	2005
1996	14.5	1998	2001
1995	15.2	1997	2000+
1994	15.0	1999	2002
1992	15.0	1994	1997
1991	16.6	1996	1999

Wantirna Estate

10 Bushy Park Lane
Wantirna South Vic 3
Tel: (03) 9801 2367
Fax: (03) 9887 0225

Warramate

27 Maddens Lane
Gruyere Vic 3770
Tel: (03) 5964 9219
Fax: (03) 5964 9219

RIESLING

Yarra Valley $$

1999	16.1	2004	2007
1998	16.6	2003	2006+
1997	15.1	2002	2005
1996	15.3	1998	2001
1995	16.7	2000	2003
1994	18.2	2002	2006
1993	17.7	2001	2005
1991	17.4	1999	2003

Region: Pyrenees Winemaker: Allen Hart
Viticulturist: Luigi Bazzani Chief Executive: Luigi Bazzani

Warrenmang is a brilliant little wine village complete with small conference centre, guest cottages and one of the best restaurants not only in provincial Australia but anywhere in Terra Australis. Its peppery, minty Shiraz is its most consistent wine, although the Grand Pyrenees has developed a loyal following for its robust and occasionally rustic and minty regional expression of Bordeaux varieties.

GRAND PYRENEES (FORMERLY CABERNET SAUVIGNON

Pyrenees $$$$

1998	16.7	2006	2010
1997	15.8	2005	2009
1995	16.7	2003	2007
1993	16.6	2001	2005
1992	16.5	2000	2004
1990	16.5	2002	2007
1989	15.0	1997	2003
1988	17.5	2000	2005
1987	13.5	1999	2004
1986	17.5	1991	1994

SHIRAZ

Pyrenees $$$

1998	14.7	2003	2006
1997	17.2	2002	2005+
1996	16.7	2004	2008
1995	14.6	2000	2003
1994	16.5	1999	2002
1993	17.0	2001	2005
1992	18.0		2004+
1991	17.0	1999	2003

Water Wheel

Raywood Road
Bridgewater-on-Loddon
Vic 3516
Tel: (03) 5437 3060
Fax: (03) 5437 3082

In its Shiraz and Cabernet Sauvignon Water Wheel makes two of
the most-recommended of all Australian red wines under $20.
Frequently embarrassing wines twice their price, they are typically
generous, plush and smooth, with a wonderfully bright, ripe
mouthful of intense berry fruit and supportive chocolate oak.

CABERNET SAUVIGNON

Bendigo $$

1998	17.4	2006	2010
1997	17.8	2002	2005+
1996	17.5	2001	2004
1995	17.0	2000	2003
1994	18.0	1999	2002
1993	18.0	1998	2001
1992	18.2	1997	2000
1991	18.0	1996	1999
1990	18.0	1995	1998

CHARDONNAY

Bendigo $$

1999	16.7	2001	2004
1998	15.0	1999	2000
1997	17.8	1998	1999
1996	15.2	1997	1998
1995	16.0	1997	2000
1994	17.5	1996	1999
1993	16.8	1995	1998

SAUVIGNON BLANC

Bendigo $$

1999	15.2		2000
1998	15.0		1999
1996	16.1	1998	2001
1995	16.0	1996	1997

SHIRAZ

Bendigo $$

1998	18.4	2007	2011
1997	17.2	2005	2009+
1996	18.2	2004	2008
1995	16.7	2003	2007
1994	18.0	1999	2002+
1993	16.6	1998	2001
1992	17.8	2000	2004+
1991	16.6	1999	2003
1990	15.8	1995	1998+

Wellington

cnr Richmond &
Denholms Roads
Cambridge Tas 7170
Tel: (03) 6248 5844
Fax: (03) 6243 0226

Region: Southern Tasmania Winemaker: Andrew Hood
Chief Executive: Andrew Hood

Andrew Hood is Tasmania's busiest contract winemaker and Wellington is his own label, a collection of pristine, fresh wines from several southern Tasmanian vineyards and made at his winery near Cambridge. The Iced Riesling is a unique and delicious dessert wine made by freeze-concentrating juice picked at normal ripeness.

CHARDONNAY

Southern Tasmania $$$$

1999	17.9	2004	2007
1998	16.4	2003	2006
1997	16.2	2002	2005

ICED RIESLING

Southern Tasmania $$$$

1999	17.9	2004	2007
1998	16.2	1999	2000
1997	16.7	1999	2002

PINOT NOIR

Southern Tasmania $$$$

1999	17.2	2004	2007
1998	17.7	2000	2003
1997	16.7	2002	2005
1994	17.0	1999	2002

Westend

1283 Brayne Road
Griffith NSW 2680
Tel: (02) 6964 1506
Fax: (02) 6962 1673
E-mail:
westend@webfront.net.au

Region: Griffith Winemakers: William Calabria, James Ceccato
Viticulturist: Anthony Trimboli Chief Executive: William Calabria

Westend is one of the smallest commercial Griffith wineries which apart from making an occasionally brilliant example of the regional dessert wine speciality, produces a 3 Bridges Cabernet Sauvignon which has entirely altered my perception of how good Riverland reds can be.

3 BRIDGES GOLDEN MIST BOTRYTIS SEMILLON

Griffith $$$$$

1998	15.3	1999	2000
1997	18.5	1999	2002+
1996	17.2	1998	2001
1995	15.4	1996	1997

Wignalls

5384 Chester Pass R
Albany WA 6330
Tel: (08) 9841 284
Fax: (08) 9842 900

Region: Great Southern Winemaker: Ben Kagi
Viticulturist: Robert Wignall Chief Executives: Pat & Bill Wignall

Wignalls is a small specialist maker of cool-climate table wines from its base at Albany in WA's Great Southern region. Recent Pinot Noir releases are recovering some of the vineyard's early 1990s form, while the latest Chardonnay and Sauvignon Blanc reflect a difficult season in 1999.

CABERNET

Great Southern $$$

1998	16.1	2000	2003+
1997	16.5	2002	2005+
1996	15.8	2001	2004
1994	17.8	2002	2006+

CHARDONNAY RESERVE

Great Southern $$$

1998	13.5	1999	2000
1997	15.0	1998	1999
1996	15.6	1998	2001
1995	15.0	1997	2000
1994	16.7	1996	1999
1993	17.7	1998	2001

PINOT NOIR

Great Southern $$$$

1999	15.8	2001	2004
1998	16.5	2000	2003
1997	16.8	1998	1999
1996	16.8	2001	2004
1995	14.0	1996	1997
1994	14.0	1995	1996
1993	16.5	1995	1998
1992	18.3	1997	2005

SAUVIGNON BLANC

Great Southern $$$

1999	15.2		2000
1998	18.0	1999	2000
1997	15.0		1998
1996	16.8	1997	1998

Region: Sunbury Winemakers: Wayne Stott, Peter Dredge
Viticulturists: Peter Dredge, Wayne Stott Chief Executive: Wayne Stott

Wildwood is a small vineyard and winery near Bulla in Victoria's Macedon region which has proven capable of some delightfully intense fruit in its Shiraz, Cabernets blend and Pinot Noir.

PINOT NOIR

Sunbury $$$

1999	18.0	2004	2007
1998	17.0	2003	2006
1997	14.5	1999	2002
1996	15.0	1998	2001
1995	15.4	1997	2000
1994	15.3	1996	1999
1993	16.8	1998	2001
1992	16.8	1997	2000
1991	13.5	1993	1996
1990	14.0	1992	1995

Region: Clare Valley Winemaker: Daniel Wilson
Viticulturist: Daniel Wilson Chief Executive: Daniel Wilson

Right out of the box, The Wilson Vineyard's wonderfully reserved Gallery Series Riesling simply oozes poise and style, following the 1998 release with another first-class effort in 1999. Like most from this maker, both wines should cellar very gracefully indeed. While the Gallery Series Cabernet Sauvignon has slipped a little in recent vintages, the Hippocrene sparkling red remains a source of fascination and pleasure.

GALLERY SERIES CABERNET SAUVIGNON

Clare Valley $$$

1998	14.6	2000	2003
1996	15.2	2001	2004
1995	15.0	2000	2003
1994	17.9	2002	2006
1992	16.4	2000	2004
1991	16.8	1999	2003
1990	15.0	1995	1998
1989	16.0	1994	1997
1988	17.5	1996	2000
1987	18.0	1995	1999
1986	17.5	1994	1998

GALLERY SERIES RIESLING

Clare Valley $$

1999	18.5	2007	2011+
1998	18.7	2006	2010+
1997	16.0	2002	2005
1996	18.0	2004	2008
1995	18.5	2003	2007
1994	17.6	2002	2006
1993	17.3	1998	2001
1992	17.5	1997	2000
1991	17.6	1999	2003
1990	18.0	1998	2003
1989	15.0	1997	2001
1988	17.5	1993	1996

HIPPOCRENE

Clare Valley $$$

1994	15.0	1996	1999
Bin 93	14.5	1998	2001
Bin 92	15.0	1997	2000
Bin 91	17.7	1996	1999
Bin 90	18.2	1998	2002

Region: Southern Tasmania Winemaker: Andrew Hood
Viticulturist: Neil Snare Chief Executive: Neil Snare

Winstead is a postage stamp-sized pinot noir and riesling vineyard near the small town of Bagdad, a little to the north of the bustling metropolis of Hobart. 1997 and 1998 display qualities more familiar in better Alsatian riesling than those we are used to experiencing in Australian wine.

Winstead

75 Winstead Road
Badgad Tas 7030
Tel: (03) 6268 6417
Fax: (03) 6268 6417

PINOT NOIR

Bagdad $$$$

1999	17.6	2001	2004
1998	17.0	2000	2003
1997	16.3	1999	2002
1996	16.5	2001	2004
1995	17.2	1997	2000
1994	18.2	1999	2002

Wirra Wirra

McMurtrie Road
McLaren Vale SA 5171
Tel: (08) 8323 8414
Fax: (08) 8323 8596

Region: McLaren Vale Winemaker: Ben Riggs
Viticulturist: Steve Brunato Chief Executive: Greg Trott

As you would expect, Wirra Wirra has used the excellent 1998 red wine vintage at McLaren Vale to its best advantage, capturing the intensity and flavour of well-ripened fruit in its most consistent selection of red wines. Few Australian wineries are as reliable as this one.

CHARDONNAY

McLaren Vale $$$

1998	16.6	2000	2003
1997	16.8	1999	2002
1996	16.7	1998	2001
1995	16.0	1997	2000
1994	17.6	1996	1999
1993	17.5	1998	2001
1992	18.2	1997	2000
1991	18.0	1996	1999

CHURCH BLOCK

McLaren Vale $$$

1998	18.0	2003	2006+
1997	18.2	2002	2005+
1996	16.0	1998	2001
1995	16.5	2000	2003
1994	18.0	1999	2002
1993	17.6	1998	2001
1992	16.8	1997	2000
1991	16.9	1996	1999
1990	18.0	1998	2002
1989	16.5	1994	1997
1988	17.0	1993	1996

HAND PICKED RIESLING

McLaren Vale $$

1999	16.4	2001	2004+
1998	15.6	2003	2006
1997	15.9	1999	2002
1996	15.0	1998	2001
1995	16.0	1997	2000
1994	16.5	1999	2002
1993	17.0	1998	2001
1992	17.9	2000	2004
1991	17.5		2003+
1990	16.5		2002+

RSW SHIRAZ

McLaren Vale $$$$

1998	18.4	2003	2006+
1997	17.2	2002	2005
1996	18.9	2004	2008
1995	17.9	2000	2003
1994	18.5	1999	2002
1993	17.6	1998	2001
1992	18.2	2000	2004
1991	18.0	1996	1999
1990	18.3	1995	1998

SAUVIGNON BLANC

McLaren Vale $$

1999	14.5		2000
1998	15.3		1999
1997	16.0	1998	1999
1996	18.0	1997	1998

SCRUBBY RISE SEMILLON SAUVIGNON BLANC CHARDONNAY

McLaren Vale $$$

1999	14.5		2000
1998	16.0	2000	2003
1997	18.0	2002	2005
1996	17.0	2001	2004
1995	15.4	1997	2000
1994	17.3	1999	2002
1993	18.3	1998	2001
1992	17.6	1997	2000
1991	18.0	1999	2003

THE ANGELUS CABERNET SAUVIGNON

McLaren Vale $$$$

1997	15.8	2002	2005
1996	18.6	2004	2008+
1995	17.5	2003	2007
1994	16.6	1999	2002
1993	18.2	2001	2005
1992	18.0	2000	2004
1991	18.2	1996	1999
1990	18.5	1998	2002
1989	16.5	1994	1997
1988	16.0	1990	1993

Wolf Blass

Bilyara Vineyards
Sturt Highway
Nuriootpa SA 5355
Tel: (08) 8562 1955
Fax: (08) 8562 4127

Region: Langhorne Creek, Barossa Valley
Winemakers: John Glaetzer, Wendy Stuckey, Caroline Dunn
Chief Executive: Terry Davis

A plethora of interesting new releases made and marketed on individual vineyards and varieties under the emergent 'Blass' label has helped breathe new life into a brand whose reds were becoming just that little too predictable. Meanwhile, despite the accolades showered on the two Wolf Blass Rieslings, both are relatively early-drinking wines to be cellared carefully.

BLACK LABEL DRY RED

South Australia $$$$$

1996	17.3	2008	2016
1995	17.0	2003	2007
1994	16.7	2000	2003
1993	18.0	2001	2005
1992	16.5	2000	2004
1991	18.6	2003	2011+
1990	18.4	2002	2010
1989	18.0	2001	2009
1988	18.5	1996	2000
1987	17.5	1995	1999
1986	18.3	1994	1998
1985	17.5	1993	1997
1984	18.2	1992	1996
1983	18.6	1995	2000
1982	17.0	1994	1999
1981	18.1	1993	1998
1980	18.4	1992	1997
1975	18.1	1995	2000

BROWN LABEL CLASSIC SHIRAZ

South Australia $$$$

1996	17.4	2004	2008
1995	16.0	2000	2003
1994	17.9	2002	2006
1993	16.7	1998	2001
1992	17.2	2000	2004
1990	17.7	1998	2002
1989	17.0	1997	2001
1988	18.1	1993	1996
1987	17.6	1995	1999
1986	18.4	1994	1998
1985	17.0	1993	1997
1984	18.1	1992	1996
1983	18.5	1991	1995
1982	17.0	1990	1994

www.onwine.com.au

Jeremy Oliver OnWine is the most authoritative, comprehensive web resource for truly independent critique, discussion and review of Australian wine.

It features:

- In depth reviews and tasting notes
- Today's wine stock prices
- Ongoing, up-to-the-minute news and interviews
- What's hot on the Australian wine scene.
- A fully searchable database of articles and tasting notes from prior issues of Jeremy Oliver's OnWine Report. This database is updated every two months and is available without charge.

This site is not a thinly veiled sales vehicle for a winery or a wine retailer, since Jeremy Oliver neithers own a winery or wine store, nor is he owned by one. Instead, Jeremy Oliver OnWine is here to provide you with 100% independent, unbiased opinion.

'Wine – with us since the earliest days of human civilisation – has come marching through to the Internet with some excellent sites. But few have more authority than Jeremy Oliver's site.

'Navigable, simple and accessible, this site stands out for those wanting information, not techno-gimmickry.'

Australian PC Authority, April 2000.

Jeremy Oliver's OnWine Report

"The most immediately attractive magazine of its kind in Australia."
— James Halliday, The Australian.

Every two months you receive twenty full colour pages packed with 'insider' information on the Australian wine industry and its products.

Information such as:

INFORMED, INDEPENDENT VIEWS FOR THE INTERESTED WINE DRINKER.

- Pre-release information and notes of new and interesting releases
- Industry and product trends
- Names to watch. New discoveries for your little black book
- Detailed and illustrated feature articles
- Wine industry facts. Who's hot and who's not!
- Cellaring tips. Bargains to buy now and enjoy later
- News and stock market comment
- Wine diary: State by state events
- Interviews with opinion leaders

"Oliver's writing is opinionated and well-informed, and although one can't expect to agree with every review of a fellow critic, I find his wine critiques have bite and accuracy."
— Huon Hooke, The Sydney Morning Herald

Subscribe at www.onwine.com.au

GOLD LABEL RHINE RIESLING

Clare Valley, Eden Valley $$

1999	17.3	2001	2004
1998	18.5	2003	2006
1997	17.5	2002	2005
1996	18.3	2004	2008
1995	16.0	1997	2000
1994	18.0	1999	2002

GREY LABEL DRY RED

South Australia $$$$

1996	17.3	2001	2004+
1995	18.0	2002	2007
1994	18.3	2002	2006
1993	16.8	2001	2005
1992	18.1	2000	2004
1991	18.3	1999	2003
1990	17.6	1995	1998
1988	17.5	1993	1996
1987	17.5	1992	1995
1986	18.3	1994	1998

RED LABEL DRY RED

South-Eastern Australia $

1998	16.7	2000	2003+
1997	16.0	1999	2002
1996	15.0	1997	1998
1995	15.7	1997	2000
1994	15.0	1996	2001

RHINE RIESLING

South Australia $$

1999	15.7	2000	2001
1998	17.9	2000	2003
1997	16.0	1999	2002
1996	16.0	1998	2001
1995	16.0	1997	2000
1994	17.4	1999	2002
1993	17.8	1995	1998
1991	17.5	1993	1996
1990	17.4	1995	1998

VINTAGE PINOT NOIR CHARDONNAY

Southern Australia $$$

1996	17.8	1998	2001+
1995	16.9	1997	2000
1992	16.4	1994	1997

YELLOW LABEL DRY RED

South Australia $$

1997	14.8	1999	2002
1996	16.5	1998	2001
1995	16.2	2000	2003
1994	15.0	1996	1999
1993	16.0	1998	2001
1992	16.9	2000	2004

Region: McLaren Vale Winemaker: Scott Collett
Viticulturist: Scott Collett Chief Executive: Scott Collett

More restrained and supple than those of its neighbours,
Woodstock's collection of McLaren Vale wines is led by its richly
textured but consistently elegant best-of-vintage label known as
The Stocks, typically made from shiraz. Its 1997 reds do Woodstock
great credit and releases to-date from the 1998 vintage
tend to suggest another fine year.

BOTRYTIS SWEET WHITE

McLaren Vale $$$

1997-98	14.8	2000	2003
1996	17.8	2001	2004
1995	18.2	2000	2003
1994	17.5	2002	2006
1993	17.1	1995	1998

CABERNET SAUVIGNON

McLaren Vale $$$

1997	16.7	2005	2009
1996	16.0	2001	2004
1995	16.2	2000	2003
1994	18.2	2002	2006
1993	17.5	2001	2005
1992	18.1		2004+
1991	18.6		2003+
1990	17.9	1998	2002

CHARDONNAY

McLaren Vale $$

1998	17.5	2001	2005
1997	16.0	1999	2002
1996	18.0	2001	2004
1995	16.7	2000	2003
1994	17.6	1999	2002
1993	18.2	1998	2001
1992	17.8	1997	2000
1991	18.3	1996	1999

GRENACHE

McLaren Vale $$

1998	15.0	2000	2003
1997	16.8	2002	2005
1996	16.4	1998	2001+
1995	15.7	1997	2000

SHIRAZ

McLaren Vale $$

1998	17.8	2006	2010
1997	17.0	2002	2005+
1996	17.9	2004	2008
1995	15.8	2000	2003
1994	16.5	1999	2002
1993	18.2	2001	2005
1992	17.8	2000	2004
1991	16.4	1999	2003
1990	18.1	1998	2002
1989	17.5	1997	2001

THE STOCKS

McLaren Vale $$$$

1997	16.1	1999	2002
1996	18.8	2004	2008
1995	17.9	2003	2007
1994	18.7	2002	2006
1993	18.0	2001	2005
1991	16.7	1999	2003

Region: Lower Hunter Valley Winemaker: Brett McKinnon
Viticulturist: Stephen Guilbaud-Oulton Chief Executive: Christian Porta

I never thought I'd be excited by Wyndham Estate's wines, which for so many years have been as bland as ice-cream. Then along came the Show Reserve Semillon and the Show Reserve Shiraz, including the wonderfully leathery 1993 vintage of this wine, a traditional Hunter classic!

Wyndham Estate

Dalwood Road
Dalwood NSW 2335
Tel: (02) 4938 3444
Fax: (02) 4938 3422

BIN 444 CABERNET SAUVIGNON

Lower Hunter Valley $$

1998	15.3	2000	2003
1997	15.3	1999	2002
1996	15.0	1998	2001
1995	16.3	2000	2003
1994	16.0	1999	2002
1993	16.7	1998	2001
1992	16.7	1997	2000

BIN 888 CABERNET MERLOT

Lower Hunter Valley $$$

1997	17.2	2002	2005+
1996	16.7	2001	2004
1995	15.8	2000	2003
1994	17.0	2002	2006
1993	16.0	1998	2001
1992	16.8	1997	2000
1991	16.6	1993	1996

SHOW RESERVE SEMILLON

Lower Hunter Valley $$$

1997	17.0	2005	2009
1996	17.2	2004	2009
1994	16.0	1999	2002

SHOW RESERVE SHIRAZ

Lower Hunter Valley $$$

1996	16.3	2001	2004+
1995	16.1	2000	2003
1993	18.6	2001	2005

Wynns Coonawarra Estate

Memorial Drive
Coonawarra SA 5263
Tel: (08) 8736 3266
Fax: (08) 8736 3202

Region: Coonawarra Winemaker: Sue Hodder
Viticulturist: Max Arney Chief Executive: Tom Park

Wynns Coonawarra is an icon in Australian red wine. That's one of the reasons I'm so disappointed by the red collection from 1997, albeit from one of the more difficult Coonawarra vintages of the 1990s. In particular, the two prestige red labels of Michael Shiraz and John Riddoch Cabernet Sauvignon are even more contrived and beefed up than one has to occasionally expect. That said, in its justly celebrated Black Label Cabernet Sauvignon, Wynns Coonawarra is traditionally considered a reliable source of affordable long-term cellaring wine. The Shiraz has a confusing and split personality, since recent vintages have been relatively quick to develop, but mature vintages from the 'seventies backwards are rightly considered to be Australian classics.

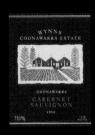

CABERNET SAUVIGNON

Coonawarra $$$

1997	16.5	2002	2005
1996	18.1	2004	2008
1995	17.2	2003	2007
1994	18.5	2006	2014
1993	18.0		2005+
1992	17.6	2000	2004
1991	18.6	2003	2011
1990	18.6	2002	2010+
1989	16.0	1991	1994
1988	18.3	1996	2000
1987	16.5	1992	1995
1986	18.2	1994	1998
1985	17.0	1993	1997
1984	16.4	1989	1992
1983	14.5	1985	1988
1982	18.1	1994	1999

CABERNET SHIRAZ MERLOT (FORMERLY CABERNET HERMITAGE)

Coonawarra $$

1997	15.8	1999	2002+
1996	16.6	2004	2010
1995	17.1	2000	2003
1994	16.8	1999	2002
1993	17.1	1998	2003
1992	17.8	2000	2004
1991	17.5	1996	1999
1990	18.0	1998	2002
1989	16.0	1991	2004
1988	18.3	1993	1996
1987	15.5	1989	1992
1986	18.5	1998	2003
1985	17.7	1990	1993

CHARDONNAY
Coonawarra $$

1999	16.8	2000	2003
1998	16.8	2000	2003
1997	16.5	1999	2002
1996	16.0	1998	2001
1995	15.0	1997	2000
1994	17.8	1999	2002
1993	16.5	1998	2001
1992	17.6	1997	2000

JOHN RIDDOCH CABERNET SAUVIGNON
Coonawarra $$$$$

1997	16.7	2005	20090
1996	17.2	2004	2008+
1994	18.7		2006+
1993	18.3	2001	2005
1992	18.0		2004+
1991	18.3		2003+
1990	18.9		2010+
1988	17.4	2000	2005
1987	18.0	1999	2004
1986	18.4	1998	2006
1985	17.0	1993	1997
1984	16.7	1992	1996
1982	19.0	1994	2002+

MICHAEL SHIRAZ
Coonawarra $$$$$

1997	16.3	2002	2005
1996	18.5		2008+
1994	18.9	2006	2014
1993	18.8	2005	2013
1991	18.3	2003	2011
1990	18.4	2002	2010
1955	19.2	1975	1985

RIESLING
Coonawarra $

1999	15.8	2001	2004
1998	17.2	2003	2006
1997	15.8	2002	2005
1996	17.2	2001	2004
1995	15.6	1997	2000
1994	17.5	1999	2002
1993	17.8	1998	2001
1992	17.0	1997	2000
1991	17.5	1999	2003

Yalumba

**Eden Valley Road
Angaston SA 5353
Tel: (08) 8561 3200
Fax: (08) 8561 3393**

SHIRAZ

Coonawarra $$

1998	16.0	2003	2006
1997	16.5	2002	2005
1996	15.3	1998	2001
1995	16.8	2000	2003
1994	16.3	1996	1999
1993	16.5	1998	2001
1992	17.6	2000	2004
1991	16.8	1996	1999
1990	17.0	1995	1998
1989	16.5	1994	1997
1988	17.5	1996	2000

Region: Barossa Winemakers: Alan Hoey, Kevin Glastonbury, Louisa Rose
Viticulturist: Robin Nettelbeck Chief Executive: Robert Hill Smith

Yalumba is a large Barossa winery owned and operated by
S. Smith & Son which serves as the winemaking centre for its
premium brands, sourced mainly from the Barossa Valley, Eden
Valley and Coonawarra. The Yalumba brand itself contains a
number of classic wines, from the under-valued The Menzies
Coonawarra Cabernet Sauvignon, to the finely crafted 'D' sparkling
wine, to the Barossa benchmark The Signature dry red and
even to that rather oaky but usually utterly charming
The Octavius Barossa shiraz.

BAROSSA GROWERS SHIRAZ

Barossa Valley $$$

1998	16.0	2000	2003
1997	17.2	2002	2005
1996	15.8	1998	2001
1995	16.8	1997	2000

'D' METHODE CHAMPENOISE

Tasmania, Victoria, South Australia $$$

1996	18.0	2001	2004
1995	17.0	2000	2003
1994	18.5	1999	2002
1993	17.5	1998	2001
1992	14.8	1994	1997
1991	18.0	1995	1998
1990	18.2	1998	2002

LIMITED RELEASE VIOGNIER

Barossa Valley $$

1999	15.7	2000	2001
1998	16.7	1999	2000
1997	16.7	1998	1999
1996	16.0	1997	1998

THE MENZIES CABERNET SAUVIGNON

Coonawarra $$$

1997	17.1	2005	2009
1996	18.4	2004	2008+
1995	16.8	2000	2003
1994	16.0	2006	2014
1993	16.8	2001	2005
1992	18.0	2000	2004
1991	18.5		2003+
1990	17.8		2002+
1989	18.0	1997	2003

THE OCTAVIUS

Barossa $$$$$

1996	16.8	2004	2008
1995	18.0	2003	2007
1994	18.7	2002	2006+
1993	17.6	1998	2001
1992	18.6	2000	2004
1990	18.8		2002+

THE SIGNATURE (FORMERLY SIGNATURE RESERVE CABERNET SHIRAZ)

Barossa $$$$

1998	18.8		2010+
1995	17.2	2003	2007
1994	18.5		2006+
1993	18.0	2001	2005
1992	18.7	2004	2012
1991	18.5		2003+
1990	18.5	2002	2010
1989	18.0	1994	1997
1988	18.3		2008+
1987	17.8	1995	1999
1986	17.5	1994	1998
1985	18.0	1997	2002
1984	16.0	1992	1996

Yarra Burn

60 Settlement Road
Yarra Junction Vic 3797
Tel: (03) 5967 1428
Fax: (03) 5967 1146

Region: Yarra Valley Winemakers: Stephen Pannell, Ed Carr, Emma Requin
Viticulturist: David Fyffe Chief Executive: Stephen Millar

BRL Hardy has a Yarra Valley base at Yarra Burn, whose wines have always been elegant, intensely-flavoured and ready to improve in the cellar. The Bastard Hill wines make a distinctively named addition to the folio, since the Pinot Noir and Chardonnay in question come from a particular slope within BRL Hardy's enormous Hoddle's Creek vineyard, whose name you can possibly fathom. Time will tell if the very extractive Pinot Noir fleshes out a little. The 1998 Yarra Burn Cabernet Sauvignon is a finely structured, classy cool-climate red.

CABERNET
Yarra Valley $$$

1998	18.1	2006	2010
1997	16.8	2002	2005
1995	18.3	2003	2007
1994	16.8	1999	2002
1993	16.8	1998	2001
1992	18.3	2000	2004
1990	16.0	1995	1998

CHARDONNAY
Yarra Valley $$$

1997	18.0	2002	2005
1996	17.0	2001	2004
1995	15.7	1996	1997
1994	15.8	1999	2002
1993	17.7	1998	2001
1992	17.5	1994	1997

PINOT NOIR
Yarra Valley $$$

1999	15.0	2001	2004
1998	16.0	2003	2006
1997	17.8	2002	2005
1994	13.5	1999	2002

PINOT NOIR CHARDONNAY BLEND
Yarra Valley $$$

1997	18.6	1999	2002+
1996	15.6	1998	2001
1993	16.0	1995	2000
1990	17.2	1995	1998

Region: Yarra Valley Winemaker: Tom Carson
Viticulturist: John Evans Chief Executives: Doug & Graham Rathbone

Yarra Edge is potentially one of the premier Yarra Valley vineyards. Today it's leased to Yering Station and its wines are made there by Tom Carson and team. As the supple and elegant 1997 edition illustrates, the Cabernets blend can become a wine of real style and finesse.

CHARDONNAY

Yarra Valley $$$$

Year	Score	Drink from	Drink to
1998	17.6	2003	2006
1997	15.2	1999	2002
1996	16.7	1998	2001
1995	18.0	2000	2003
1994	16.0	1999	2002
1993	16.3	1995	1998
1992	18.5	2000	2004
1991	16.2	1996	1999
1990	18.2	1998	2002

YARRA EDGE (CABERNETS)

Yarra Valley $$$$

Year	Score	Drink from	Drink to
1997	18.5		2009+
1996	15.2	1998	2001
1995	16.5	2003	2007
1994	18.7		2006+
1993	15.4	1998	2001
1992	18.3	2000	2004
1991	17.1	1999	2003
1990	18.1	1998	2002

Region: Yarra Valley Winemaker: Nick Walker
Viticulturist: Damien de Castella Chief Executive: Terry Davis

One of the most successful of the wide array of Mildara Blass brands, Yarra Ridge presents early-drinking, flavoursome and typically reliable table wines priced for the bistro market. Its Reserve wines offer an extra dimension of concentration and oak treatment. Many have done very well on the wine show circuit.

CABERNET SAUVIGNON

Yarra Valley $$$

Year	Score	Drink from	Drink to
1998	16.3	1999	2002
1997	15.0	1999	2002
1996	15.3	1997	1998
1995	15.5	2000	2003
1994	17.7	1999	2002
1993	16.7	1998	2001

Yarra Edge
**Edward Road
Lilydale Vic 3140
Tel: (03) 9730 1107
Fax: (03) 9739 0135**

Yarra Ridge
**Glenview Road
Yarra Glen Vic 3755
Tel: (03) 9730 1022
Fax: (03) 9730 1131**

CHARDONNAY

Yarra Valley $$$

1999	15.8		2000
1998	16.2	1999	2000
1997	16.7	1998	1999
1996	16.8	1998	2001
1995	16.5	1997	2000
1994	17.0	1996	1999
1993	17.3	1994	1995

MERLOT

Yarra Valley $$$

1998	16.8	2000	2003
1997	16.8	1999	2002
1996	16.0	1998	2001
1995	18.1	1997	2000
1994	16.7	1999	2002
1993	15.0	1995	1998

PINOT NOIR

Yarra Valley $$$

1999	15.5	2000	2001
1998	15.3	2000	2003
1997	16.0	1999	2002
1996	17.1	1998	2003
1995	17.6	2000	2003
1994	18.1	1999	2002
1993	15.6	1998	2001

RESERVE PINOT NOIR

Yarra Valley $$$$

1998	16.8	2000	2003
1997	16.7	1999	2002
1996	16.5	1998	2001

SAUVIGNON BLANC

Yarra Valley $$$

1999	15.0		1999
1998	15.4	1998	1999
1997	17.0	1998	1999
1996	17.8	1997	1998
1995	16.5	1996	1997

Region: Yarra Valley Winemaker: Ian Maclean
Viticulturist: Ian Maclean Chief Executives: Ian & Anne Maclean

Yarra Yarra is a tiny Yarra Valley vineyard (not that you would have guessed) which specialises in dry red and white wines from the Bordeaux varieties. Its point of difference is that its red wines marry some of the structure and depth of a Cullen cabernet with the fineness and elegance of Mount Mary. That said, its wines are utterly distinctive and reflect the season experienced by the individual vineyard. It's also pleasing to see another emergent high-quality blend of semillon and sauvignon blanc.

Yarra Yarra

**239 Hunts Lane
Steels Creek Vic 3775
Tel: (03) 9830 4180
Fax: (03) 9830 4180**

CABERNETS

Yarra Valley $$$$

1997	17.4	2002	2009+
1996	16.0	1998	2001+
1995	19.0		2007+
1994	18.2	2002	2006+
1993	17.3	2001	2005
1992	17.5	2000	2004+
1991	18.7	1999	2003+
1990	18.8	2002	2010+
1988	18.7	2000	2008
1987	17.6	1995	1999
1986	16.0	1994	1998
1985	17.2	1997	2005
1984	18.0	1996	2004

RESERVE CABERNET SAUVIGNON

Yarra Valley $$$$

1997	16.7	2002	2005+
1995	18.6		2007+
1994	16.9	2002	2006+
1993	16.8	1998	2001

SAUVIGNON SEMILLON

Yarra Valley $$$$

1998	16.5	2003	2006
1997	18.3	2002	2005
1996	17.8	2001	2004
1995	18.7	2003	2007
1994	16.3	1999	2002
1993	15.7	1995	1998
1992	18.7	2000	2004
1990	16.3	1995	1998
1989	16.6	1994	1997

Yarra Yering

Briary Road
Coldstream Vic 3770
Tel: (03) 5964 9267
Fax: (03) 5964 9239

Region: Yarra Valley Winemaker: Bailey Carrodus
Viticulturist: Bailey Carrodus Chief Executive: Bailey Carrodus

When they are good, they are very good indeed. Bailey Carrodus creates some of the most opulently concentrated and fine-grained of all Australian red wines, most frequently from cabernet sauvignon and shiraz. The best are simply great wines, capable of developing over a very long period. Yarra Yering's white wines appear to lack protection against oxidation and excessively rapid advancement and seem at odds with some fundamental tenets of modern white wine production.

CHARDONNAY
Yarra Valley $$$$$

1997	15.0	1998	1999
1994	16.5	1999	2002
1993	17.2	1998	2001
1992	17.1	1997	2000
1991	18.0	1996	1999
1990	17.0	1998	2002

DRY RED NO. 1
Yarra Valley $$$$$

1998	17.6	2006	2010
1995	14.5	2000	2003
1994	18.2	2006	2014
1993	18.5	2001	2005
1992	17.4	2000	2004
1991	18.6	1999	2003
1990	19.0	2002	2010+
1989	17.5	1994	1997
1988	15.8	1993	1996
1987	16.5	1995	1999
1986	18.0	1994	1998+

DRY RED NO. 2
Yarra Valley $$$$$

1994	18.5	2002	2006
1993	18.0	1998	2001
1992	18.4	1997	2000
1991	16.0	1993	1996
1990	18.2	1998	2002
1989	17.5	1997	2001
1988	16.4	1990	1993
1987	15.5	1992	1995
1986	16.0	1991	1994
1985	17.5	1993	1997

DRY WHITE NO. 1

Yarra Valley $$$$$

1998	14.6	1999	2000
1995	15.4	1997	2000
1994	17.2	1999	2002
1993	17.0	1998	2001
1992	15.9	1997	2000
1991	17.2	1999	2003
1990	15.3	1998	2002
1989	15.1	1991	1994

MERLOT

Yarra Valley $$$$$

1994	18.8	2002	2006
1993	18.3	1998	2001
1992	17.6	1997	2000
1991	18.1	1996	1999
1990	17.3	1995	1998

PINOT NOIR

Yarra Valley $$$$$

1996	15.8	2001	2004
1995	16.2	2000	2003
1994	17.0	1999	2002
1993	15.0	1998	2001
1992	18.8	2000	2004
1991	18.7	1999	2003
1991	18.6	1996	1999
1990	17.0	1995	1998

UNDERHILL SHIRAZ

Yarra Valley $$$$$

1994	17.0	1999	2002
1993	16.8	1998	2001
1992	18.9	1997	2000
1991	17.5	1993	1996

Yarrabank

38 Melba Highway
Yering Vic 3775
Tel: (03) 9730 1107
Fax: (03) 9739 0135

Region: Yarra Valley Winemakers: Claude Thibaut, Tom Carson
Viticulturist: John Evans Chief Executives: Doug Rathbone & Laurent Gillet

Yering Station has linked up with Devaux Champagne and its winemaker Claude Thibaut to fashion this very complex and creamy sparkling wine, made equally from Yarra Valley and Mornington Peninsula fruit. The wines each display a mouthfilling creamy texture, lingering flavours and clean, refreshing acidity.

YARRABANK CUVÉE

Yarra Valley, Mornington Peninsula $$$$

1996	17.7	2001	2004
1995	18.6	2000	2003
1994	18.6	1996	1999
1993	18.2	1995	1998+

Yellowglen

White's Road
Smythesdale Vic 3551
Tel: (03) 5342 8617
Fax: (03) 5333 7102

Region: Bendigo Winemaker: Charles Hargrave
Viticulturist: Damien de Castella Chief Executive: Terry Davis

Yellowglen is one of the more ubiquitous mid-market to premium brands of Australian fizz whose home at Smythesdale is the headquarters of Mildara Blass' sparkling wine production. Even though its name suggests it might come from elsewhere than South Australia, I've always had a soft spot for the very elegant, classy Cuvée Victoria.

CUVÉE VICTORIA

South Australia (?!) $$$$

1996	18.0	2001	2004
1995	17.0	1997	2000
1994	18.2	1996	1999
1993	17.0	1995	1998
1992	18.0	1994	1996

VINTAGE BRUT

South-Eastern Australia $$$

1997	16.5	1999	2002
1996	16.7	1998	2001
1995	17.6	1997	2000
1994	16.0	1996	1999
1992	17.4	1994	1997

Region: Yarra Valley Winemaker: Tom Carson
Viticulturist: John Evans Chief Executives: Doug & Graham Rathbone

Yering Station

38 Melba Highway
Yering Vic 3770
Tel: (03) 9730 1107
Fax: (03) 9739 0135

Yering Station seems ready to fill the dearth of high-quality new Yarra Valley wineries. Despite the plethora to have set up shop in there over the last two decades, not enough are rising to this level. Its 'standard' wines understandably reflect the youth of the vines from which they are made, while the releases so far under the Reserve label include some excellent Chardonnay, Shiraz and Pinot Noir. Yering Station's winery, cellar, restaurant and cellar door complex is one of the most impressive in Victoria.

CHARDONNAY

Yarra Valley $$$

1999	16.2	2000	2001
1998	18.0	2000	2003+
1997	17.0	1999	2002
1996	14.5	1997	1998
1995	14.8	1996	1999
1994	14.4	1996	1999
1993	18.0	1998	2001
1992	18.1	1994	1997

VICTORIA's
Est. 1838
FIRST VINEYARD
YERING
Station
1997
Yarra Valley
CHARDONNAY

PINOT NOIR

Yarra Valley $$$

1999	15.3	2001	2004
1998	16.7	2000	2003
1997	16.0	1998	1999
1996	16.5	1998	2001

VICTORIA's
Est. 1838
FIRST VINEYARD
YERING
Station
1997
Yarra Valley
PINOT NOIR

Yeringberg

Maroondah Highway
Coldstream Vic 3770
Tel: (03) 9739 1453
Fax: (03) 9739 0048

Region: Yarra Valley Winemaker: Guill De Pury
Viticulturist: Guill De Pury Chief Executive: Guill De Pury

It might come as a surprise to most Australian wine drinkers how well and for how long the comparatively refined wines of Yeringberg actually cellar, lasting in some instances for well over a century. The 1998 Yeringberg red blend is just another example. If anything, Yeringberg's recent vintages have actually managed to raise the reputation of this stellar small vineyard to an even higher plane.

CHARDONNAY

Yarra Valley $$$$

1999	16.8	2004	2007
1998	18.6	2003	2006
1997	18.3	2005	2009
1996	18.3	2004	2008
1995	17.8	2003	2007
1994	17.8	2002	2006
1993	18.6	2001	2005
1992	18.3	2000	2004
1991	17.5	1996	1999
1990	18.6	1998	2002
1989	16.0	1991	1994

MARSANNE ROUSSANNE BLEND

Yarra Valley $$$$

1999	18.2	2007	2011
1998	18.0	2003	2006
1997	18.5	2005	2009
1996	17.5	2004	2008
1995	16.5	2003	2007
1994	18.3	2002	2006
1993	18.4	1998	2001
1992	17.9	1997	2000
1991	17.2	1993	1996
1990	17.5	1995	1998

PINOT NOIR

Yarra Valley $$$$

1998	15.0	2000	2003
1997	18.9	2005	2009
1996	18.4	2004	2008
1995	17.3	2000	2003
1994	17.8	2002	2006
1993	17.6	1995	1998
1992	18.0	1997	2000
1991	17.8	1996	1999
1990	18.5	1998	2002
1989	16.8	1994	1997
1988	16.7	1993	1996

(RED, FORMERLY CABERNET SAUVIGNON)

Yarra Valley $$$$

1998	18.8		2010+
1997	18.6	2005	2009+
1996	18.1	2004	2008
1995	16.6	2003	2007
1994	18.5	2006	2014
1993	17.6	2001	2005
1992	18.8		2012+
1991	17.3	1999	2003
1990	18.7	2002	2010+
1989	15.8	1994	1997
1988	18.7	2000	2008+
1987	15.6	1992	1995
1986	16.5	1994	1998
1985	17.0	1993	1997
1984	18.5	1996	2004
1983	15.2	1988	1991
1982	18.6	1994	2002
1981	16.6	1993	2001
1980	19.0	1992	2000
1979	18.8	1991	1999
1977	17.3	1989	1997
1976	18.6	1988	1996
1975	18.7	1987	1995+
1974	17.8	1986	1994

Region: Coonawarra Winemakers: Matt & Nick Zema
Viticulturist: Nick Zema Chief Executive: Demetrio Zema

Zema Estate

Riddoch Highway
Coonawarra SA 5263
Tel: (08) 8736 3219
Fax: (08) 8736 3280

Zema Estate is a red wine specialist located in the heart of Coonawarra. The Zema family prunes its vineyard by hand, thereby avoiding the intense leafy/mulberry flavours developed in several larger Coonawarra vineyards. They enjoyed their best vintage ever in 1998, creating wines of rare individuality, class and character. The Shiraz is an absolute Coonawarra classic, simply crammed with intense spicy fruit but handled with oak and tannin so cleverly that despite its sweetness, it's long, fine, tight-knit and stylish. Don't miss it.

CABERNET SAUVIGNON

Coonawarra $$$

1998	18.3	2006	2010+
1997	16.7	2002	2005
1996	16.0	2001	2004
1995	17.2	2000	2003
1994	17.8	1999	2002
1993	17.5	2001	2005
1992	18.3	2000	2004
1991	17.8	1999	2003
1990	18.0		2002+

CLUNY

Coonawarra $$

1998	18.0	2006	2010
1997	16.2	2002	2005
1996	15.1	1998	2001
1995	16.6	2000	2003
1994	16.0	1999	2002
1993	15.4	1995	1998

FAMILY SELECTION CABERNET SAUVIGNON

Coonawarra $$$$

1996	18.3	2004	2008+
1994	18.4	2002	2006
1993	17.5	2001	2005
1992	16.8	2000	2004
1991	17.9		2003+
1990	16.8	1998	2002
1988	17.7	1996	2000

SHIRAZ

Coonawarra $$$

1998	18.7	2006	2010
1997	16.0	1999	2002
1996	16.6	2001	2004
1995	17.0	2003	2007
1994	16.4	1999	2002
1993	18.4	2001	2005
1992	16.8	1997	2000
1991	18.0		2003+
1990	18.5		2010+
1989	16.7	1997	2003
1988	18.2		2000+